VALUE-DIRECTED MANAGEMENT

VALUE-DIRECTED MANAGEMENT

Organizations, Customers, and Quality

Bernard Arogyaswamy and Ron P. Simmons

Q

Quorum Books
Westport, Connecticut • London

Library of Congress Cataloging-in-Publication Data

Arogyaswamy, Bernard.
    Value-directed management : organizations, customers, and quality /
Bernard Arogyaswamy and Ron P. Simmons.
        p. cm.
    Includes bibliographical references and index.
    ISBN 0–89930–797–3 (alk. paper)
    1. Management—United States.   2. Quality of products—United
States—Management.   3. Customer service—United States—Management.
I. Simmons, Ron P., 1957– . II. Title.
HD70.U5A8   1993
658—dc20   92–1749

British Library Cataloguing in Publication Data is available.

Library of Congress Catalog Card Number: 92–1749
ISBN: 0–89930–797–3

First published in 1993

Quorum Books, 88 Post Road West, Westport, CT 06881
An imprint of Greenwood Publishing Group, Inc.

Printed in the United States of America

The paper used in this book complies with the
Permanent Paper Standard issued by the National
Information Standards Organization (Z39.48–1984).

10 9 8 7 6 5 4 3 2 1

To Lita and Tarini, whose fortitude and understanding have been
invaluable and remarkable, and to my parents for their
guidance and encouragement—BA

and

To Diane, Lyndsey, Lauren and Leyla, who endured with patience,
surviving the many miles, hours and logistics during
this book's creation—RS

CONTENTS

FIGURES

PREFACE

If *excellence, total quality, competitiveness, global strategy*, and *empowerment* have been among the most popular buzz words of the eighties, what are the most likely buzz words of the nineties? We don't really care. What we *do* care about is the articulation of an approach for firms to achieve ever stronger market positions through an unquenchable thirst for improvement. Within these pages we present a management package tailored to do just that. All this probably sounds very familiar—as it should—since most firms obviously seek to be successful by stimulating high commitment among their employees. What may not sound very familiar is the route we employ to get there from here. The concept of value takes center stage in our presentation. It is the elixir that can bring a new vitality to the practice of management. Starting from Porter's concept of the *value chain*, we propose a simplified version of the chain to clearly illuminate the process of value creation in products and services. When coupled with our detailed analysis of important customer needs (the *components* of value, as we term them), what emerges is a potent technique for strategic management characterized by a constant striving to maximize value delivered to customers.

With continuous improvements in value as a launching pad, we shift gears to a *how-to* mode. We consider the concept of value in light of the actions and experiences of world-class business firms, particularly those of Japanese and American origin. Rather than provide our readers with a laboriously compiled list of practices successfully adopted by the giants of global competition, we have tried to distill the essence of value management from their actions. The result is a systematic and coherent framework for realizing value enhancements regardless of the dynamics of customer needs, competitors' strategies, and product changes. Just in Time Manufacturing, Total Quality Control, semiautonomous work teams, Strategic Business Units, value teams ("Structure Busting Teams" in our terminology), job rotation and the concept of the holographic organization are among the important techniques we have woven into our tapestry of the high value organization. The mix of ideas and realism that we bring to the how-to stage of our work provides a clearer understanding of the rationale underlying these practices, especially when viewed against the exciting backdrop of customer value.

Customer value creation is indeed organizational alchemy and the transformation process is addressed in detail in the how-to part of the book. However, we are, if nothing, conscientious guides. As any traveler knows, nothing is quite so reassuring on a long journey than to periodically determine that he or she is on the right track. Signposts and landmarks provide measures of the progress a firm makes toward its mission of value. Time-based yardsticks such as response time and time to market, indices for job rotation and team management, and indicators of employee commitment are just a few of the tracking mechanisms that can assist in locating a firm on its value map and enable corrective action.

If superior value is to be more than a short-lived phenomenon, the effort exerted for improvement must be unrelenting. Our traveler never reaches his or her destination since there is none! There are only way stations to briefly halt at and survey one's progress, spot one's competitors, and to track innovative changes since the last stop. Value is a moving finish line and any satisfaction felt at delivering the very best value should be tempered by the knowledge that the race is unending and those who do not improve are losing ground. Getting managers and employees to buy into the concept of high value, long haul management is critical to establish a wellspring of value-driven ideas and actions. Building a *culture* of value through the use of symbols, hero(in)es and recognition systems serves as the culmination of our effort, the final piece in the working prototype of the value creating organization.

Ideas and experiences mingle freely in our account of the day-in, day-out, year-in, year-out value achieving firm. Pragmatism is the name of the game and only what has been found to work has found its way into our bedrock principles of value. We are not ashamed to admit that we have borrowed some ideas from successful Japanese practices. After all, the Japanese were not exactly bashful about serving themselves large portions of Western technology in the late nineteenth century. Nor were they embarrassed by the liberal importation into Japan of foreign, particularly American, technology and management ideas after World War II. The *globally* competitive firm we envision in this book must be able and willing to combine the best that Japanese and western management have to offer and bring this powerful weaponry to bear in the single-minded pursuit of value. Much of this book is devoted to making the weaponry and the target easily accessible. Value is a cause that unites and strengthens *any* organization, supplier or customer, small venture or large, high growth or no growth industry. The ground spanning and connecting the successful corporations of the world is an exciting place to be. Join us.

ACKNOWLEDGMENTS

One wintry afternoon not long ago, we were sitting in Ron's office in Syracuse, New York, watching the snow pile up at an alarming rate on the asphalt outside. We weren't sure which was more depressing, the snow or the story being recounted to us. A product manager's deteriorating performance rating had brought him as close to corporate disaster as he could come without losing his job. As we tried to grapple with his problems and advise him on his missed opportunities and misconceptions, we realized that we were trying to preach a doctrine we had not articulated fully ourselves. We stumbled around mentally, searching for authors and authorities to commend to our troubled friend, and others like him, too. We realized we knew of none. That evening we decided to do something about it.

During the course of our sometimes direct, but often meandering progress we have talked to, bounced ideas off, persuaded and been persuaded by executives, entrepreneurs, consultants and academics. We truly regret we cannot thank all of them by name for their contribution to this work. We appreciate all the time they spent and interest they showed in the project.

We must identify a few prominent contributors, though. We would like to thank Arlyn Melcher who has never failed to stimulate, encourage and, yes, criticize. John Doult's insistent queries ("What went wrong at XYZ, Inc.?") have spurred some of our thinking on national and corporate competitiveness. Paper industry executives have provided us with a diversity of insights on how organizations can be revitalized: special thanks to David Klausmeyer of Mead Specialty Papers, Doug Mele of International Papers, Don LaTorre of Engelhard, David Hearne of Champion, and David Corder and Ed Thompson of Black Clawson. Sharyn Knight's dedication and perseverance in word processing have provided tremendous support throughout our endeavor, and we owe her much for her hard work.

While we obviously cannot claim all the credit for this work, any mistakes and misstatements that have made their way in are solely our responsibility.

VALUE-DIRECTED MANAGEMENT

1

FOUL PLAY OR FAIR GAME?

HOME FIELD ADVANTAGE

For over a decade there has been increasing concern and discussion of how companies based in the United States have taken a beating from companies based in East Asia—initially and primarily Japan, but now including South Korea, Taiwan, Hong Kong, Singapore and, perhaps, Malaysia, Thailand and Indonesia. The industries surrendered to the East Asian wave include shipbuilding, automobiles, steel, VCRs, TVs, cameras and electronic chips. Composite materials, information technology, entertainment, communications and even services currently appear to be the target industries.[1]

Obviously, this systematic conquest of major industries has shocked both companies whose markets have been directly attacked as well as those who fear they could be next on the "hit list." Another affected group has been the workers rendered jobless by the success of foreign competitors. These two powerful constituencies, defeated companies and upset workers, combined in the face of a common threat, have often spurred governmental action such as "voluntary" restrictions in auto imports, sanctions against dumping of electronic chips, and so on. The general reasoning underlying such a response has been that conditions in the foreign firms' home nations combined to give them an unfair advantage. For example, the argument goes, Japanese automakers benefitted from many aspects of Japanese business conditions which were not available to U.S. automakers—lower labor costs, lack of pollution controls, cultural tendencies to group cohesion and loyalty, the government's cooperative relationship with business firms, and patient stockholders. The case often made by business executives, union leaders, politicians, and journalists is that these countries, particularly Japan, have given themselves a tremendous "home field advantage" by tailoring (doctoring?) the playing field to suit themselves, recruiting inexpensive talent, building cohesive teams, etc. "The cold war is over, and Japan won" reflects the emotions, ranging all the way from wry humor to bitter frustration, that pervade this issue.[2] The question of how we can turn the tables on our unfair competitors naturally arises. The answer is to give them a taste of their own medicine, of course! Change the rules of the game so that no "visiting" team could possibly win here. Some of the actions proposed or already adopted are:

• Setting limits on imports, industry by industry, particularly for the most vulnerable ones;
• placing obstacles in the way of foreign firms that wish to buy property or stock in the United States;
• retaliating against countries (against specific industries in such countries if necessary) where American firms report that access has been denied or made difficult for them;
• exhortations to pay greater attention to the country of origin ("Buy American") rather than how well they meet consumers' needs.[3]

All this could of course prove extremely effective in giving the home team a winning record. It might also result in turning the local fans off the game, in keeping the paying customers away. After all, who wants to see two lesser-caliber teams play even if they are homegrown? Can you imagine what baseball in New York City would be like if the entire season consisted of the Yankees playing the Mets, 81 games at the Bronx and the other 81 at Shea Stadium? Not only would fan interest wane, but player quality would start going down due to reduced competition and limited customer options. In a nutshell, then, proposals to set up islands of home field advantage could destroy fan interest and the game itself. The results achieved by the 1983–84 Detroit Tigers are worth thinking about and emulating. They own the longest road winning streak in sports (21 games) and demonstrated that an excellent product can and will stand on its own.

PENALIZING THE CONSUMER

Undoubtedly, projecting sports as a metaphor for business or national affairs could prove to be misleading or counterproductive if taken to an extreme. However, the negative impact on local fans (of protecting home teams in a sport such as baseball) pales in comparison to the impact on buyers of goods or services when *industries* are sheltered. Most of us buy a product such as a TV or camera when we feel a need for it. Typically we try to establish a match between our needs and what is available, keeping in mind factors such as the price, manufacturer's reputation, warranty, etc. If we cannot get what we want—and are unlikely to be able to do so *in the near future*—most of us are likely to compromise and settle for the best available. Forcing customers to buy what's available is an injustice to them, particularly if they have gotten used to buying the best. Limiting customer choice is not a fruitful policy either for American firms to recommend or for American policymakers to pursue. It would reward inefficiency and ensure the survival of the feeblest. So-called public sector (government owned) firms in England, France, India and other countries will testify to the debilitating effect of governmental help.[4] When viewed from the customer's perspective, taking action against foreign firms or groups of firms does not seem a sensible option. It's like cutting off one's nose to spite the face. It makes even less sense when one considers that a cycle of retaliation could ensue, thus hurting the American consumer even more. The fact that it would also affect consumers in other countries is little, if any, consolation.

The only way we can even begin to deal with the problem is by admitting that some of the successful foreign firms *may* be doing things right, or at any rate, doing them better than most of our firms have. After all, if even when the yen's value rose relative to the dollar, imports into the United States continued to climb (when, logically, they should have plummeted), there must be more than *costs* (fairly or unfairly derived) at work here.[5] This is driven home even more by the fact that wage rates in Japan are comparable to, if not higher, than in the United States (as are the costs of fuel and most other raw materials).[6] When we consider further the continued success of the Xeroxes and the IBMs in the Japanese market,[7] we might come to the conclusion that the playing conditions were, perhaps, not the main reason for our team's poor showing. Our relative lack of interest in foreign markets could be one reason. Thailand is a case in point. It has a minuscule economy compared to that of the United States, but one that has achieved startlingly high annual GNP growth rates during the 1980s. One might expect that American firms would exhibit some interest in an awakening market, but one would expect wrong. Thailand has, in the recent past, invested more in the United States than the other way around. In fact, Thailand has established facilities in the United States in spite of the manufacturing costs being higher than in Thailand, as have the Koreans and Japanese. [8] The reason is that tariffs make it prohibitively expensive to import goods in a wide range of industries. This example illustrates the reluctance of our firms to explore new territories and our tendency to complain about protectionist trade practices abroad when our hands are not quite clean either.

TRANSFORMATIONS, DISCOVERIES, AND
CONSTANT CHANGE

The Oakland A's arguably have been baseball's dominant team of the late 1980s. They were expected to win just by showing up at the 1988 and 1990 World Series. Imagine their surprise when the Dodgers in 1988 and the Reds in 1990 decided not to play the part of sacrificial victim. Some of the Oakland players, fans, and media had so thoroughly convinced themselves of their superiority that they could not admit to being outplayed. In a sense we in the United States have, relative to our foreign competitors, fallen victim to the same pattern of thought. We are unwilling to admit that our (undeniable) past superiority in products and services has either been eroded, or disappeared, or become a handicap. Our successes in various fields may have desensitized us to the major strides other countries, notably Japan, have made, particularly in technology and management during the past decade or two.

American achievements from the mid-nineteenth century to the present day are too numerous to be listed here. For example, Edison's inventiveness, Carnegie's pragmatism, Morgan's organizational wizardry and Ford's manufacturing genius helped to create an awesome economic engine. However, we know by experience and through received wisdom that the only constant in the world is that it is constantly changing. The international situation, for example, has changed dramatically during this century: many countries have become independent, particularly in Asia and Africa; the world has gone through two World Wars and a Cold War; the nuclear threat has waxed, waned and waxed again; much of Western Europe is uniting to form the 12 nation European Community, and so on. The changes and discoveries in science and technology have been as, if not more, dramatic. Relativity and the space-time continuum, the existence of subatomic particles, antimatter, and black holes, the nature of time itself, space travel and exploration, string theory and other Grand Unification Theories (GUTs) have caught our imagination and changed our lives.[9] The list includes just a fraction of the achievements in physics and does not even broach the revolution that has swept through the other natural sciences and the life sciences.

MANAGEMENT OF THE "SCIENTIFIC" AND
"HUMAN" VARIETIES

In the midst of so much change driven by exponential growth in knowledge about our world and ourselves, surely the way in which organizations are managed must have undergone corresponding changes. This is not necessarily so. The two dominant philosophies of management in the 20th century have been the Scientific Management (SM) perspective and the

Human Relations/Resources (HR) movement. Scientific Management is based on the premise that

- tasks can and must be designed in great detail, based on which
- standards can be established in order to
- reward or punish employees.[10]

On the other hand, Human Relations oriented managers proceed on the assumption that

- employees need social interaction at work;
- consideration and humanity in dealings with employees makes them satisfied on the job;
- motivation is best accomplished by job characteristics (e.g., being aware of one's contribution to the completed product) rather than by external means alone (e.g., money).[11]

These contrasting styles of management have held sway for the better part of the 20th century in the United States. Scientific Management has tended to stress efficiency achieved through control as a measure of an organization's success while Human Relations has emphasized harmony through employee satisfaction.

Firms embracing SM in its totality discovered that even if tasks were performed as designed, employees began showing signs of boredom and alienation. On the other hand, in pure HR firms, the efficiency that goes with predesigned, precisely monitored tasks is missing in spite of employees being more satisfied. Employees are happy but unproductive. The differences that divide them call for great care to be exercised in combining them to get the best features of both.

MANAGEMENT ON THE OUTSIDE

Both these systems of management are inward directed. That is, their primary purpose is the optimal use of human, material, and informational resources available *within* the firm. Strategic management, which acquired increased importance beginning in the 1960s, has, on the other hand, tried to focus attention on the firm's external environment (competitors' actions, technological change, governmental regulations, and so on.) While strategy has long been studied and used in warfare (Sun-Tsu and Clausewitz being two of its better known exponents),[12] its application to business decisions has been relatively recent. In essence, strategy in business helps firms forecast and successfully deal with their present and future environments by judiciously deploying their capabilities. Identifying environ-

mental opportunities (new market segments, product changes and innovation, competitors' moves) and transforming weaknesses into strengths
(allocating resources, building a cohesive organization, and so on) are
integral parts of strategy.[13] Strategy has been an effective means for firms
to be sensitive to the needs of their constituents. Disc brakes,
the use of environmentally "neutral" materials, and the emergence of
financial full-service "supermarkets" are some instances of need sensitive
strategies. In general, strategy was originally and continues to be primarily
an outward-looking activity, with both conceptualization and decision
making falling within the domain of top management. While the formulation of strategy is typically carried out by the Chief Executive of a firm
and his or her select advisors, actually implementing the plans of action
chosen devolves upon all the employees, more so those at the lower levels
of the organization. Translating strategy-as-conceived into strategy-as-
implemented calls for methods of organizing and inspiring employees
using means such as organizational structure, standards and rewards,
communication, empowerment, and shared values and beliefs. In effect,
therefore, organizations need to invoke either the HR or SM philosophies
or an alloy of them for optimal use of their *internal resources* in order to
best meet the needs of a demanding, constantly changing *external environment*.

A STRATEGY OF VALUE

A gap could obviously exist between externally driven, top management
initiated *ideas* and internally focused, subordinate-level *actions*. One may
visualize ideas and actions as sources of almost inexhaustible energy
which need to be in step with each other if they are to combine for the
good of the firm. In an eight-cylinder car, if the timing and sequence are
not precisely set, not only will the car experience a loss of power, it could
also result in more serious problems (vibrations, increased wear and tear,
etc.) A firm whose strategic ideas and employees' actions do not converge
is, similarly, likely to be disorganized and suffer from a lack of focused
effort. *Delivering value to customers* is a glue that can bind internal and
external perspectives together into a *unified whole*. A firm's relationship
to its external environment centers around its ties to its customers. As
shown in Figure 1.1, the product (we use product to include and be
interchangeable with service throughout this book) binds a firm to its
customers and is the basis for the firm's existence and its role in society. How companies reward their employees, what dividends are paid
to shareholders, the nature of a firm's position in the local community,
its conformity to regulations, etc., are all predicated upon the company–
product–customer nexus. Value is a "gravitational force" that could attract toward it both internal (employee driven) and external (strategic)

Figure 1.1
Value as a Binding Force

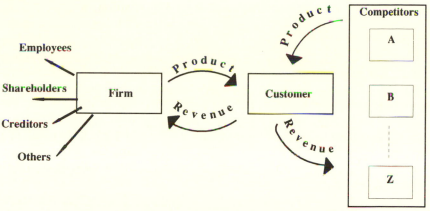

energies generated by the organization. A focus on customer value would also result in both energies continuously increasing through a process of feeding off each other—higher achieved value results in more being sought and in new ways of achieving value, which then leads to more intensified efforts at implementation, and so on. Gravity is again an apt analogy since it causes acceleration or a continuous increase in velocity just as a value focus will elicit ever-increasing levels of conceptual and actional energy.

In this book we take the position that if American firms wish to compete on an equal footing with their foreign competitors, dedication (or re-dedication) to providing customers with the value they seek is imperative. The three dimensions of value—the product, the customer, and the firm—have to be actively and creatively managed if the customer, the firm, and the rest of society are to benefit in the long term. Systematically targeting customer value as the overriding mission of a firm goes a long way to ensure that a firm meets with enduring success. Its customers keep coming back or, in the case of first-time buyers, they don't feel they're involved in a game of Russian roulette. Attempting to lower customers' standards by eliminating competitors, foreign and domestic, will certainly do little to deliver more value.[14] Whoever the beneficiaries of curbing foreign competitors might be, customers aren't going to appear anywhere on the list.

While customer value is the centerpiece of our design for success many questions obviously remain to be answered. What is customer value and how does one deliver it? Does the notion of value differ from industry to industry and, if so, how? Does the value delivered vary from one time period to another within the same industry? We hope to address these and related issues in this book. We offer a *strategy of value*, a comprehensive approach to building and sustaining excellence measured by the yardstick of customer value.

WHAT LIES AHEAD

In the next two chapters we provide an overview of value beginning with what it means, alternative ways of providing it, its importance and how it may be improved—in short an "everything you always wanted to know about value, but didn't know existed" guide to the subject. The need for a coherent strategy and the forms such a strategy could assume are highlighted, as are the conditions under which such a strategy may need to be changed. The actual *execution* of a strategy directed to providing customer value is then taken up in chapters 4 through 9. We develop a framework centered around:

> **INTERDEPENDENCE**
> **INTEGRATION**
> **INVOLVEMENT**
> **INDICATORS**
> **INGRAINING**

These INs are essential to providing increasing value since they are the crucial connection between a firm's strategy for dealing with its external stakeholders and the way in which it manages its material, informational and human resources. They constitute different but mutually reinforcing elements of the edifice of value and are each critical to its attainment. The INs are analogous to a five-number combination to a safe. In the absence of even one number, the contents (value) are beyond reach. The INs may be described as follows:

- **Interdependence** is the extent of linkage that exists between two successive activities or events. The activities may be as varied as receiving and communicating orders in a fast food restaurant, drilling and stamping in a machine shop or product promotion and customer contact in a marketing department. Irrespective of the context, we argue that tighter linkage (stronger interdependence) builds more value. Chapter 4 tells why and how. Techniques such as set up reduction, lower capacity increments and Quality Function Deployment which help achieve greater value through interdependence are introduced and discussed.

- **Integration** denotes the nature and level of communication between activities or operations *not* directly or obviously linked to each other, both within and external to the firm. These are some of the gaps that we address in chapter 5 in making a case for stronger connections as a means to enhance value. Methods to build better, more durable communication channels are offered, as well as a

Figure 1.2
Integration

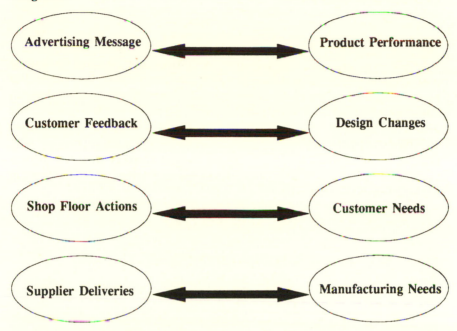

review of coordinating mechanisms to ensure that a unified view of value prevails within the firm.

- **Involvement**, very simply, is a process by which employees voluntarily and actively pursue increments to value. If Interdependence and Integration are to have their desired effect on customer value, the employees of the firm must be totally convinced of the need for them and be involved in their implementation. Achieving total commitment to the first two **IN**s is discussed in chapter 6 along with methods to encourage individual and group-based participation. The flat organization, flexible job designs, suggestion systems, incentive schemes (including ESOP) and management through work teams are some of the techniques analyzed and recommended.

- **Ingraining** is a process by which people at work develop norms and beliefs. Certain ways of thinking and doing become taken for granted even though they have not been explicitly stated. We view ingraining (in chapter 7) specifically as a set of long-term actions by which the first three **IN**s and the Indicators become second nature to the employees. Without ingraining, the practices suggested by the other four **IN**s will typically be short-lived and the firm will revert to the status quo ante.

- **Indicators** provide monitoring and control—continuously checking progress, informing others and initiating corrective action if needed. Problems arising from design deficiencies, delays in delivery, defective parts and machine breakdowns are some of the areas in which information needs to be regularly collected, distributed, and used. Wherever called for, *good* performance (e.g., a sharp reduction in the defect rate, improvement in customer response time, etc.) also ought to be noticed and recognized. Anything that relates to implementing Interdependence, Integration and Involvement would be included under the category of Indicators. Indicators are, in a sense, the guardian angel of the first three INs: they keep watch over actions and achievements, counseling restraint or redoubled vigor where necessary. They serve as a mirror that reflects not only the level of performance but also the processes, behaviors, and assumptions that are beneficial in the long run. We deal with Indicators in two parts, one covering general measures of value (chapter 8), the other (chapter 9) evaluating more specific achievements.

In chapter 10 we evaluate the viability of our value management action plan in the context of cultural, corporate and industry differences. We conclude that the principles developed are universal though they might need fine-tuning to the needs of the firm.

LEARNING—MAINLY FROM OURSELVES

In presenting our vision of value through the five INs we uncover or rediscover ideas and principles, many of which first came to prominence in the United States. Most of us are aware that the Japanese implemented the principles of statistical process and quality control as laid out by Dr. Deming and Dr. Juran which helped them, by their own admission, tremendously in the improvement of product quality and in market conquest.[15] However, many of the *principles* underlying the Japanese management of operations, exemplified by Just-in-Time (JIT), Total Quality Control (TQC), and so on, were also first developed, by and large, in the United States. For example, the use of teams for performing entire tasks, greater freedom on the job, job rotation, and the centrality of the customer, are some of the foundations of JIT "imported" into Japan.[16] Many of these ideas were ignored, or tried and discarded in this country, primarily due to the relatively plentiful state of raw material and other resources, particularly prior to the oil embargo of 1973, but also because we had not expected foreign, particularly Japanese, competitors to be as successful in garnering chunks of our markets as they have proved to be. Since many of our recommendations—such as the notion of product value and the supremacy of the customer, strategy and a vision of the firm in the long term, participative management and its therapeutic value, to mention just a few—involve concepts that are indigenous to the United States, accepting and absorbing them may not prove troublesome. However, other practices, such as our traditional preference for "Management by Separation," that is, separating operations and activities from each other so that each can function with undisturbed efficiency, may have to be unlearned due to the waste and disunity they encourage. Wherever we recommend a course of action that is likely to prove troublesome in the non-Japanese context we try to provide ways to ease into it, mitigating at least some of the possible side effects.

This book, therefore, stands at the confluence of two influential streams of management thought—the "Atlantic" stream, exemplified by Scientific Management, Human Relations, Strategic Management, and the notion of value, on the one hand, and the "Pacific" stream, best illustrated by techniques such as JIT, TQC, cooperative vendor linkages, and employee involvement, on the other. While some chapters are predominantly one or the other (chapter 3, for instance, is more "Atlantic" in its emphasis while chapter 4 leans toward the "Pacific") ideas and illustrations from both streams are fairly evenly distributed throughout the book.

NOTES

1. Japan's Ministry of International Trade and Industry (MITI) projects phenomenal growth in the market for composite materials, and companies such as Kyocera Corporation and Toray Industries are gearing up for the estimated $13 billion market in the year 2000. (See *Business Week*, November 11, 1991, pp. 168–69.) Japan's venture into service businesses by adapting principles of manufacturing to the needs of service industries such as tourism, insurance, distribution, and finance is outlined in *The Economist*, October 20, 1990, pp. 83–84.

2. As reported in *Time*, February 10, 1992, p. 17.

3. For a succinct review of the trade issues and emotions bedeviling relations between the two countries, see Daniel Metraux, *The Japanese Economy and the American Businessman* (Lewiston, NY: Edwin Mellen Press, 1989), pp. 101–24 and Thomas K. McCraw, "From Partners to Competitors: An Overview of the Period Since World War II," in Thomas K. McCraw, ed., *America Versus Japan* (Boston, Mass.: Harvard Business School Press, 1986).

4. While public enterprises are no doubt established for sound reasons, they generally tend to constrain customers' options. An extreme example is India, where they were established to help develop an industrial base but led in most industries to the stifling of private producers. Their 1500-fold growth between 1951 and 1985 resulted in protectionist monopolies that are being dismantled, albeit rather slowly, today. Francis Cherunilam's *Business and Government* (Bombay: Himalaya Publishing House, 1990) provides a broad overview of this and other problems arising from governmental intervention. For an update on the privatization of public enterprises in Russia, Eastern Europe, and Latin America, see *Business Week*, October 21, 1991, pp. 49–56.

5. The value of the dollar fell from a rate of 357.60 yen in 1970 to 133.48 yen in mid-1989. That is, the yen appreciated to nearly 250% of its 1970 value in the course of about 20 years. (*Statistical Abstract of the United States*, Washington, D.C.: U.S. Bureau of the Census (110th ed.), 1990), p. 858. The depreciation in the dollar's value was not, as one might expect, accompanied by an increase in U.S. exports to Japan and/or lower Japanese exports to the U.S. On the contrary,

the merchandise trade balance rose in Japan's favor almost every year, and in 1988 was about $52 billion, more than 5 times what it was in 1980 (p. 808).

6. As James Abegglen and George Stalk, Jr. observe in *Kaisha* (New York: Basic Books, 1985), p. 194, the United States averaged 7 metric tonnes of steel per 100 man-hours in the mid 1960s compared to 2 metric tonnes (mT) for the Japanese. In the mid 1970s, the Japanese production rate of 9 mT was ahead of the United States figure of 8 mT. In spite of rapidly increasing wages in Japan, the cost differential in favor of the Japanese widened from $45 to $74 per mT. Better use of equipment and greater energy-efficiency through the use of continuous casting technology and less dependence on oil are some of the explanatory factors (pp. 75, 76). While wage rates in the steel industry remain lower in Japan than in the United States, the average earnings of the typical Japanese worker has kept rising and, in fact, by 1982 was about on par with those of their American counterparts.

7. Besides Nippon IBM and Fuji Xerox, other foreign-based firms that have done well in Japan include Coca Cola, Hewlett Packard, and Nestlé (Ibid., p. 216).

8. *The Economist*, December 22, 1990, p. 89; the extent of non-tariff protection in the United States has been estimated to have risen by about 25% between 1981 and 1986 (*The Economist*, February 11, 1989, p. 63).

9. The GUTs attempt to unify the four main forces in physics. See, for example, Stephen Hawking's *A Brief History of Time* (Toronto: Bantam, 1988), which is remarkable for its lucid treatment of a complex subject. GUTs in physics are still nowhere near being realized or agreed upon. They are, however, being discussed and argued over. This stage has yet to be reached in management GUTs.

10. While Frederick Taylor was undoubtedly the apostle of the SM movement, he was ably supported by other thinkers cast in the same mold, notably the Gilbreths, and Gantt. See Frank Gilbreth's *Motion Study* (New York: Van Nostrand Reinhold, 1911) and John Kelly's *Scientific Management, Job Redesign and Work Performance* (London: Academic Press, 1982) for a thorough treatment of this important aspect of management thought, past and present.

11. Among the influential writers in this phase of the development of management thought were Douglas McGregor (*The Human Side of Enterprise*, New York: McGraw-Hill, 1960), Rensis Likert, (*New Patterns of Management*, New York: McGraw-Hill, 1961), and Frederick Herzberg ("One More Time: How Do You Motivate Employees?" *Harvard Business Review*, Jan.-Feb., 1968), pp. 53–62.

12. Sun-Tzu. *The Art of War* (New York: Oxford University Press, 1971). Carl von Clausewitz. *On War* (Harmondsworth, U.K.: Penguin, 1985).

13. Groundbreaking work by Igor Ansoff (*Corporate Strategy*, New York: McGraw-Hill, 1965) and Kenneth Andrews (*The Concept of Corporate Strategy*, Homewood, IL: Irwin, Third Ed., 1987) are classics that provide historical background and an excellent introduction to the field. Ansoff's recent work, *Implanting Strategic Management* (New York: Prentice-Hall, 1990), brings the reader up to date in the field and is a fascinating study of how far strategic management has travelled in a quarter of a century.

14. Denying customers access to competitors' high value products lowers standards and is quite different from Milind Lele and Jagdish Sheth's strategy of lowering customer expectations in order to exceed them (*The Customer is Key*,

New York: Wiley, 1987). This strategy brings the firm's capabilities in line with expectations unlike standard lowering which lowers capabilities.

15. W. Edward Deming's *Quality, Productivity and Competitive Position* (Cambridge, Mass.: MIT Center for Advanced Engineering Study, 1982) articulates his views on quality—views that have undergone considerable revision from the statistical quality control message the Japanese received twenty-five years earlier. J. M. Juran's *Quality Control Handbook* (New York: McGraw-Hill, 1979) preserves much of the original message preached to the Japanese.

16. Included in this list would be some of the investigations conducted on sociotechnical systems and team-based work at the Tavistock Institute in England, notably E. L. Trist and K. W. Bamforth's "Some Social and Psychological Consequences of the Longwall Method of Coal Gettings," *Human Relations* 4 (February 1951) pp. 3–38, and E. J. Miller and A. K. Rice's *Systems in Organization: The Control of Task and Sentient Boundaries* (London: Tavistock, 1963), as well as research carried out in the U.S. on job design and improvement. Richard Hackman and Greg Oldham's *Work Redesign* (Reading, MA: Addison-Wesley, 1980) and "Development of the Job Diagnostic Survey," *Journal of Applied Psychology*, April 1975, pp. 159–70 are outstanding examples of pragmatic inquiries in this field.

2

THE MANY FACES
OF VALUE

VALUE—THROUGH ANALYSIS AND CHAINS

Automobile dealers scream until they're blue in the face that the cars they feature will provide you with superior value. The neighborhood discount store claims that its goods give you the best value for your dollar. And a rock singer's fans assure you that their hero delivers value at his concerts as no other singer can. Most of us have a fairly good idea what *value* means in each of the preceding contexts, though some of us might have trouble explaining what value consists of, suggesting how it may be achieved and determining whether it exists in a specific case.

Economists have been using the term value for a few centuries. They employ the term *value-in-use* to describe how functional or useful a product is and *value-in-exchange* to convey some idea of its availability and price. Jeremy Bentham[1] used the word *utility* to denote value-in-use as well as the aspects of value-in-exchange that are related to timely and geographic access to the product. Attempts to quantify, compare, and measure utilities have led to enormously complicated computations (with, we regret to say, little utility!). We prefer to use *worth* rather than utility so as to avoid the conceptual baggage associated with the latter. Moreover, two of the more prominent attempts to come to grips with the idea of product value use *worth* almost synonymously with utility.

The first of these approaches, value analysis, was originally developed by Miles[2] while working for General Electric and it has subsequently been widely applied particularly in manufacturing firms. Fallon,[3] who became value analysis' most eloquent crusader, defined it as a method to determine customer needs and deliver a product to satisfy them. In fact, Fallon went so far as to say that "the customer is the source of all industrial value" (p. 48). That is, value creation in any society is best served by maximizing value delivered to customers.

Product worth and cost are the twin components of value, and value analysis explores them in detail. Product worth derives from a product's ability to satisfy precisely identified customer needs. For example, if the important properties that customers seek in a vacuum cleaner are

- effective cleaning
- noiseless operation
- a range of attachments
- lightness and mobility
- sleekness of styling

the firm should target these properties in designing and manufacturing its cleaners. In addition, the same *relative importance* should be assigned to these components of product worth as customers desire. If, for instance, market research reveals that "effective cleaning" and "lightness and mobility" are dominant criteria, product worth would be enhanced by improving upon performance in these two areas. Any perceived short-comings in them would need to be attended to first, before working on other features of the product.

Apart from directing efforts toward enhancing product worth, value analysis also argues for cost reduction while keeping worth constant. In fact, many of the earlier applications of the technique concentrated on performing the same function at an ever-decreasing cost (e.g., lowering the cost of the materials used in building the motor and supporting frame for the vacuum cleaner). And, in value analysis' best of all possible worlds—not an unlikely prospect, through the adoption of designs involving fewer parts, substituting cheaper though not necessarily inferior materials, standardization of parts and materials for various products—worth could be increased and cost reduced simultaneously.

Over the years, value analysis has lost some of its initial shine. Its practitioners have tended to focus mainly, if not exclusively, on cost reduction as a means of increasing value. While we have nothing against chipping away at costs—material, manufacturing and otherwise—it tends to result in the dangerous virtue of incrementalism. A single-minded pursuit of cost reduction could, over time, result in a low-priced product that few want—a triumph in terms of cost, and a bust in terms of worth![4] The predominately inward focus increasingly leads to isolation from customers' needs, competitors' capabilities, and other shifting trends in the external world.

Michael Porter wrote two very influential books in the eighties. The first, *Competitive Strategy*, laid out Porter's conceptualization of *generic strategies*—strategies that encompass all possible actions a firm may undertake—which he labeled cost leadership, differentiation, and focus.[5] Cost leadership flows from becoming the lowest cost competitor while differentiation entails creating real and/or perceived differences from other available offerings. Firms employing a focus strategy, on the other hand, direct their products/services toward a narrow range of market segments, presumably reaping the benefits of market specialization. People Express attempted and successfully achieved, for a few years, a strategy of cost leadership in the airline industry. Few frills on board, minimum baggage handling, and cash payment were some of the means employed to do so. More recently, airlines have sought to differentiate themselves from one another based on the availability of Frequent Flyer programs, punctuality of departures and arrivals, more direct flights, etc. A strategy of focus is exemplified by airlines that offer special "deals" to business travelers, commuter airlines operating flights along the rim of a "hub and spoke" system, and so on. Similar strategy "compartments" consisting of firms adopting the three generic strategies can be found in almost every industry. In *Competitive Advantage*, published in 1985, five years after his initial venture, Porter explores more fully the origins and bases of generic strategies.[6] He suggests that generic strategies follow from the source(s) of competitive advantage (the things the firm does better than its competitors to the satisfaction of important constituents such as customers, suppliers, the government, and distributors) enjoyed by the firm.

Porter's major contribution to the understanding of competitive advantage is his notion of the *value chain*. The value chain is the sequence of activities, from start to finish, by which the product or service is transformed from an idea to a consumable form. If the product is steel, the chain would start, say, with the mining of coal and iron, and end with delivery to a customer such as a manufacturer of steel cans. If the firm were not fully integrated backward (or the mill were a steel minimill), the value chain would commence with the receipt of raw materials, and if forward integration were incomplete, the chain could end with manufacture and warehousing. While our view of the value creation process differs slightly from that of Porter's, we have essentially tried to capsulize his value chain to better develop our strategy of value and its successful execution.

There are, in our view, three dominant activities in the creation of value: Conceptualize it, Construct it, Communicate it. We refer to these activities or stages as the 3Cs of value. (We shall also, on occasion, refer to these 3Cs as C1, C2, and C3, respectively.)

Figure 2.1
The 3Cs of Value Creation

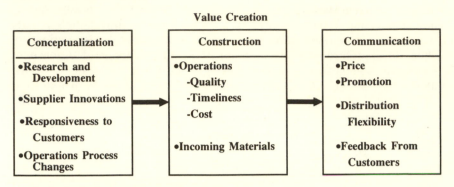

VALUE CONCEPTUALIZATION

As Figure 2.1 illustrates, the first-stage of value creation comprises the generation of ideas leading to value enhancement. Modifications to an existing product or process are a part of value conceptualization. The idea of switching from a multi-line to a single line system at a teller counter or machine would fit this value category as would the development of a reliable filmless camera. Making suppliers a part of value creation could also be initiated at this stage of the process by placing additional responsibility on them for improving the part of the product they provide. In the vacuum cleaner example cited earlier, the motor manufacturer could be coopted into developing quieter and lighter motors appropriate to the range of equipment offered by the firm. Some of the methods that could be employed to foster greater creativity in product ideas follow.

- **Self-contained Research and Development (R&D) groups**. Creativity becomes the responsibility of R&D, which is staffed by specialists in visualizing and realizing marginal or major product changes. Ever since companies such as Dupont and Bell Labs first took, and successfully traveled along, this road, setting up a separate R&D group has been a popular way to enhance value at the concept stage.

- **Extended design teams**. Given the diversity of external demands (competitors' actions, governmental regulations, and technological advances, in addition to pressing customer requirements) depending upon a single group, such as the self-contained R&D, could prove to be inadequate and dangerously myopic. An extended design team could be formed in which individuals belonging to marketing research, vendor management, legal affairs, and so on are made part of a group such as a Product Council, whose role it is to generate ideas for product improvement and bring them to fruition. The team could also be informally constituted where the channels for networking are indicated but no further attempt is made to structure the team's membership or responsibilities. We shall encounter both types of teams later (chapter 5).

- **Responsiveness to Marketing Research data**. The essence of value unquestionably lies in providing products or services that fulfill customer needs. The long term success of a firm in the marketplace is predicated upon its ability to react to, anticipate, and even create needs. While BIC was creating a need for a low cost disposable writing instrument when it introduced its nineteen-cent Crystal ball-point pen, Gilette's competing brand was a bid to react to needs of customers.[7] Walt Disney, on the other hand, was clearly anticipating the needs of millions of future visitors to his theme parks when he articulated the concept of the amusement park and combined it (Disneyworld) with futurism (EPCOT). Spectacle, efficiency and safety are combined to design the service provided. As Disney himself is reported to have said, "You know what the people want and you build it for them."[8] Marketing research inputs are invaluable in product design since they ensure that R&D's feet are firmly planted on the ground. It is less likely that a product will end up out on a limb, as a result of numerous incremental improvements, made with scant attention to the market, when Marketing and R&D are tied together.

- **Empowerment of employees**. Another way to achieve a value focus early in the value chain is by eliciting suggestions from and delegating decisions to lower level employees. Rather than adhering to a system of rigidly compartmentalized functions, where, for instance, R&D is the Designated Innovator while Operations performs the "grunt work," the excitement could be spread around. Innovation is sometimes viewed as comprising three stages—need recognition, initiation, and implementation.[9] Need recognition follows from the realization that something is wrong. Customers, employees, regulators, and other stakeholders could be the source of information about gaps in performance. Marketing Research is the organizational function generally entrusted with this function. Initiation, or the generation and testing of new ideas, is typically the purview of R&D while implementation is assigned to Operations. There is often a rigid separation between the need recognizers and initiators on the one hand and implementors of innovation on the other.

Demarcation among the three activities results not only in a slower diffusion of new product/process ideas, it also lowers the acceptance level for new ideas. Opening up need recognition and initiation possibilities to the "run of the mill" employees is also a powerful motivator and a source of numerous ideas. The separation of the phases of innovation is not only a philosophical one (creativity and experimentation versus routine and subordination) but frequently a geographical divide as well—the farther apart they are, the less likely one will influence the other. One of the reasons for locating Xerox's Research Center in Palo Alto when most of its operations were nowhere near the West Coast was surely to keep groups with apparently divergent aims far apart. This, incidentally, succeeded only too well: the Palo Alto Research Center's (PARC) development of an early version of the microcomputer was not accepted by top management partly, in this case, due to inadequate communication between the initiators and the implementers. Much of the other research work conducted at PARC (which housed perhaps some of the best scientific minds of the day) was also not implemented in part due to the separation between the initiators and implementors. One of the highly successful applications—the linking of micro-processors in a copier by adopting the configuration of the office automation system, Ethernet, that PARC had been working on—arose when the copier group in Rochester specifically contacted PARC and requested their help.[10]

Kipling penned the famous and often-quoted lines

> Oh, East is East, and West is West,
>   and never the twain shall meet[11]

which might seem to argue that entities that are so different from each other as R&D and Operations ought to stick to what each does best. Such an interpretation might, at first blush, seem to be supportive of initiators, acceptors, and implementors not straying out of their chosen areas. How-ever, just as "War is much too serious a thing to be left to military men!,"[12] value conceptualization is too important a task to be left entirely to R&D. Kipling, himself, in the lines immediately following the ones cited, cor-rected any impression he might have conveyed of advocating separation:

> But there is neither East nor West,
>   Border, nor Breed, nor Birth,
> When two strong men stand face to face,
>   though they come from the ends of the earth![13]

There is neither East nor West where R&D and Operations are con-cerned either. In fact, R&D and Operations functions should not just communicate with each other, they should infringe on each other's ter-ritories! Designing for Operations (on the part of R&D) and suggestions for product design and process (provided by Operations) can only help in better delivering value by providing a better product. Minimizing parts variations (operational variations in the case of a service), adopting mod-ular designs and the incorporation of multiple use capability are some of the guidelines Schonberger[14] recommends in designing for ease of man-ufacture or for better services. A second opinion (from other activities) is more useful when the patient (or firm) is still alive.

We shall address in subsequent chapters the issues of communication between R&D and operations (*Integration*) and the "hows" and "whys" of empowering employees and inducing them to shoulder greater respon-sibilities (*Involvement*). It is, however, no exaggeration to say that since final value often depends heavily upon how it was originally visualized, multiple inputs to the conceptualization process are to be welcomed, even if they need to be actively canvassed.

VALUE CONSTRUCTION

Webster's dictionary defines *construction* as making or forming by combining parts. In a literal sense, value construction *is* putting parts of a product or components of a service together in a total value package. For example, for a business or vacation traveler value is constructed by combining services, such as

- courteously receiving the prospective traveler's initial request for information
- quickly providing the information needed
- ticketing at a satisfactory fare and with a convenient routing
- comfortable, punctual, and safe travel conditions
- convenient arrangements for rental cars, hotel accommodations, and sightseeing, if necessary

While individual airlines would be concerned about value construction from the time of entry into the terminal to when the passenger exits, travel agents would typically delve into how value may be enhanced by the actions of value providers all along the chain. The diverse sources of customer value would therefore be of prime importance to travel agents in selecting the respective providers (e.g., transportation to and from the airport, contractual arrangements with rental car companies, hotels, and airline reservation systems).

Undoubtedly, in product as well as service businesses conceptualization is indispensable to achieving high levels of value. After all, whether the firm provides vinyl binders or fast foods, automobiles or software, visualizing how value will be provided, how this will afford the firm a competitive advantage relative to its rivals, and constantly seeking to enhance the value concept, are critical to its continued success. Just as important, however, is making the concept come to life. A painter or sculptor or musician does not touch our sensibilities merely by his or her powers of imagination. The ability to communicate these images through sight, touch or sound counts for at least as much. Actually converting an idea, therefore, into a form by which others can realize value lies at the heart of value creation.

While we reiterate that barriers should not be erected between the visualizers and constructors of value it is also beneficial to think of value construction as being concerned primarily with developing better ways of *building* value into a product, of vesting the product with the characteristics envisioned for it.

COST REDUCTION—NOT THE ONLY WAY TO CONSTRUCT VALUE

The value construction phase (often the domain of production and production-related functions such as machine operation, material handling, shop floor supervision and maintenance) has typically been expected to aspire to one overriding objective, cost minimization. Though perhaps unintended by Taylor, one of the enduring results of adopting the efficiency philosophy of Scientific Management has been a preoccupation with costs. No doubt the initial and primary thrust of Scientific Management was to increase productivity. But, since productivity is usually reckoned as Output divided by Input, attempts to raise productivity levels tended to gravitate toward maximizing outputs at a given input or minimizing inputs to achieve a certain output. While overall productivity has remained high in the United States over the past four decades (whether measured against input measures of labor hours or dollars of capital invested),[15] a continuing focus on productivity has served to make production an inward looking function, content to develop techniques to increase outputs or lower costs, or both. Exacerbating this autistic tendency, so to speak, has been the fact that Chief Executives, drawn in far greater numbers from the ranks of Marketing and Finance professionals than from a shop floor persuasion, have not encouraged production people to look at or deal with, the external environment.[16] (After all, that might be bad for efficiency!) Moreover, conventional wisdom in the discipline has also tended to concentrate on efficiency issues. For example, the transportation problem, aggregate production planning, location decisions, large batch manufacturing, and the famous—rather, infamous—EOQ (Economic Order Quantity) method for calculating order or batch sizes are all formulated to minimize costs.[17]

Are we trying to overturn this long tradition of cost-directed action that has developed in value construction? Certainly not. We are not arguing that the cost reduction perspective is wrong, merely that it does not go far enough. Surely there is more to production than cost and quantity concerns? Surely people in production cannot be expected to get excited over meeting quantity and cost targets? We consider it imperative that value construction be clearly seen to encompass not just cost and quantity, but also criteria essential to value such as quality and response time. Making quality and time-related performance an integral part of operations not only imbues the latter with a (hitherto absent) external vision, it also provides an effective way to bind value conceptualization to value construction. In other words, the rationale for value delivery articulated by R&D/Design is picked up on and given expression to by Production/Operations, without necessarily getting caught up in frenzied efforts to maximize volumes or minimize costs.

COMMUNICATING VALUE

Peter Drucker once wrote that the essence of marketing is to create a customer,[18] which includes finding more buyers for the product and/or suggesting multiple uses for it. Baking soda in refrigerators and in tooth-paste, the use of wines in cooking in addition to direct consumption, and sneakers for sporting uses and casual wear are some examples of the multiple use approach. Obviously, marketing is a critical element in com-municating value to customers. The value envisioned in the conceptual-ization stage and given substance to in the construction stage has to be communicated to the customer. Value communication includes both pro-viding access to the product and the exchange of information.

Customer access, in the case of a tangible product, includes:

- Transporting, and, if necessary, storing the product in warehouses.
- Deciding on distribution channels to be employed, transportation to distributor locations, helping with displays, and arranging for shelf space.
- Getting the product message across to customers through advertising, publicity at points of sale, providing detailed instructions for assembly and/or use, and direct contact between customer and salesperson.
- Staying in touch with customers in order to make sure that the value delivered is in fact being received. The use of surveys, focus groups, comments and complaints received in writing and at any toll-free number set up for this purpose, and statistics on repairs during the warranty period are some of the ways in which value shortcomings may be rectified and capabilities reinforced.

SERVICE FIRMS AND VALUE COMMUNICATION

One might, at first glance, be tempted to conclude that the first two (distribution-related) value communicators listed have little relevance to service businesses. After all, services, unlike goods, are typically not transported to customers. The latter often have to travel to avail them-selves of services—as in the case of restaurants, video parlors, law offices, retail establishments, grocery stores, educational institutions, hotels, and so on. But even though services have little portability, physical access is still a significant factor in value. For instance, the convenience store industry was the fastest growing segment of the retailing industry in the 1980s, with sales quadrupling in the period 1978 to 1988,[19] primarily due to the time-value they provide customers due to the stores' locations (being nearer residential neighborhoods than grocery stores generally are). Location is a similarly potent source of value in the case of most of the other services mentioned above, too. Some firms that are unable to mul-tiply their customer service outlets (due to the prohibitive expense in-volved) take the franchising route, or bring the service to the customer, as in the case of Federal Express, and UPS pickup and delivery service for overnight mail and parcels, respectively. Home shopping and library services attempt to overcome the "access barrier" to communicating value. Home banking has tremendous potential in this regard too.

Exchange of information with customers can also differ markedly depending on whether the firm is a product or service business. Promotion of services can follow traditional lines. Advertising, for instance, is commonplace for all types of services while point-of-sale publicity (hairdressers suggesting alternative styling, auto mechanics who offer discounted rates to customers who have come to them for preventive maintenance, temptingly displayed desserts at your favorite restaurant, etc.) also often follows a parallel track to retailers' efforts, with which most of us are familiar, to encourage impulse buying.

In the fourth aspect of value communication, direct two-way information transfer between customer and firm, service businesses enjoy an edge, because the customer is *in* the system. Their needs are therefore not remote and to be inferred but right here and given expression to. The likelihood of a firm being able to match customer needs exactly is correspondingly higher, provided the firm can customize its services. An interactive relationship with customers often develops in many service arenas *while the service is being rendered*. The customer could explain his/her needs—air travel routing with stopover, variations on a dinner order, advice from a securities analyst—and often receive service in real time. Again feedback could also be instant, resulting in high communicated value, provided responsiveness, flexibility, and learning ability are incorporated into the system.

Firms that have staked their success on standardized services *must* offer customers enough to replace personalized attention. Lower prices as in the case of routinized legal counsel, a combination of prices and quality/cleanliness provided by fast food firms like McDonald's, and speed of service offered by quick oil change specialists are some of the compensatory benefits customers are often willing to settle for.

Paul Hawken is right on the money when he asserts that every product should be reduced to its essence. The essence is providing a service, since customers generally are interested not in the product itself but rather what it can do for them.[20] To illustrate: if a revolutionary method of indoor cleaning were to be made available, (provided it met the requirements of effective cleaning, quietness, mobility, etc.) the best conceived, constructed, and communicated vacuum cleaner in the world would probably come off second best. Similarly, if a more effective and convenient method of joining metals together were to be invented, arc welding would likely become an anachronism. (Plasma arc and inert gas welding, while extremely beneficial in specific applications, are no more than minor ripples in the relatively unchanging development of the welding industry over the past sixty years.)

Products and services are therefore undoubtedly similar as far as the "bottom line" of need satisfaction is concerned. However, another essential distinction separates them further. Typically, customers do not use products in the presence of their vendors, unlike services in which the customer or user is an integral part of the operations. The mingling of value construction and communication that occurs in businesses in which the customer enters the system is worth striving toward in manufacturing firms as well. Since operations personnel are familiar with the caliber of product value built in to the product/service, who better to communicate value to customers and receive feedback than those who installed the value in the first place? While we do not advocate the abolition of Marketing Departments everywhere, the establishment of direct links between producers and buyers of a product facilitates not only quick, accurate feedback and responsiveness to market needs but also provides operations personnel a higher purpose (value enhancement) stimulated by direct contact with the beneficiary of this value, the customer.

BRINGING THE Cs TOGETHER

In sum, the 3Cs comprise a *unified* process by which product value is *actively* pursued and is *constantly* being created. It is imperative that the process be unified since ideas for value creation have to be adequately matched by the actual value achieved and passed on to customers. Kodak's revolutionary idea for a disc camera was not accompanied by an acceptable constructed value.[21] Similarly Polaroid's instant movie system, Polavision, when introduced, fell short in the value communication stage, particularly in dealing with initial feedback regarding picture quality.[22] While it is therefore critical that each C be constantly worked at in order to enhance value, a balance among the Cs has to be maintained. This may even require value at one or more stages be reduced. For example, if a firm's promotional efforts result in an image that the product is unable to match—an electric shaver that is neither smooth nor comfortable in its performance or a portable cassette player with tinny reproduction—the firm would be well advised to scale back on its communication strategy and/or enhance conceptualized/constructed value to avoid abnormally high expectations and a collective customer turn-off. On the other hand, not communicating the value built into the product would result in foregoing business due to potential customers not being aware of the product's true capabilities. Not only is a value balance among the 3Cs to be continuously monitored, the balance between them and external elements is also a matter of utmost concern.

Figure 2.2 depicts the three *interfaces* at which a value balance is to be achieved. These occur

- among the 3Cs;
- between each of the Cs and their external environments;
- within each of the Cs.

Figure 2.2
Interfaces Among, Within, and Outside the 3Cs

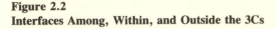

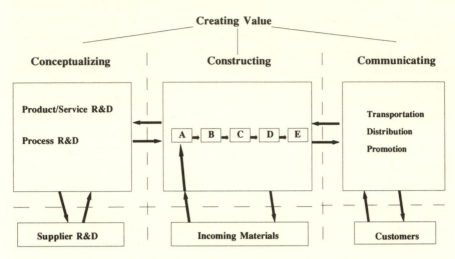

We have earlier dealt with the interface among the Cs (and shall continue the discussion later in chapter 5). Attaining a value balance with vendors (who, for the sake of illustration are the only external elements, apart from customers, shown in Figure 2.2) calls for the firm and its vendors to be on the same wavelength. If a firm seeks to succeed as a cost leader, it should have suppliers with the same drive; if a firm prides itself on flexibility of product styling and volumes, so should its suppliers; if a company is obsessed with quality, its suppliers should be similarly preoccupied. An imbalance in any of the dimensions of value between a firm and its vendors could result in an overall diminution of value.

The activities within each of the 3Cs also need to be coordinated to achieve a leveling of value. Again, for purpose of illustration, one of the Cs (constructing) has been selected to demonstrate the notion of balance. Let us assume that incoming materials are processed at operations A, B, C, D and E which represent Material Handling, Cutting and Welding, Machining, Painting, and Assembly (using parts received from vendors as well as parts processed internally), respectively. Value of the finished product is intimately related to each of these operations. Regardless of how well the painting is performed, if the welding has been done haphazardly or the machining is not carried out as specified, value constructed into the product is eroded. Even an activity such as material handling can contribute to or detract from value depending on its timeliness, responsiveness to schedule changes, and so on. (We explore the achievement of value balance within each stage of the value creation process in greater detail in chapter 4.)

THE MANY FACES OF VALUE:
COMPONENTS AND CAPABILITIES

We have tried, thus far, to give fuller substance and meaning to value creation in the case of both products and services. After reviewing value analysis and Porter's value chain, we laid out a model to maximize value delivered. Let us now take a step back and, in light of our 3C model, rediscover, if you will, the important components of value that firms may selectively deploy to satisfy customer needs, outdo competitors, and function in harmony with their external environment. Among the important components of value (see Figure 2.3) are product/service *functionality* (or performing the use for which it is intended), *quality* (which includes reliability or repeated trouble free operation, durability, safety, and, unless disposable, ease of maintenance) and *appearance*. The bars alongside these properties indicate the role played by each of the 3Cs in achieving these three value dimensions. For all three components, functionality, quality, and appearance, the three Cs are equally important. Unless designed into a product, quality is just not attainable at the construction stage. Quality not conceived or constructed cannot be communicated for fear of the customer backlash we talked about earlier. (For a closer look at quality see *Time for Quality* in chapter 9.) This total dependence on *each* stage, C1, C2 and C3, applies not only to every aspect of quality but also by extension to functionality and appearance/styling. In the case of services, such as hairdressers, airlines, or fast food restaurants, appearance refers not so much to the tangible offering—such as a hamburger—but to the accoutrements of the service itself, the locality, the external and internal decor, the comfort of the waiting areas, and so on. For the first three components of value, therefore, the 3Cs are of considerable significance and need to be coordinated—hence the continuous bars in Figure 2.3. (This reasoning applies to the next three factors and the continuous bars therefore appear next to environmental concerns, costs, and flexibility as well.)

Environmental issues have, over the past few years, increasingly aroused our concern both as members of the public and as consumers. To the voice of the former, one can be assured policymakers have been and will continue listening; and consumers make a potent force for change. Whether the issue be global warming as a result of burning fossil fuels or accelerated air, land and water pollution caused by producers and consumers alike, or opposition to the use of animal extracts for perfumes and colognes, the effect is, and will probably continue to be, a preference for products which are environmentally neutral (that is, do not have any impact on the environment). How is environmental neutrality related to product value? Very simply, consumers are beginning to factor into the price of a product, the long term environmental impact associated with

Figure 2.3
Value Components and Capabilities

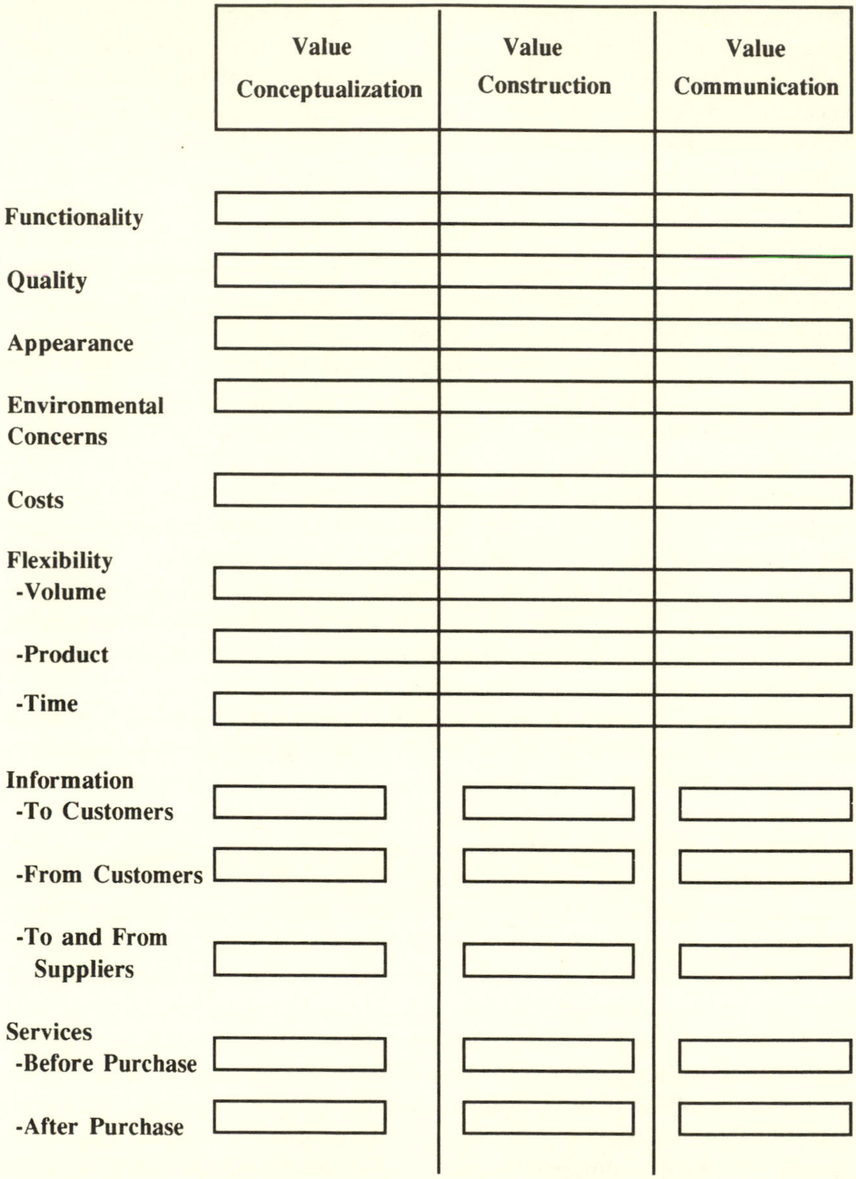

	Value Conceptualization	Value Construction	Value Communication
Functionality			
Quality			
Appearance			
Environmental Concerns			
Costs			
Flexibility -Volume			
-Product			
-Time			
Information -To Customers			
-From Customers			
-To and From Suppliers			
Services -Before Purchase			
-After Purchase			

it. True, the costs thus estimated by consumers are likely to be based more on impressions than on precise figures but their impact will nonetheless be very real.[23] Firms whose products and/or production methods damage, or have the potential to damage, the environment will benefit from carefully designing and building their products to reduce what is presently a *virtual* cost, and by telling consumers about their achievement. Though it does not appear that consumers will forgo products and services they have grown accustomed to like refrigerants, disposable diapers and personal transportation, a marked preference for products that strive toward environmental neutrality is discernible. The trend toward recycling in the paper (grocery bags, newsprint) and container (metal cans, bottles) industries, the increasing popularity of "biodegradable" materials (household chemicals, garbage bags), and a refusal to patronize products perceived as environmentally negative (tuna caught in fishing grounds that abound in dolphin), indicates the value implications of environmental neutrality and the need for firms to take a holistic approach to it.

Flexibility, in a physical sense, is the ability to take various shapes and forms, while mentally it denotes resilience, a capacity to adapt to change. Value is created through flexibility[24] if the organization is capable of

- delivering the product/service in the variety needed—cars made to individual preferences, varied fare in restaurants, grocery stores willing to provide items on request;
- dealing with variations in the quantity ordered—pump manufacturers who can fill orders for ten pumps or one thousand pumps (almost) equally well; university departments that can change teaching methodology to suit fluctuating class sizes and students' abilities;
- giving customers both the above without any delays—waiting less than a week for a customized new car, eliminating the "float" between check-in and check-out times at most hotels.

Flexibility as a means of delivering value can be achieved best through coordination between the concept and construction of value. (Obviously, where it is an important component of value, it is also necessary to effectively communicate this aspect of a firm's contribution to value.)

Overall cost is an inseparable part of all the value activities. The design affects the materials and process used (and vice versa) while the message of value conveyed to customers has to be tailored to the value constructed. Cost reduction efforts, therefore, should not focus exclusively on any one part of the value process. Attempts to slash manufacturing costs, for example, without considering the need to modify product design, outsourced material, quality standards, and promotional effort could well result in a poorly made product with a superior image! Again, the costs that concern us here are not just the obvious ones—direct materials and labor, and indirect/allocated costs, but also hidden costs such as those incurred in rework, warranty claims, redesign (of the product and/or process), tarnished reputation and lost orders, etc. If the product derives its value primarily from its low price, it may be immune to these hidden costs if customers expect little beside flexibility from the product. Customer expectations may be suitably lowered through communication: for example, the preceding costs may not apply in the case of disposables.[25] For durables, life cycle costing from the viewpoint of consumers could be performed to determine the total cost to them over the life of the product in purchasing a product. While we do not address life-cycle costing further in this book, we try to come to grips with the rather complex topic of costing later (chapter 9).

Information to and from customers as shown in Figure 2.3 is also served by all 3Cs. However, the separation among the stages of the process indicates that information to customers may be provided directly by R&D, Operations, and Marketing—and vice versa. That is, while functionality, quality and appearance must be achieved, enhanced, and delivered in a unified *flow* of activities within the firm, the dissemination of information/advice and the soliciting of feedback is not the sole preserve of any one function. Of course, the information given or received needs to be shared internally (see chapter 5).

Services rendered before purchase of the product are typically provided at the communication phase for consumer goods while all 3Cs are involved in the case of industrial goods, particularly customized ones. For services after purchase, all three phases could be involved depending on the severity of the problem—major, widespread failures could involve the entire organization while an isolated incident of damages in transit may be dealt with by the relevant department.

APPLYING THE COMPONENT-CAPABILITY CHART

We close this chapter with a brief illustration of how the 3C framework may be applied to enhance value and gain an edge over one's competitors. Using the framework developed earlier, the components of value felt to be important to customers are marked X, as in Figure 2.4. Customer surveys provide the basis for determining the most important aspects of value. Next, the firm's ability to meet customer needs in regard to each of the 3Cs is evaluated. For example, since functionality is a critical constituent of value, to what extent do the Cs measure up to the task? In this case, value appears to be successfully constructed into the product but is not being effectively transmitted.

The firm's performance in regard to environmental concerns appears to be disappointing while in the cost department, value construction and communication appear to be slightly more efficient than the conceptual-

Figure 2.4
Implementing the Component-Capability Technique

	Value Conceptualization	Value Construction	Value Communication
Functionality*	X	X	X
Quality*	X	X	X
Appearance	X	X	X
Environmental Concerns	X	X	X
Costs*	X	X	X
Flexibility			
-Volume		X	X
-Product		X	X
-Time		X	
Information			
-To Customers			X
-From Customers			X
-To and From Suppliers	X	X	
Services			
-Before Purchase			X
-After Purchase*			X

ization stage. As far as volume flexibility goes, the firm seems to be deficient in production although it seems to have conveyed the opposite impression to its customers. Exactly the reverse seems to have happened in product flexibility—customers don't know of the company's ability to provide a variety of products—though the response seems to occur after a considerable time lag (low time flexibility).

Areas in which the firm's value performance is deficient need to be targeted for improvement, focusing resources where most effective. Designing for producibility so as to achieve a cost reduction through a coordinated effort between R&D and manufacturing; analyzing and addressing the environmental impact of the firm's product, processes and philosophy, and reducing set up times to improve volume flexibility are some of the actions that suggest themselves. Customer inputs would be invaluable in assessing, at the very least, how capably the firm meets their important needs. Since customers might not want to, or have enough information to, review the firm's performance on each of the Cs, this would be conducted internally, possibly by a Product Value Council (or some such group), if one has already been constituted as part of the extended design team mentioned earlier, or by forming such a team specifically to help the firm become more aware of and competitive in delivering the best value to its customers.

Refinements of the component-capability matrix are certainly possible. One extension would be to assign weights to each of the value components to indicate their relative importance. Environmental concerns, for instance, would merit greater significance at the C2 stage of the value chain in the paper industry than in, say, the small appliance business. And within the paper industry, quality would generally rate higher than, say, volume flexibility. Other value components may need to be enumerated depending on the industry. In the airline industry, for instance, safety and punctuality would merit attention as distinct factors. Also, instead of X marks, ratings on a scale of 1 to 10 could be used to provide a more precise picture of the firm's capability in the important value components. Similar value component-capability charts could be drawn up for each of the major competitors to provide an assessment of the firm's value-deficiencies and the nature of corrective action needed. In a nutshell, the component-capability technique brings a value focus to bear in better serving customers and achieves an input-output analysis of the firm's value stance, by weighing the (output) needs of customers against the (input) 3C levels that can be pressed into service. The matching of the components and capabilities of value is a critical way to determine what a firm needs to do to improve its competitive position. (Capabilities, incidentally, can exist or be lacking at *any* stage of the value chain and obviously encompass a wide range of activities.) In that sense they are, as Stalk, Evans, and Shulman[26] point out, a much broader and more versatile notion than that of core competency which was typically restricted to technical and production competence. The specific actions taken to enhance value must, of course, be viewed against the backdrop of the firm's overall strategy. We now turn our attention to what strategy means in a value framework.

NOTES

1. In emphasizing the pleasure individuals and groups derived from a particular action (like buying a product), Bentham's perspective corresponded more closely to the modern perspective on value than did the more popular cost- and labor-based theories of value. See Catlin's *The Progress of Economics* (New York: Bookman, 1962), pp. 145–48 for a fuller evaluation.

2. Lawrence Miles, *Techniques of Value Analysis and Value Engineering* (New York: McGraw-Hill, 1961).

3. Carlos Fallon, *Value Analysis to Improve Productivity* (New York: Wiley-Interscience, 1971). Fallon's overview of the discipline is an excellent one notwithstanding his forays into mythology and his references to "the little woman."

4. Value analysis, in its incarnation as value engineering, progressively developed a preoccupation with cost reduction, a preoccupation that often marginalizes the customer. Glimmers of such an emphasis are evident in Miles's work. In fact, years later Richard Schonberger (*Japanese Manufacturing Techniques* (New York: The Free Press, 1982)) refers to Value Analysis primarily in terms of its cost reduction focus.

5. Michael Porter, *Competitive Strategy: Techniques for Analyzing Industries and Competitors* (New York: Free Press, 1980).

6. Michael Porter, *Competitive Advantage* (New York: The Free Press, 1985).

7. While BIC no doubt rejuvenated the anemic writing instrument market in the early 1960s, Gilette was quick to respond to the customer expectations that BIC had stimulated. Gilette's thirty-nine cent retractable, twenty-nine cent fineline porous point and nineteen cent non-retractable pens were introduced to take advantage of the booming low-price end that BIC successfully tapped into. See "BIC Pen Corporation (A)" in Roland Christensen, et al., *Policy Formulation and Administration* (Homewood, IL: Irwin, 9th ed., 1985), p. 292.

8. Ron Zemke with Dick Schaaf, *The Service Edge* (New York: Penguin, 1990), p. 530.

9. See Daniel Robey's *Designing Organizations* (Homewood, IL: Irwin, 2nd ed., 1986), pp. 467–69.

10. Gary Jacobson and John Hillkirk, *Xerox: American Samurai* (New York: Collier, 1987), pp. 256–60.

11. Rudyard Kipling "The Ballad of East and West," *Collected Verse of Rudyard Kipling* (New York: Doubleday, Page & Company, 1916), p. 136.

12. Attributed to the French statesman Talleyrand though the lines were also spoken by Clemenceau without acknowledgement.

13. Rudyard Kipling. "The Ballad of East and West." *Collected Verse of Rudyard Kipling* (New York: Doubleday, Page & Company, 1916) p. 136.

14. Richard Schonberger, *Building a Chain of Customers* (New York: The Free Press, 1990).

15. Productivity measured as output per hour has climbed continuously since 1960. The rate of increase has eased off somewhat but productivity is *not* declining (*Statistical Abstract of the United States*, Washington, D.C.: U.S. Bureau of the Census, 1990, p. 406). While the fact that productivity has risen faster in Japan has, in effect, placed many U.S. firms at a disadvantage, the introspective nature of a preoccupation with productivity hasn't helped either.

16. Only 9% of the 1000 CEOs surveyed by *Business Week* (November 25, 1991, pp. 174–90) had a production/operations background and even among those some had a dual background. Nearly half the surveyed sample had taken the Finance/Accounting and Marketing paths.

17. Textbooks are generally a reliable barometer of accepted knowledge in any discipline and cost minimization appears to be the most important criterion in that sense. See, for example, Everett Adam and Ronald Ebert's *Production and Operations Management* (Englewood Cliffs, NJ: Prentice Hall, 5th Ed., 1992).

18. Peter Drucker, *An Introductory View of Management* (New York: Harper's College Press, 1977), p. 88.

19. Jeffrey Bracker, *Circle K Corporation*, in John Montanari, Cyril Morgan, and Jeffrey Bracker, *Strategic Management* (Chicago: The Dryden Press, 1990), p. 589.

20. Paul Hawken, *Growing A Business* (New York: Simon & Schuster, 1987), p. 73.

21. Not only were the negatives so small that they needed to be greatly enlarged but the pictures themselves were relatively grainy as well. See Seth Lubose, "Aim, Focus and Shoot," *Forbes*, 26 November 1990, p. 67.

22. The picture was grainy and could only be seen clearly if positioned directly in front of the screen. Moreover, the camera's bright light tended to annoy small children. The lack of sound clearly didn't help either. While Polaroid's value conceptualization could be apportioned part of the blame, the product was a revolutionary one and needed careful two-way communication with customers to see it through its troubled infancy. (Peter Bernstein, "Polaroid Struggles to Get Back in Focus," in Alan Rowe, Richard Mason and Karl Dickel, *Strategic Management & Business Policy*, Reading, MA: Addison-Wesley, 1986).

23. Paper companies, 60% of whose output ends up in landfills, are actively engaged in finding ways to use less material—in disposable diapers and in liner-board for packaging, improved conservation, composting possibilities for diapers, and recycling for an increasing range of papers. An important part of the "greening" is consumer preference (*Standard and Poor Industry Surveys*, February 21, 1991, pp. 77–78.) Consumer pressure has most recently been exerted on Mc-Donald's (to change from plastic to paper packaging), disposable diaper manufactures, and on cosmetics makers (for natural cosmetics and to use refillable containers.) See Jacqueline Scerbonski, "Consumers and the Environment: A Focus on Five Products," *Journal of Business Strategy*, September/October 1991, pp. 44–48.

24. The dimensions of flexibility in terms of volume, product and time, are derived from Suresh Kotha and Daniel Orne's framework outlined in "Generic

Manufacturing Strategies: A Conceptual Synthesis," *Strategic Management Journal*, 1989, *10*, pp. 211–31.

25. Milind Lele ("How Service Needs Influence Product Strategy," *Sloan Management Review*, Fall 1986, pp. 63–70) offers a framework juxtaposing high and low extremes of fixed and variable costs of product failure against each other. Disposable products typically are associated with low fixed as well as low variable costs resulting from product failure.

26. George Stalk, Philip Evans, and Lawrence Shulman, "Competing on Capabilities: The New Rules of Corporate Strategy," *Harvard Business Review*, March-April 1992, pp. 57–69.

3

A STRATEGY AND VISION OF VALUE

DELIVERING VALUE TO CUSTOMERS—AND TO EVERYONE ELSE

Many of our readers are probably more than a little nonplussed and perhaps uncomfortable with our almost exclusive focus on value delivered to customers. Is customer value the sole rationale for a firm's existence? Granted, customers are important and satisfying their needs through a variety of means (including the 3Cs) is indispensable for a firm's survival and success. But if providing top value is necessary, is it also sufficient? After all, firms have owners (shareholders), employees, regulatory agencies, and other vital constituencies to satisfy, in addition to customers.

Does that mean that, in addition to customer value, shareholder value, employee value, governmental value, and a range of assorted value concerns need to be constantly monitored? If so, we could become like the (no doubt apocryphal) painters of the Golden Gate Bridge in San Francisco. Just as soon as they've completed painting the bridge, they have to start all over again at the other end! We would have to go from one value angle to another and by the time we reach the last one we'd have to start all over again with customer value, since tinkering with components of shareholder or employee value, inevitably would affect customer value (e.g., reducing the scale of after-sale services could reduce costs and increase profits, thus increasing shareholder value while diminishing customer value; increasing wages could increase employee value, raising prices and diminishing customer value, and so on).

If we treat the different types of value as being irreconcilable, we are indeed faced with a Gordian knot. If, on the other hand, we see the benefits that customers, shareholders, employees and others reap as flowing from the same "reservoir of value" no dilemma exists. The Gordian knot is neatly sliced in two, as Alexander did over two thousand years ago. While conflicts can undoubtedly arise, for instance, between customers' needs and those of shareholders, *in the long run*, shareholders' needs are best fulfilled by satisfying customers' requirements. Without a market for its product or service, a firm has no reason to exist; a firm that continues to deliver the worth and cost combination that customers need will inevitably be able to maximize shareholder wealth as well.

Lincoln Electric has been immensely successful in the arc welding industry. Established in 1906, it has become a world market share leader, fending off assaults from domestic and foreign rivals. James Lincoln, who was its CEO for over fifty years and molded the firm to his philosophy, firmly believed that the customer's interests came first and employees were next in importance. He felt shareholders were relatively unimportant and would automatically be taken care of if customers and employees were.[1] We do not discount shareholders' importance as much as James Lincoln did (his firm was, and has increasingly become, largely family- and employee-owned). On the other hand, we do feel that by striving toward customer value *continuously*, a firm will be able to fulfill its obligation to all its various constituents eventually, if not immediately. For instance as William Copulsky[2] points out, sustainable value flows from the "top line" of sales and customer value to the "bottom line" of profit. Merck has, through much of its history, exemplified this stance. Not by coincidence has it been among the most successful firms in the world pharmaceutical industry.

However, Keynes's admonition about our being dead in the long run is worth keeping in mind, particularly since patience isn't a strong suit as far as shareholders and even employees are concerned. An obsession with customer value may not be given time to succeed by these, and perhaps other, important constituents. The situation parallels that of a baseball team carefully cultivating a crop of young pitchers in its farm system. In the long run, the pitching staff might well carry the team to a championship. In the short run, however, fans could get disillusioned and key players might "test the market" and switch to a team that can win in the near future, both developments possibly leading to turnover in the managerial and administrative positions. As in baseball, so in business: short term concerns could jeopardize long term interests. What's needed, in addition to a single-minded pursuit of value, is an overall strategy of value, a broad vision and articulation of how a firm will, while pursuing constantly rising customer value, simultaneously meet the expectations of its other stakeholders.

STRATEGY: MILITARY AND SPORTS METAPHORS

Strategy, as we observed in chapter 1, is an area of management decision making linking the organization to its external environment. It is a field that has been extensively studied, mainly due to its absorbing interest to Chief Executives and to others in central management. In military matters, strategy has been around for many years—Caesar's strategy for driving a wedge of his infantry through enemy ranks, Rommel's "pincer" strategy, and the successful British "search and destroy" strategy used to counter the Communist insurgency in (then) Malaya illustrate the military notion of strategy being the means employed to achieve a goal. The strategy adopted in warfare may be in place for a long period of time—as was the Allied strategy to deny the German forces access to fuel supplies as well as the painstaking and costly British effort in Malaya—or it may be a short term affair. Examples of the latter include the amphibious landings at Normandy that led to victory in Europe, the Israeli "surgical" preemptive strikes which decimated the Egyptian air force in 1967, and, more recently, the successful air-softening, land-hammering strategy pursued by the Allied coalition in the war with Iraq. (Shorter term strategies in the military context are generally referred to as tactics.)

Strategy is also a popular concept and term in sporting circles. A baseball team, for example, may combine speed around the bases and strong starting pitching with a strategy of stringing hits and stolen bases together into runs, while holding the opposition to fewer runs. (The St. Louis Cardinals have tended to exemplify such an approach.) Another team might prefer (as the New York Yankees have often seemed to) to go out and get the best talent available in an attempt to maximize their returns in the course of a year. In football, the San Francisco 49ers, whose playoff exploits are fast becoming legendary, have managed to combine a rugged and quick-moving defense with a flexible, primarily aerial offense. During the 1980s, the New York Giants and the Chicago Bears, on the other hand, based their strategy on a defense that is not only stingy but also creates opportunities (such as good field position) to be exploited by highly conservative offenses. Effective strategies are evident, though not as complicated as those in football, in individual sports too. Borg's high percentage play while anchored at the baseline revolutionized tennis although McEnroe did manage on occasion to pierce Borg's armor with crisp volleying and superb touch.

The use of military and sports metaphors is extraordinarily apt in business strategy, except that military and sports strategies are almost obsessively directed to getting the better of the enemy and opponents respectively. While military means often serve political ends and sports teams are paid to entertain, success is generally measured by a general's or coach's ability to defeat the opposition. Of course, competition is also a fact of life in the market place for goods and services (if we ignore monopolies). But competition is not the *reason* for a firm's existence, the customer is. Though few firms relish or actively seek competition, it is not necessarily a deterrent to success. Large, well-established rivals may help increase demand for a product, while the very need for survival could hone the skills of those left in the fray. Moreover, many highly competitive industries support a range of firms that are successful according to their own yardsticks, much as a jungle, grassland, or field can support many competing forms of life. Business is, therefore, not always a zero-sum game where one firm's gain is another's loss. Not only can a firm's success create demand for a product (as Apple did for microcomputers and Xerox did for copiers) or whet it (Texas Instruments for hand-held calculators and BIC for low-price pens), thereby increasing each firm's sales potential, it is possible, even commonplace, for companies to occupy various niches. General Motors and Toyota share the automobile industry with BMW and Mercedes Benz. However, the latter pair of firms do not go head-to-head with the former pair. Differences in product type and market segments targeted dictate that the components of customer value will also vary. The same obviously also applies to differences across the range of models offered by Toyota or General Motors. Each division has a distinct notion of how value may be created using the 3Cs. By the same token, Motel 6 is not engaged in direct competition with the Hilton group of hotels. Though technically in the same industry, each firm has quite distinct approaches to the creation of value. And yet, Toyota, GM, BMW, Volvo, Hilton, and Motel 6 have survived and achieved a fair degree of success (GM's recent problems notwithstanding). In fact, over a period of time, organizations may come to depend upon the activities on which their past strategies were based to be the driving force for their strategies of the future. Melcher, Arogyaswamy and Gartrell[3] identify operations (including technology), marketing and finance as the three activities that can and do guide and direct a firm's strategies. They term them "leading strategies" since they, in effect, lead a firm to continually build upon its successful value-maximizing strategies be they in new products or regions, for new customers or with new technologies.

There are no standard, surefire strategies for success. Firms target certain value components and seek to deliver them through an appropriate combination of the 3Cs. Of course, the basis of value delivery could change over time and even vary at the same point in time at different locations. Porter's generic strategies (which we referred to earlier in connection with his insights on competitive advantage and product value) of cost leadership, differentiation and focus may be (and often are) adopted by competitors in any given industry. Cost leadership (achieving the lowest cost position) is obviously not within every firm's ability to strive toward and attain. In fact, not more than one or two firms in any industry can provide value arising predominately from cost-effective operations. By far the majority of firms succeed through the adoption of one of the other two strategies. Even in the case of so-called commodities, companies strive to increase other dimensions of value provided to consumers rather than seeking just to compete on a cost basis. Mobil and Exxon are among the petroleum firms that attempt to position their gasoline as being superior in quality (anti-clog, non-freeze, etc.), in addition to which their service stations stock an increasing array of convenience items. Mercedes Benz focuses on the prestige and image-conscious end of the automobile market, while Toyota's manufacturing efficiency gives it a cost and quality springboard which is reinforced by its marketing wizardry. Combinations of these strategies are also possible, as when instant oil change (focus) specialists seek to establish a low-cost position due to the high volume of business generated by a timely response to customer's minor automobile service needs.

STRATEGIES TO SHARE VALUE

The generic strategies make the assumption that the company intends to persist in a concentration mode, that is, limit its horizons to a single product/service or achieve a predominant portion of its sales in one industry. Few large or medium size firms confine their product horizons. Typically it is small businesses that start with such a focus. With success and growth generally comes a desire to reduce dependence on any one product/market. Diversified firms have more stable sales and earnings. Risk reduction unquestionably helps enhance shareholder value.[4] Most firms have historically been uncomfortable about "sticking to their knitting" lest they knit a sweater that's no longer in style or that someone else can make at half the price (perhaps with a machine they've just invented). The reluctance to place all one's eggs in one basket is quite understandable since it could result in binding the company's future to just one product, a product that might be rendered obsolete or substituted by alternate products. Also, competitors could prove to be more competent at value creation by identifying the desired components of value more accurately or delivering them more effectively. Continuous value enhancement in a single product area is certainly laudable, but prudence dictates that other stakeholders' needs (shareholders, employees, creditors, and suppliers, for instance) also be taken into consideration. Diversification is an important strategy in assuring that the needs of a variety of stakeholders are given careful enough attention to merit their strong approval. Moreover, expanding the product and market scope of the firm widens its spectrum of customers, providing even more opportunities for delivering value in completely novel ways. Much of the rest of this chapter, therefore, addresses the various faces of diversification from the value perspective.

Diversification has, of late, come under fire for being the cause of many firms' declining ability to compete with domestic and foreign rivals. It is, however, conglomerate diversification that distracts a firm from its mission of value. When a firm has numerous product and service offerings, few of which have any relationship to each other, the objective becomes to maximize shareholder value (stock price and/or dividend). Commitment to a product line or to its customers is conspicuously *absent* at the corporate level.[5] Conglomerates not only keep their eggs in different baskets, they often forget where their baskets are! On the other hand, concentrically diversified firms—General Electric, Matsushita, Procter and Gamble, IBM, and Honda, to name a few—seek new product or market opportunities with a view to continuing their prior success in value creation. IBM, for example, has excelled at providing engineering, installation, maintenance and other types of services to customers. This source of value has been consciously developed and maximized regardless of whether the product be a mainframe computer, a microcomputer or peripheral equipment.[6] Procter and Gamble, whether in consumer nondurables or in its more recent food/pharmaceutical ventures has, undoubtedly, always been known for its clear conceptualization and faultless construction of value. However, its ability to unerringly communicate the value residing in its products—through timely and well-planned distribution, superb promotion, and rapid assimilation of customer comments—is what enables P & G to maximize value in its erstwhile as well as new product areas.[7]

A BIOLOGICAL ANALOGY

Diversification into concentric or related areas to deliver value in new and numerous ways is not uncommon in the natural world. Animal species often successfully survive changes in their environments through *adaptation* and *variation*. Adaptation occurs over many generations and typically involves the development of characteristics that increase the likelihood of survival. Coloration that enables prey such as rabbits and birds to blend in with their surroundings in order to escape detection by potential predators is a common phenomenon. Species of fish and eels that live at great depths where little light penetrates have developed sensory capabilities which are not dependent on sight. Similarly those individuals in any species that become even a little superior to their peers in speed, strength, or reach, are more likely to survive and reproduce. When some of these improvements increase the ability of a species to survive, the variations become permanent features as in the case of monkeys with prehensile tails, the membrane that enables certain species of squirrels to fly, and so on. Nature's way of dealing with a hostile environment appears to lie in acquiring features that enable successful continuance of the species and/or the emergence of species and sub-species (diversification) with superior survival capabilities.[8]

Corporations could, within reason, reap the benefits of emulating nature. Pursuing a single-minded strategy of delivering and enhancing value to customers in a given product through continuous and rapid adaptation to customer needs could prove successful if the external environment does not turn nasty. The extreme uncertainty that prevails in many business environments and the possibility of rapid, unforeseeable change makes diversification, the equivalent of variation, an attractive course of action. We are rather wary of overextending the natural science analogy. After all, in business we often *create* parts of our environment, customers being an example, which is rare in the ecological context. In fact, the concept of a customer, or the lack thereof, clouds many analogies of business to the natural sciences unless one views the customer as our entire planet, for whose overall benefit all species exist and compete. However, as long as firms stay within the confines of an environment, part or all of which is familiar to them, providing product variations and responding to changing demands, the ecological model appears to be a fairly sound parallel.

VALUE SHARING—ACQUISITION AND INTERNAL DEVELOPMENT

Diversification itself can be accomplished either internally or through an alliance. Many of P & G's product introductions are the result of its search for better ways to serve customer needs. This applies both to its "proliferation" strategy in which "New and Improved" products supplant or compete with the "traditional" ones as well as to its "Innovation" strategy of seeking entirely new products like Simplesse, the fat substitute. P & G has also, on the other hand, adopted an alliance strategy by acquiring Vicks, the British pharmaceutical firm. Acquisition is not an evolutionary approach, and is often preferred when a particular value creation mode is difficult to activate (as was Vicks's reputation and distribution access) quickly enough to suit the firm's needs. Ideally, acquisition should be undertaken not just to accelerate sales or asset growth but primarily to facilitate the firm's value mission. That is, acquisition as a means of diversification is most desirable not only when it adds to sales and increases market share but also when it provides ways to successfully replicate value creation methods in new product/service areas and incorporate new methodologies of value into existing products. Figure 3.1 illustrates the two forms of value exchange that are possible. The 3Cs are represented as C_1, C_2, and C_3 and the shaded vertical bars indicate the

Figure 3.1
Value Sharing Between Existing and New Products

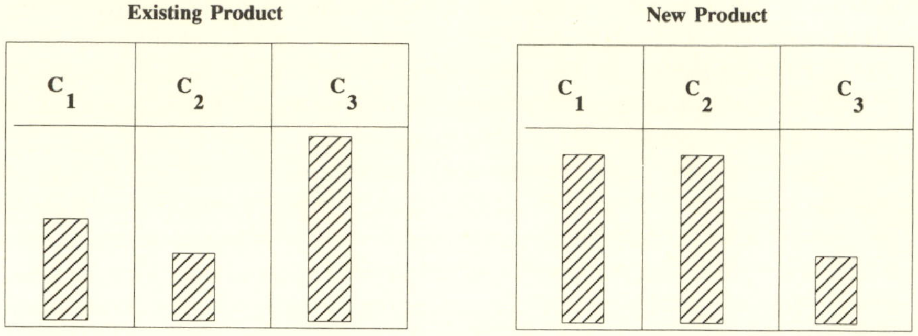

Existing Product   New Product

capabilities possessed by the firm in each value component. In this instance, the new (acquired) business offers skills in R&D and Manufacturing to the present business while the latter could seek to share some of its Value Communication capabilities with the recent acquisition. Such an approach could be used not only to maximize value-sharing after acquisition but also to evaluate possible acquisition candidates.

Even when a firm seeks to diversify through internal development of new product and/or market areas value may be transferred in both these ways. For example, Campbell's diversification efforts were initially almost completely internally driven.[9] Each new product introduced by the firm had access, wherever necessary, to Campbell's dedicated sources of supply, motivated retailers, and the company's sterling reputation. Those elements of the 3Cs that helped Campbell's succeed were pressed into action to do the same for new products. Conversely, any value focus successfully applied in an extension product generally also benefitted the original lines (e.g., frozen and dehydrated food technology, developed for other product areas, being employed to produce single desserts and dry soups respectively). (Figure 3.1 may be applied to good effect in this context as well.) In fact, part of Campbell's recent problems and the ouster of its CEO McGovern in 1989 may be attributed to the spate of acquisitions on which the firm embarked in the 1980s. The rate of aggregation of new products exceeded the value absorption capabilities of the firm.

The process of transferring the essence of value from existing to potentially lucrative products could take time, thereby making evolutionary, internally based diversification less attractive. Gulf Oil's painstaking progress toward the number two position in low-density polypropylene was rendered almost a totally wasted effort by Union Carbide's development of a less costly production process.[10] General Motors's rather tepid interest in small cars (in spite of having, prior to the oil embargo of 1973, done much research and developmental work in the area) allowed its competitors, notably those from Japan to steal a significant march over it.[11] On the other hand, the acquisition route is not riskless either. The need for the parties to the merger to acquiesce in the union and work cooperatively often is a major barrier to successfully accomplishing a strategy of value combination. General Motors's acquisition of EDS, Exxon's acquisition of Reliance Electric and General Electric's brief dalliance with Utah Electric speak to the caution necessary in attempting to weld disparate entities together even when they have much in common, and much to gain from helping each other. In spite of EDS's relative success after being acquired by GM, it has never quite fit in with the culture of the larger parent. Nowhere is the difficulty in extracting "synergy" (the transfer of resources or more specifically, the transfer of *value-creating* resources) more evident than in the financial services industry, the marketplace for securities, insurance, deposits, loans, credit cards and related offerings. American Express typifies the experience of firms that seek to offer one-stop shopping. While its ventures into investment banking (Amex Banking Corp.), securities (Shearson Lehman Hutton) and information services (IDS) performed relatively well, its insurance wing (Fireman's Fund) fell upon hard times and had to be divested. At any rate, American Express has had considerable trouble fostering cooperation among its constituent units.[12] It had been expected that, given the specialized skills required in some businesses (e.g., licensing for securities analysts, knowledge of local regulations for insurance sales) at least client lists ought to be exchanged as a starting point. Even this has proved to be a thorny issue for Amex, as it did for other firms in the industry.

While concentric diversification can indeed run into glitches and even end in disaster, we hasten to point out that numerous examples of successful combination exist—

- Maytag's acquisition of Magic Chef, which rounded out Maytag's product line with the addition of kitchen appliances and almost doubled its market share between 1985 and 1990[13];
- Honda's diversification from motorcycles to automobiles and subsequently into lawnmowers and generators was fueled by its value delivery capabilities in the design and manufacture of small engines and their successful incorporation in a variety of equipment[14];
- International Paper's acquisition of Hammermill has given IP a strong position in the fine and specialty papers segments complementing its commodity and reprographic papers, and paperboard business.[15]

SHARING VALUE THROUGH JOINT VENTURES

Certainly, there are risks involved in diversification. But there are also risks attendant upon staying put. An environmental niche in which continuous value enhancement is the goal may not always be an unassailable refuge. For those firms that seek to expand their bang for the value buck, so to speak, joint ventures could be a viable and less risky option. Originally embraced by oil firms to mitigate the financial and political risks associated with exploration in the Middle East, joint ventures have gained in popularity particularly during the last decade. The most common rationale for joint ventures nowadays is to unite the *bases* for value that each party to the joint venture possesses and has successfully deployed. The IBM-Rolm alliance sought to bring IBM's service orientation and Rolm's expertise in specific areas of manufacturing technology under one roof. The GM-Toyota joint venture to produce Novas in California, on the other hand, was set up with the express purpose of providing Nova buyers the benefits of Toyota's expertise in design and manufacture, with GM bringing to bear its considerable distributional and promotional weaponry. In essence, the parties to a joint venture, as do those in a merger, hope to achieve an optimum value balance among the 3Cs. Toyota's capabilities in the first two Cs complement GM's in the third one, particularly in the context of the North American market. IBM's capabilities both in conceptualizing and communicating value through service provide an apt foil to Rolm's manufacturing know-how.

Since the joint venture is a separate entity formed by resources contributed by the parent organizations, its success or failure does not necessarily have a major impact on them, unlike in a merger, where the consenting parties' assets, performance, and future become one. Though a joint venture is less risky than a merger (both, incidentally, are irreversible) it sometimes is subject to the same causes of failure as those that beset mergers. The most common cause of a breakdown is the inability of the partners to agree upon a course of action for their protegé, even when the broad outlines of a strategy have been settled in advance. Moreover, if the newly created entity is composed of employees drawn from the partners, divergent perspectives on product value may lead to confusion and contradiction in the joint venture. While prior agreement on strategies to be adopted by the new entity would help address the first failing, particularly if top management were recruited from outside so as to avoid even the hint of a bias, the second deficiency is more difficult to deal with. Recruiting all the employees from other firms to mitigate the clash of cultures could negate the very basis for the proposed venture, a complementarity of value focus. Unless the strategies selected reflect such a complementarity and the employees are in turn driven by the need to enhance value (through combination and/or exchange), acquisitions and joint ventures will undoubtedly experience all sorts of post-union pathologies.[16]

EXPANDING THE HORIZONS OF VALUE

The old admonition to "Go West, young man!" was, as we know all too well, taken very seriously by the Japanese, South Koreans, Taiwanese and Singaporeans. To firms based in these countries exports and, more recently, joint ventures and direct investment abroad have been their lifeblood. American firms, blessed with a large, lucrative market at home have not been as eager to gain a vantage point in foreign markets. Of course there are conspicuous exceptions like IBM's and Xerox's exceptional success not only in Japan but also in markets the Japanese eye wistfully (China, for one). Procter and Gamble's successful European operations have encouraged it to expand further in parts of Asia and Africa. Goodyear, in defending its leadership position in tires has established tire plants worldwide. While there is less of a sense of urgency to the expansion of American firms abroad, "going international" could be a very lucrative proposition indeed. Ford's European operations have not only added considerably to the company's coffers, they have helped make a winner out of the Escort. General Electric's and Westinghouse's sales of power generation equipment, McDonalds's successful conquests of the European and Japanese markets, and International Paper's successful entry into the European market all speak to the potentially immense rewards that accompany expansion abroad.

Much of the international market expansion initially undertaken was done by "multidomestic" firms, whose international operations were independent of those at home. Each international group was therefore like a separate domestic operation—hence the label. While the multidomestic firm increases total sales, the relative separation of the various foreign operations from each other and from their home base affords little opportunity for a common value focus.[17] For example, if a firm (whether in audio/video electronics, pharmaceuticals or fast foods) pursues a multidomestic strategy, its carefully nurtured expertise (say in material procurement and high quality manufacturing) might atrophy in its autonomous foreign locations. Multidomestic firms became popular because it was felt that each nation/society needed tailor-made products, marketing strategies, personnel practices, and so on. This was true up to a point. Automobiles in England, Japan and India, for example, have the steering on the right unlike in most other parts of the world. Similarly, pollution control specifications vary from country to country, average gas consumption of the fleet is far lower in Japan and Europe than in the United States, and so on. Obviously, a single design of car would not work everywhere; even the same model would need to be modified. Again, a product such as cooking oil is not the same the world over, the composition depending on traditional preferences or the most easily available

raw materials, etc. A single oil type is unlikely to be successfully mar-
ketable worldwide.

A UNIFYING VISION OF VALUE

Undoubtedly, customer needs must be discovered and fulfilled. After
all, that has been the entire refrain of our tune of value. But firms that
try to deliver value in different countries with little or no attempt to build
on value capabilities previously accumulated elsewhere are, in effect, like
conglomerates whose different products have no conscious value relationship to one another. And just as conglomerates, so to speak, *devalue*
a firm's mission to its customers, multidomestic firms do not take advantage of potentially significant sources of value. Sharing and thus multiplying value are ignored in both types of organization.

The emergence of the global firm is a recent phenomenon and one that is
consistent with the notion of value exchange and maximization. Whether
the value emphasis be in conceptualization, construction or communication, endowing all foreign operations with the same attributes could prove
to be a decisive factor in repeating the success enjoyed at home. Xerox's
successes in designing a copier (starting with its 1045 model) which inte-
grates the many microprocessors used for control and is versatile in using
different paper qualities, and its evolution into a Just-in-Time manufacturer
are significant sources of value in the United States which are shared by the
firm's affiliates worldwide.[18] Unilever's extensive operations in less-
developed countries not only increase its revenues and earnings, they have
increasingly moved away from their earlier role of value *absorbers* and are
becoming value *originators*. For example, their product development activities in countries such as India have proved to be extremely fertile in gen-
erating ideas for improved process design and better materials, which have
turned out to be extremely beneficial elsewhere.[19] To borrow a term from
thermodynamics, foreign subsidiaries need not always be "sinks" of
value. They can also develop into "sources."

Quite obviously it would be easier to become a global firm (that is,
adopt a uniform value focus worldwide) in some products than in others.
Commodities are obvious candidates for globalization. The steel, chemicals, cement and mining industries display a high degree of similarity in
finished products and in processes employed and stand to gain tremendously through a coordinated effort to establish the same foundations of
value. Of course, minor variations arising from differences in materials,
worker capabilities, customer preferences, and governmental regulations
are always possible, though they should not detract much from the ac-
centuation of shared value. A global view of value is not a far-fetched
notion in consumer goods either. Even though the need for responsiveness
to local preferences is likely to be much more pressing, the potential for

sharing value certainly exists. Cases in point are disposable razors, automobile tires, watches, pens, electronic goods and electrical appliances. Levitt argued that the cost advantages of globalization (worldwide *cumulative* experience leading to more effective designs, higher manufacturing efficiency, improved customer service, etc.) would persuade customers to modify their preferences where necessary to take advantage of lower prices.[20] While this scenario has not yet been fully realized, the fact that many firms in consumer goods and services appear to be acquiring increasingly global characteristics (General Electric, McDonalds, BIC, Goodyear, Phillips, and Proctor and Gamble) suggests that his view could yet prove realistic.

Easing multinational firms' transition from a multidomestic to a global posture are the revolutionary changes in communication technology that have occurred in the recent past and continue to occur. Drawings under preparation in Germany could be viewed on line and modified (in real time) in the United States and in Brazil. Software for computer-aided manufacturing could be transferred from one facility to another making it relatively simple to enhance the value achieved in manufacturing at all locations. Instant inventory updates, finding and transferring personnel and materials urgently needed at one or more far-flung operation, and the ability to transmit images and documentation provide an incentive to move from a multidomestic to a global posture. Additionally, with the fluctuations that almost continually occur in exchange rates, strategic coordination could provide "windfall" profits to firms that, say, step up production in countries whose currency is experiencing depreciation and cutting back in locations where the currency is appreciating. Another opportunity arising from exchange rate fluctuation that can be exploited, particularly by the global firm, stems from the fact that the origin(s) and the destination(s) of funds need not be identical. That is, if funds (for operating or capital expenditures) are needed in Argentina, the money may be raised in France (say, due to the favorable interest rates) and transferred electronically (and instantly) to Buenos Aires. If the global firm's home base is in the United States, hedging contracts between the franc and the dollar may be entered into to guard against exposure due to possible appreciation of the franc during the currency of the loan. While such actions would amount to little more than speculation if the firm undertook coordination only to exploit exchange rate differentials, treating the benefits flowing from the latter as lucrative "perks" from directed and coordinated international expansion certainly makes the effort even more worthwhile.

Bartlett and Ghoshal, after an exhaustive study of nine multinationals, observe that the need may arise for firms to acquire a combination of the traits of global and multidomestic firms.[21] While reaping the benefits of a global strategy (design coordination to share findings, economies of scale in materials if not in operations, funds transfers, production scheduling, and so on) such a firm may also have to be responsive to localized customers' needs. Customers may want to have their cake and eat it too (which they're quite entitled to do). Bartlett and Ghoshal label this sort of firm a 'transnational.' In value terms, it appears that the transnational's emphasis has to be on the conceptualization stage. Designing the product so that variations can be incorporated to meet local needs is one of the keys to transnational functioning. The use of modules or platforms from which product variety can be launched to satisfy local needs epitomizes the product flexibility/resource efficiency that is the hallmark of transnational firms. While the C2 stage of the chain emphasizes uniformity over all the firm's locations so that the modules themselves are universal, specific needs are incorporated much as options in an automobile are. They are added on. While value communication is best left to local discretion, the transfer of design and development information will typically be accompanied by information that can be passed on to customers or, equally important, received from them. Caterpillar's ability to acquire a transnational coloring has been an essential feature of its strategy to take back market share from Komatsu.

VALUE-INTENSIVE VS. VALUE-EXTENSIVE STRATEGIES

In a corporation-wide sense, value maximization (as we have seen in this chapter and in the preceding one) results from employing a diversity of methods. The basic notion of determining and fulfilling customer needs, while seeking continuously to improve upon past achievements, is the bedrock upon which customer value rests. However, there are different paths to these desired ends. These different approaches are not necessarily exclusive of one another. They may be employed in unison just as an army may employ aerial bombardment, flanking attacks and political pressure to defeat the enemy or as a baseball team may use good pitching, publicity for an outstanding player, and promotional tickets ("Kids' Night") to kindle fan enthusiasm. In essence, the firm needs to evaluate its ability to satisfy customer needs by implementing Figure 2.3 (or some variation of it) in which the 3Cs are arrayed against the detailed needs of its customers. The stages of the value creation process must be both *separately* and *collectively* attuned to the needs of customers.

Concentrating on a single product and market segment and seeking to continuously enhance value delivered by improving worth and/or reducing cost is a perfectly viable strategy until opportunities arise to expand the firm's scale/scope of operations or threats to its limited domain develop. As we have seen, various diversification strategies open up to allow the firm to transfer its value basis to new businesses, through internal development or acquisition, by entering into joint ventures, establishing a globally integrated firm with windows of responsiveness, and so on. A strategy of concentration, with value increases being confined to a single product market area, may be termed *value-intensive*. On the other hand, a strategy of diversification, of products and/or markets where value is in effect multiplied, is *value-extensive*. Whether a firm's strategy be value-intensive, value-extensive, or a combination of the two, the analysis starts with the abilities-needs (input-output) chart of the previous chapter. Subsequently, the analysis proceeds to evaluate how best to extend the value competence of the firm to other domains, the details of value sharing, and so on.

STRATEGIC THINKERS AND DOERS: LESSONS TO BE UNLEARNED

While a firm's strategy must therefore be firmly rooted in considerations of value, the concept of strategy itself needs some explanation, and perhaps some change too. Strategy is perceived as encompassing

- the articulation of a vision and mission for the firm,
- goals and the means for achieving them,
- the rationale for resource allocation, policies and guidelines,[22]
- the achievement of a "fit" between the firm and its environment,[23]
- a "pattern in a stream of decisions,"[24] and
- the long term "intent" of the firm.[25]

When the word strategy is mentioned, one or more of these meanings are likely to be visualized whether the audience consists of managers or academics or, volatile though it be, some mixture thereof. The story about the seven blind men who, on touching an elephant, pronounced it to be a rope, a tree, a house, and so forth, depending on the part touched, seems to be very apropos where strategy is concerned. The concept of value, however, provides a unifying structure to these diverse views of strategy. Value provides the fit between the firm and its environment, is the pattern underlying a firm's actions, is the basis for an organization's mission, and can help decide where to allocate resources. We shall pick up on these and other themes of value throughout the rest of this book.

While value maximization provides a unifying perspective on strategy, there is one aspect of strategy that needs little orchestration since it is almost consensually shared. Few question that strategy is the responsibility of top management just as in war strategy is the sole preserve of the general.[26] In the rigidly stratified configuration of the typical military organization, the overall strategy for the conduct of the war is typically carried out at the topmost level by the Chairman of the Joint Chiefs and his team while battle plans designed to dovetail into the war strategy are developed at the level of the local commander(s). Similarly, a football team's strategy is conceived, fleshed out, and brought to life by the owner, general manager, and the head coach. Whether the campaign be a military or sporting one, strategy takes shape at the top and makes its way down. This is not to say that soldiers and players are pawns to be moved about at will. Just as an army marches on its stomach, and must be kept happy and in high morale, athletes are often extremely sensitive and can be as cantankerous as any prima donna. It is therefore extremely important to ensure that both troops and players remain enthusiastic and committed to the cause.

In both instances the level of commitment and dedication among the rank and file depends upon the operating conditions (climate, terrain, rations, air cover; salary, supporting staff, fans, location) and on the success achieved. Winning, regardless of whether it's an army or a basketball team, is great motivation. In a sense, armies and sports teams differ greatly from the business enterprise. Armed conflict carries a life and death urgency, thus providing a built-in, supreme motivation to faithfully carry out the orders handed down and hence, indirectly, the overall strategy. Success in competitive sports, on the other hand, calls for eliciting enthusiasm and zeal from a relatively small group—the full complement of players rarely exceeds fifty in any sport.

Few, if any, organizations can focus their employees' minds by posing the choice in "perform-or-die" terms (as the military can), nor can they limit their firm's size, hold out the potential for multimillion-dollar contracts, or the possibility of a few years of public adulation as the sports team often does. The routine nature of many jobs in industry typically makes working a painful ordeal due to the need to constantly accept and follow instructions. Strategy is, as we noted earlier, a top-down process. However, by the time it reaches the lower echelons, strategies may as well be pronounced dead on arrival. By the time it trickles down to the rank and file, most of the inspiration and excitement that may have attended its formation at the upper reaches, has generally trickled out. The enthusiastic Chief Executive stands all too often in marked contrast to the indifference and even hostility that characterizes the business firm at the operative level. Vogt and Murrell[27] identify six crises that face us on the national and individual levels. While the crises of energy, of confusion, of conflict, and of stress are indeed important and need managing, most apropos here are the crises of alienation and of spirituality. Vogt and Murrell argue that autocratic systems create dependencies but little connectedness and belonging. The spiritual crises, on the other hand, arise from a lack of purpose and meaning in the work itself. While ideas to carry the firm to the pinnacle of excellence (say, in value delivered) may continue to flow downward, the energy needed to bring these ideas to fruition is long gone, if it was ever present. The situation is analogous to a person whose brain is functioning perfectly while his body is incapable of responding to the stimuli received.

How does one instill a sense of strategy achievement and generate the driving force of a *strategy of value* in the entire workforce? Certainly not by adhering to the traditional top-down strategy paradigm. Rather, a vibrant spirit of oneness with the firm and its strategy must be encouraged and created. Awareness, acceptance, and active pursuit of the firm's strategy have to be consciously and constantly cultivated. Moreover, and equally importantly, a cadre of zealous and imaginative workers driven by the value metaphor needs to be established in order for strategy to link the firm at all levels to the external environment. Strategy will then become a tangible, exciting activity with customer value as its prime mover, its living core.

In the next two chapters we accord top priority not only to the details of how value can be maximized, but also how the notion of value can be introduced into and permeate organizations. Subsequently, we discuss approaches to get employees to buy in to the need to assiduously enhance value and to participate in the strategy process, in developing and not just executing it.

NOTES

1. James Lincoln's preoccupation with customer needs continues to be a cornerstone of the firm's strategy. Lincoln Electric has successfully maximized customer satisfaction while providing job security and encouraging participative decisions within the work force. See Arthur Sharplin, "The Lincoln Electric Company," in John Montanari, Cyril Morgan, and Jeffrey Bracker (eds.), *Strategic Management* (Chicago: Dryden, 1990), pp. 807–20.

2. William Copulsky, "Balancing the Needs of Customers and Shareholders," *Journal of Business Strategy*, November/December 1991, 44–47.

3. Arlyn Melcher, Bernard Arogyaswamy and Ken Gartrell, "Leading Strategies: The Trade-offs of Financial, Production and Marketing Activities," in William Guth, ed., *Handbook of Business Strategy 1986/1987 Yearbook*, (Boston: Warren, Gorham and Lamont, 1986), pp. 501–18.

4. This argument applies to diversifications into related product areas (e.g., Matsushita's diversification into a range of electronics products and Procter and Gamble's ventures into a variety of consumer goods) and not to the type of product line expansion carried out by ITT. See Charles Hill and Gareth Jones, *Strategic Management* (Boston: Houghton Mifflin, 1992) p. 226.

5. Of course, this lack of commitment is not necessarily a disadvantage. In firms whose value creation ability is highly specialized and/or difficult to transfer to new product lines conglomerate expansion—commitment or no commitment—could be the only option. (Ibid., p. 228.)

6. Peter Drucker in *Innovation and Entrepreneurship* (New York: Harper &

Row, 1986) terms the strategy "creative imitation"—waiting till a competitor is about to introduce a new product before swinging into action to develop a similar one, (p. 220–21), and delivering better value through superior service at all stages of the chain.

7. Drucker (ibid.) describes P&G's strategy in its soap, detergent, and toiletries lines as similar to IBM's. "Creative imitation" in this case is woven around a theme of value communication.

8. See, for example, Julian Huxley's *Evolution in Action* (New York: Harper, 1953) for a description of the biological process. Bill McKelvey and Howard Aldrich's "Populations, Natural Selection, and Applied Organizational Science," *Administrative Science Quarterly*, 28, 1983, pp. 101–28 offers an excellent review of natural selection in biology compared to that in organizations. It appears that much of the variation that takes place in organizations, as in nature, is blind rather than purposeful.

9. Sheila Brock, et al. "Campbell Soup Company," in Charles Hill and Gareth Jones's *Strategic Management* (Boston: Houghton-Mifflin, 1992), pp. 631–59.

10. *Business Week*, December 18, 1978, pp. 62–68.

11. See James Brian Quinn's synopsis of GM's actions, "General Motors Corporation: The Downsizing Decision," in Arthur Bedeian's *Organizations: Theory and Analysis* (Chicago: Dryden 2nd ed., 1984).

12. William Wilsted, "The American Express Company," in Montanari, Morgan, and Brecker *Strategic Management* (Chicago: The Dryden Press, 1990).

13. *Business Week*, October 14, 1991, p. 86.

14. *The Economist*, October 13, 1990, p. 71.

15. *Business Week*, October 28, 1991, pp. 140–41.

16. Strategic alliances can become costly misadventures. The experience of Metheus Corporation (a software firm) that sought an alliance with Computervision provides an illustration of the conflict that could emerge. Marketing executives at Computervision refused to work with Metheus, didn't involve the latter in their marketing efforts, and even signed a development contract with their ally's competitor. Expectedly the marriage soon ended. A similar fate befell the Acme-Cleveland and Multi-Arc Vacuum System Inc. alliance. Value sharing though a laudable mission, has to pass the crucial test of human, group, and organizational compatibility. (*Business Week*, July 21, 1986, pp. 100–5).

17. See Charles Hill and Gareth Jones, *Strategic Management* (Boston: Houghton-Mifflin, 2nd ed., 1992), p. 253.

18. Starting with the 10 Series, consisting of the 1045, 1075 and 1090 models, Xerox has enhanced its value worldwide by designing copiers on a multinational basis, thus reducing acceptance time in its various markets. In fact Xerox even won a Grand Prize Award for industrial design from the Japanese government! See Gary Jacobson and John Hillkirk, *Xerox: America's Samurai* (New York: Collier, 1986), p. 250.

19. See Christopher Bartlett and Sumantra Ghoshal's *Managing Across Borders* (Boston: Harvard Business School Press, 1989), pp. 35–37.

20. Theodore Levitt, "The Globalization of Markets," *Harvard Business Review*, May-June 1983, pp. 92–102.

21. Christopher Bartlett and Sumantra Ghoshal, *Managing Across Borders* (Boston: Harvard Business School Press, 1989).

22. In addition to Kenneth Andrews and Igor Ansoff cited earlier, Alfred Chandler's *Strategy and Structure* (Cambridge: MIT Press, 1962) helped formulate these perspectives on strategy.

23. See, for example, Danny Miller, "The Genesis of Configuration," *Academy of Management Review*, 1987, 12(4), pp. 686–701. Miller explores four *imperatives*—environment, structure, leadership and strategy—and their relationship.

24. Henry Mintzberg, "Patterns in Strategy Formation," *Management Science*, 1978, 24, pp. 934–48.

25. See G. Hamel and C. K. Prahalad, "Strategic Intent," *The McKinsey Quarterly*, Spring 1990, pp. 36–61. The authors view strategic intent as sitting somewhere between the organization's mission and its goals (in terms of its time frame), and fortified with generous doses of willpower and staying ability. Komatsu's pledge to "Encircle Caterpillar" and Canon's desire to "Beat Xerox" are prime instances of strategic intent, simply stated and almost as single-mindedly pursued as Captain Ahab's pursuit of his quarry.

26. Carl von Clausewitz, *On War*. (Harmondsworth, U.K.: Penguin, Reprinted 1985.) Clausewitz asserts that political ends underlie all military action and the top officers are therefore the strategy makers.

27. Judith Vogt and Kenneth Murrell, *Empowerment in Organizations* (San Diego, CA: University Associates, 1990), pp. 12–22.

4

INTERDEPENDENCE: ELIMINATING INSULATION

INDIVIDUALISM AND THE FREE ENTERPRISE SYSTEM

When the Berlin Wall was breached and torn down far more was accomplished than the reunification of Germany. Communism as a guiding philosophy lost much, if not all, of its luster, particularly in Eastern Europe, and the latent hostility of the cold war went down a few notches. While subsequent events may have rendered the accompanying optimism and celebration premature it seems quite unlikely that an economic system founded on state ownership of both capital and the means of production will ever find favor on the scale that it once enjoyed. It is equally unlikely that a political ideology advocating the curbing of individual freedoms and the adoption of centrally directed plans will attract a large following anywhere.

No doubt the various recent developments in the Soviet Union and Eastern Europe are a vindication of the political and economic principles which are the cornerstone upon which societies such as the United States, Western Europe, and Japan are built. If there is a dominant metaphor underlying the working of the economies of most developed countries it is that of Adam Smith's "invisible hand." Self interest and individual effort are central to Smith's vision of an ideal economic system, resulting in a price and resource allocation mechanism of unparalleled efficiency. At the heart of this free enterprise system is the *individual* and his or her right to choose among products, among employers, and among investment opportunities. Ayn Rand, in her voluminous works extolling capitalism constantly stressed the importance of individual effort not only in achieving a feeling of self-worth but also in maximizing the good of society.[1] She sharply criticized governments that, no matter how well-intentioned, seek to institute programs to benefit segments of society rather than allow the market to take care of them.

Obviously, nowhere in the world does a free enterprise system exist in such pristine purity. In countries such as France, England, Holland, Japan, and West Germany capitalism has been "socialized." Health care, electricity, unemployment benefits, transportation, and child care are some of the areas in which governments provide subsidies, if not the service itself. The so-called "public sector," in fact, consists of government-owned corporations competing with privately run ones, often on preferential terms. Even in the United States, the government administers social programs, monitors the status of foreign trade, and maintains and regulates public services, to mention a few of its responsibilities. While capitalism "with a heart" is perhaps an inevitable development, the fact remains that individual effort and achievement continue to underpin the economic and political institutions of free enterprise. Logically, one might expect that individualism would be similarly highly valued in organizations.

INDIVIDUALISM WITHIN THE FIRM

Paradoxically, however, within organizations individualistic behavior could work to the detriment of the organization. Employees who seek to further only *their* ambitions and interests might, and often do, jeopardize their colleagues' legitimate aspirations as well as the goals of the firm at large. Organizations, almost by definition, cannot emulate the freedom that prevails in society and in the marketplace. For example, manufacturing operations are typically not farmed out if they are already an integral, essential part of the manufacturing process and the capacity to perform them exists within the firm. That is, the discretion to outsource certain components and products may be curbed or even eliminated. Similarly, the marketing department is *bound* to promote and distribute its own products and is typically not free to deal with the product offerings of other companies. In other words, once a function or activity is performed in-house, the free market is generally not an option, even if it is a substitute for the activity in question. In fact, there is a school of thought that believes organizations are formed when markets "fail." The failure of markets could result from buyers not being able to trust suppliers (unreliability in terms of materials deliveries and information), from there being too few suppliers, or from buyers requiring specifically designed ("idiosyncratic") products.[2] Once a set of activities comes within a firm's purview (whether they consist of manufacturing, marketing, personnel, or engineering) the ties that bind the parts of a corporation together within the same product/service area are strong indeed. The independence that flows from the ethic of individualism and characterizes the relationships among individuals and groups in society as well as among firms in the free market is therefore *not* a hallmark of organizational relations. The need for unity and a coordinated response to external challenges creates *interdependent* groups, which *cannot* allow unalloyed self-interest to guide their thoughts and actions.

Since the individualism and independence that characterize democratic societies and free markets are difficult to recreate in organizations, how can we reconcile the apparent contradiction? Is it at all possible to successfully constrain individuals within a firm when they generally have a free hand outside it?

THE RESPONSE TO DEPENDENCIES: INSULATION

The tension between societal freedom and organizational restraints is one that exists in most democratic systems, particularly those where individual effort is encouraged and rewarded. (Japan may not completely conform to this pattern partly due to the group norms fostered in its institutions.[3]) As consumers, we do not take kindly to being dependent on one or a few makers for any product, whether clothing or appliances. The more numerous the choices we are presented with, the less constrained we feel. Corporations reflect this need for alternatives by trying to reduce dependence on any one supplier, customer, shareholder or employee. Since similarly unfettered behavior is neither possible nor advisable between individuals and groups in corporations, dependencies are a reality to be confronted and dealt with on a day-to-day basis.

Thompson's ideas on interdependence and on managing it are fairly representative of the attitude toward interdependence within firms.[4] Thompson, who wrote persuasively during his all-too-brief career was a clear-minded pragmatist. To begin with, he advocated "sealing off the technical core," by which he meant that the part of the firm where its *essential work* gets done (this would be the manufacturing process in a firm making a product) must be *isolated* from internal and external disturbances. Accordingly, marketing departments are established primarily to handle issues relating to the customer (and secondarily to keep the customer at arm's length). Separating the customer from the production process (or at least reducing their access to it) helps increase the productivity of the manufacturing function, thus enhancing output and, presumably, profits. A similar rationale holds for the creation of a Materials Management department to handle issues and problems regarding all incoming materials. Both these "insulators" have, over the years, evolved into complex entities in their own right. Functions such as Promotion and Advertising, Marketing Research, Transportation, and Channel Management have sprouted and flourished as part of Marketing while Inspection,

Material Substitution, Vendor Assessment, and Inventory Management are integral parts of many Materials Management departments. In spite of the relatively sophisticated nature of both these functions, in essence they constitute "shock absorbers" placed between an efficiency-maximizing activity (production) and supposedly efficiency-reducing influences (such as suppliers and customers). The intent is to allow production to focus on the conversion of inputs to outputs while the provision of inputs and disposal of outputs is left to others. Dependency on external forces is replaced by a dependence on other departments which are charged, in particular, with moderating the effect of the external factors.

How do these shock-absorbers or cushions deal with or mitigate dependence on the outside world? Thompson cites buffering, forecasting, smoothing, and scheduling as some of the more popularly used methods.[5]

- **Buffers** include inventories of raw materials and finished goods which protect against input and output shocks, respectively. Production can thus continue uninterrupted by the vagaries of supply and demand. Similarly, the use of reliable equipment and well-trained employees can also buffer a production process from input uncertainties.

- **Forecasting** of demand and of input capabilities helps cope with reliance on external factors by being prepared for variations in them when they do occur. Demand forecasting applies not only to the *quantities* expected to be sold but also the types of changes likely in the market—higher quality standards, lower prices due to more intense competition, a desire for more customization, and so on. Any discontinuity that could upset the flow of production has to be forecasted and appropriate action taken.

- **Smoothing** or leveling entails strategies to reduce demand during peak periods and increase demand during off periods. Examples are "happy hours" at bars, discount rates offered at night by telephone companies, and weekend fare packages offered by airlines.

- **Scheduling** of production/operations covers detailed planning of quantities and times, facilitating the efficient and continuous operation of the process. Where smoothing is difficult to achieve, scheduling could play the role of a cushioning device. For example, it is difficult to make customers change their buying behavior, to buy toys in May or June, say, instead of in November or December. Instead of smoothing demand (externally) companies try to deal with the problem *internally* by producing at a constant rate throughout the year and building up inventories or by stepping up the production rate as the seasonal peak in demand occurs.

All these dependence-reducing techniques have been widely practiced in industry. Buffering through inventory, scheduling production in predetermined quantities, trying to get customers to change their requirements through smoothing, and so on, have done their share to make our organizations even more allergic to interdependence. We revert to the path-

Figure 4.1
Pooled Interdependence

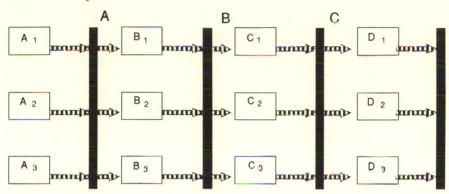

Figure 4.2
Sequential Interdependence

ologies often induced by these practices after a brief review of the nature
and character of interdependence.

INTERNAL DEPENDENCIES

Dependencies occur not only on external factors but internally as well.
Thompson distinguished among three types of interdependence[6] which
apply both to the external and within-organization connections.

- **Pooled interdependence** arises when inputs are contributed by many different
  sources (Figure 4.1). Secretaries tied to a common data base, and airlines that
  rely on travel agents to function like in-house selling agencies provide examples
  of this form of interdependence.
- **Sequential interdependence** is a slightly more intense form of dependency and
  occurs when an activity has only one source of inputs. As shown in Figure 4.2,
  A has to be completed before B starts, B before C, and C before D; that is, the
  operations are sequentially dependent. This is more intense than the pooled
  type since the latter allows alternate input sources (A_2, A_3; B_2, B_3; C_2, C_3; D_2,
  D_3) for each operation. The outputs from each operation are combined in pooled
  interdependence to form the (less uncertain) input for the next operation, effectively reducing the level of dependency.
- **Reciprocal interdependence** arises when a mutual or two-way dependency exists.
  Typically such a situation occurs when tasks and/or inputs are unpredictable as

Figure 4.3
Reciprocal Interdependence

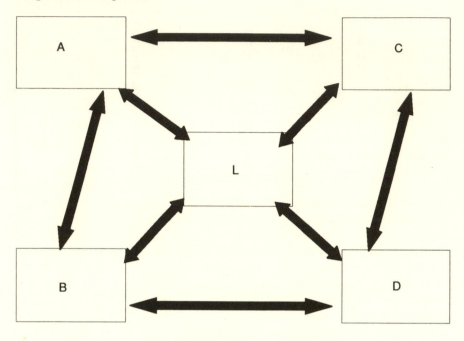

in the case of a patient undergoing tests in the emergency wing of a hospital. The nature of the complaint, the age and history of the patient, and the results of initial investigations are some of the factors that determine where the patient goes next. Similarly, when a company such as Xerox sets up a New Product team consisting of individuals with varied backgrounds (Design, Engineering, Production, Marketing, Finance, and Personnel are some of the disciplines typically represented), the interactions among team members and the team leader cannot be anticipated, much less programmed or specified. As shown in Figure 4.3, interactions could occur between any two of the parties at any time. For convenience, the dependencies between B-C and A-D have been omitted. For example, if the team were working on an improved vacuum cleaner, information provided by Marketing about the advent of a new competitor would be passed along to Design and the team leader (marked L), along with details as to the new rival's expected strategy, product features, and so on. The need to speed up introduction of the new product and to increase promotional efforts to counter the unforeseen challenge might be some of the concerns that would involve most, if not all, the members of the team. The transfer of resources (primarily information in this instance) takes place in an essentially unpredictable fashion. Activities could be sources and recipients of resources depending on the stage of the project and the nature of external developments.

INTERNAL INSULATORS

On comparing the three types of interdependence, a few differences among them are obvious. As pointed out, the degree of dependency increases from pooled to sequential to reciprocal interdependence due to the progressively higher *uncertainty* or *unpredictability*, and the *frequency* and *urgency* of the transactions involved. In the case of sequential interdependence, the relationship is one-sided or asymmetrical. Earlier operations consequently possess power, the power of work continuance or stoppage, over subsequent activities. In reciprocal interdependence, the relationship is two-sided, which results, so to speak, in twice the uncertainty, frequency, and urgency in the transactions entered into.

The most common reaction to greater interdependence has been, as we have pointed out earlier, to try to reduce it. Buffering, forecasting, smoothing, and scheduling are regularly used to lower the level of interdependence from reciprocal to sequential and from sequential to pooled. If feasible, organizations would like to minimize internal and external interdependencies, even to the point of eliminating them. As individuals, we are accustomed to being relatively independent of others, to having "our space." Most of us would prefer to drive ourselves to work than share a ride with others, own a house than live in an apartment, and be rewarded completely on the basis of our own efforts than be dependent on others for all or part of our remuneration.

As with individuals, so too with organizations. If dependencies lead to an unreliable process (since the "chain is only as strong as its weakest link") and create conflicts and stress between individuals and/or groups, the solution is obvious: cut or, next best, loosen the links. Cutting the links would generally not be feasible since the sequence in which most tasks are carried out would need to be preserved. Disconnecting tasks from each other would only lead to a lot of confusion. However, *loosening* the links, or reducing the *degree* of dependence is feasible and indeed often the preferred option.

One of the most commonly used methods to achieve a slackness of the links between tasks (performed by individuals or groups) is through the building up of inventories. We have already mentioned finished goods and incoming material inventories as effectively buffering the firm against the vagaries of demand and supply. We will address these external linkages and those of dependencies among departments in chapter 5. Within the firm too, inventories can and do serve the same purpose. Rather than cushioning the *firm* against external shocks, work-in-process inventories buffer one *operation* from another. Just as insulating the technical core was meant to increase its efficiency, delinking successive operations from each other takes the argument to its logical (illogical?) extreme. If, in Figure 4.4 operations A, B, C and D represent, say, welding, drilling,

Figure 4.4
Inventory as Buffer

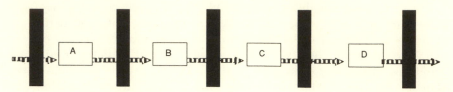

machining, and painting respectively, B's dependence on A, C's dependence on B, and D's dependence on C could be disruptive and stressful to B, C, and D, particularly if A, B, and C respectively failed to deliver materials when needed. The tendency to disagreement and conflict would be higher if workers at each of these work centers were rewarded on the basis of their output rates. The "fire-fighting" solution would be, and has typically been, to establish buffers such as inventory between work centers to insulate them from each other thus, hopefully, maximizing their efficiency.

INVENTORY—SOWING THE SEED OF WASTE AND COMPLACENCY

One result of creating "islands of efficiency" through the use of inventory has been the introduction and acceptance of many different types of waste. Inventory itself is essentially a waste since it consists of excess material that would not normally be needed if operations are performed as planned. In addition to the obvious waste associated with inventory such as storage, deterioration, and opportunity cost of capital are some hidden and generally ignored costs. Included among these less obvious costs are

- the cost of rework, which could be high when materials are produced in large batches to be held in inventory;

- the space occupied on factory floors by inventory which often impedes free movement of people and materials;

- the greater requirement for material handling in quantities proportionate to the increased inventory.[7]

While these undoubtedly add to the already excessive waste and heavy burden associated with inventory, we feel that the damage done by inventory goes beyond waste and cost. Inventory is insidious. It makes people and groups *complacent*. It is a reassuring feeling to know that if things go wrong there is something to fall back on.

It's easy to see how the virtues of individualism and buffering the core have combined to produce not just a passive acceptance of inventory but an active pursuit of it. And as long as customers had products of similar or lower value to choose from, firms were under no pressure to jettison profligate manufacturing principles. However, the eclipse of many American and European firms by their Japanese counterparts makes it imperative that we see inventory for what it is:

- a security blanket, which absolves us of the necessity and responsibility for maintaining cooperative, long-term relationships with customers and suppliers;
- a barrier between successive operations, creating the illusion that each operation can be "micromanaged" with great efficiency, in disregard of others;
- an encouragement to commit mistakes (or at least, no penalties attach to them) since excess material will always be there to rescue us;
- an active ingredient in splitting the organization in many different parts which are *indifferent* to the fate of their counterparts within the firm.

If we were asked to identify *one* villain in the saga of our declining competitiveness here and abroad, it would be inventory. By encouraging the use of large batches, it deters a firm from becoming flexible in responding to changing customer needs (unless these needs occur in high volumes too). By severing links within and outside firms it effectively obscures, even eliminates, the very *idea* of the customer. Products gradually come to represent the results of the firm's activities and not the essence of customer need satisfaction. Elevating the concept of efficiency-through-isolation to the level of a doctrine hurts the firm's integrity and prevents adoption of a coordinated program of action. In general, therefore, inventory strongly hinders the achievement of customer value both by reducing product worth and raising its cost. At the same time, it works toward destroying the unity of an organization that seeks to deliver value. The overriding purpose in targeting inventories for reduction is symbolic—the realization that interdependencies have to be accepted and managed rather than eliminated. While "action plans" for banishing inventory from the shop floor may meet with early success, the success is likely to be short-lived unless it is preceded, accompanied or followed by a change of heart. Others in manufacturing, as well as in those other departments, must be viewed as essential partners in fulfilling the firm's mission of value to its customers. As someone once said, "If we don't hang together we shall most certainly hang separately!" If others' mistakes, breakdowns and slip-ups affect us (our work, pay, peace of mind) adversely, we have to see clearly that emulating the ostrich is no solution. When we raise our heads out of the sand after having ignored everything that's been going on around us, we may have no customers or colleagues left.

SPREADING THE BLAME AROUND—BATCH SIZES AND SETUPS

To be sure, inventory is not the only culprit in the shocking drama of declining U.S. competitiveness. If a movie were made it would have to be rated R due to explicit scenes of disregard for the customer and the firm. Inventory's villainy has been supported in its erosion of firms' capabilities by an able cast of characters. A factor that has contributed almost as much as inventory to our inability to respond to the challenges of foreign manufacturers, even when we know *something* has to be done, is the tendency to "Think Big!" We have nothing against thinking big when it comes to thinking about one's career and personal goals or when a Chief Executive visualizes the long-term future of the firm. However, when it comes to production quantities, the days when Henry Ford could exclaim that his customers were welcome to any color Model T "as long as it's black" are numbered in a growing list of industries. Obviously, producing something in large numbers whether it be automobiles, electronic components, air transportation, or hotel services, helps lower the *manufacturing* cost of each unit made or each customer served. But a company that produces 10,000 cars or TVs of a particular styling when only 1,000 are needed incurs obvious as well as hidden inventory costs (ten times as much rework if a defect is found, confusion and clutter on the shop floor). Typically, the hidden costs of high-volume manufacture stay hidden, while the complacency that often sets in when inventories are held persuades us that manufacturing in large quantities is far more cost-effective than low-volume manufacture. In effect, the belief that large batch scheduling and production is the lowest cost mode becomes a self-fulfilling prophecy since inventories provide backup and help avoid the "trap" of costly changeovers.

Obviously high set up costs amplify and reinforce the belief that large batches are most cost effective. If set up costs are high, scheduling short runs is indeed a forbidding prospect. Large batch scheduling affords an easy but expensive way out with its false and myopic promise of low costs. A way out of this seeming vicious circle is to try to reduce the time and cost of changeovers. The reductions effected by firms such as Toyota (in some cases, from a few hours to less than ten minutes) have become legendary and have unquestionably been a critical part of the simultaneous cost reduction and quality improvement these firms have achieved.[8] As we said earlier, an obsession with *quantity* hinders our ability to deliver value. This is particularly true of industries where the product or service is *not* totally standardized. Even in the case of standardized products or commodities, producing only as much as is needed would be the value maximizing approach in the long run. Set up times would not matter much since few changeovers would be required.

Where customers' needs are not uniform and product variation is desirable (either because competitors are providing it or even more importantly because they *aren't*) batch sizes become a significant component of a firm's production effectiveness in providing value at the construction stage. Figure 2.3 shows that batch volumes, hence set up reductions, assume tremendous importance when a product's value is determined by, or hinges around

- quality, particularly where differences among competing products is discernible or obvious;
- flexibility, in terms of being able to offer product variations, fill orders for small quantities, etc.;
- time economy as displayed by its responsiveness to customers' needs and its competence in dealing with customers' service and information needs quickly, irrespective of order sizes.

OF LAYOUTS AND SIGNALS

Since smaller batches go hand in hand with inventory reduction, buffers and barriers between operations and between the firm and its external stakeholders—notably its suppliers and customers—will diminish considerably. A further reduction in the internal barriers may be achieved by *rationalizing* the layout of the manufacturing operations. Adoption of a cellular layout is one such prominent option. A cellular layout is one in which all the operations that go toward manufacturing a particular product and its variations are *grouped together* physically in a way that emphasizes the *interconnections* among the operations, and facilitates the *flow* of the product. A process layout, on the other hand groups *similar operations* together thus emphasizing the *specialization* inherent in the different processes, facilitating achievement of greater *expertise* in each process.[9] The difference between the two types of layouts is illustrated in Figure 4.5. The upper half of the figure shows a cellular layout for two products (A and B) with each product being manufactured in separate groups of machines, while the lower half shows a process layout. Obviously, the latter is appropriate in a job shop situation where the sequence of processing is unpredictable. However, apart from this situation (one of a kind/custom made products) the cellular configuration is feasible for most types of consumer products. The cellular layout is likely to be more expensive no doubt, since it calls for the use of dedicated (dedicated, that is, to the particular product being made) machines and hence, perhaps, necessitates the use of more machines than in the process mode.

Figure 4.5
Cellular and Process Layouts

CELLULAR

For A

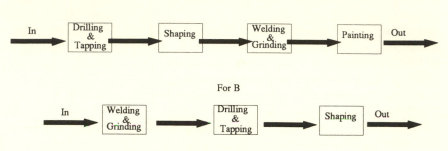

For B

PROCESS

For A and B

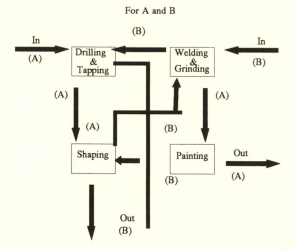

However, in order to achieve greater value through reductions in both batch volumes and in barriers between operations, it would also be worthwhile and cost effective in the context of machine capacity to "Think Small." That is, the alternative to establishing a process-based facility (in which each machine incorporates the *sum* of the processing needs for all the products to be manufactured) is *not* a product layout with the same high-capacity machines. Rather, the machines in a product configuration

Figure 4.6
Intensifying Interdependence Through Kanban

should be of far lower capacity than in a process shop, if the flexibility and quality aspects of product value are to be fully realized.[10] Deciding how much capacity to install at each work center therefore has important implications for a firm's progress toward value maximization and needs to be coordinated with its set up, inventory, and layout.

Inventory depletion lowers barriers, and set up reductions encourage contractions in batch size. Both these big steps toward value enhancement are undoubtedly further reinforced by the use of smaller capacity machines and cellular or dedicated layouts. The result is a product-centered and customer-driven approach to operations. All in all, these four techniques seek to enhance value delivered to customers by *intensifying* dependencies within manufacturing, not by moderating or eliminating them. A fifth vehicle also exists to ratchet interdependence up another notch. The Japanese refer to it as the Kanban; very simply, it is a signal, sent by one operation to the *preceding* one to produce more components.[11] While layout, set up/small batch scheduling, minimum inventory, and small capacity decisions stimulate value-through-interdependence, the Kanban forces the issue. As shown in Figure 4.6, the flow of material is from A to B to C to D. On the other hand, A *does not* produce anything until B sends information (represented as ←) back to A to actually process and deliver more output. Lot sizes are typically kept small, with a batch of one as the ideal. The implementation of a Kanban system is an indicator of how effectively interdependence has been created and managed. We introduce the notion of Kanban here to emphasize the importance of bringing inherent dependencies to the surface and exploiting rather than suppressing them in order to maximize delivered value.

INSULATION IS EASY, INTERDEPENDENCE IS A PAIN

If interdependence is indeed the key to value, why has it been avoided and sought to be eliminated, particularly in a firm's operations? Partly because it is much easier to create efficiency in separate parts than in the whole, but mainly because when the parts of a *social* system (that is, one that involves human beings) are tightly linked to each other, they impose severe stresses upon the system. As Thompson put it, when groups are dependent upon each other (reciprocally interdependent) they have to function through a process of *mutual adjustment*.[12] In other words, routines and standard operating procedures (SOPs) will not suffice. Decisions and actions will have to be conditioned on the situation at hand. No longer can a batch of 10,000 be run off at a work center regardless of the status of other operations. Under the new regimen of interdependence, even a batch of 100 will have to be interrupted if *any* operation experiences a slow down or breakdown. Operators at idle machines would be expected to perform maintenance on their own machines or help out at the defective one, depending on the relative needs of both. Product quality or process control problems would also lead to the line shutting down, possibly multiplying the level of dissatisfaction and even resentment felt by the workers.

MODERATING THE PAIN

In trying to avoid the pitfalls of interdependence, firms have tended to choose the easy, if expensive, way out. How, then, does one deal with the disruptive stress-inducing effects of interdependence? By instituting measures that can help set the stage for accepting greater interdependence. Some of the measures that can help moderate the effects of tight dependencies follow.

- **A reasonably well *balanced* sequence of operations**. If, for example, in Figure 4.6, A consumed 2 minutes per part and B 10 minutes per part, and C, again 2 minutes per part, even small batch manufacture would cause work-in-process inventory pile-up at B and waiting time for C. Process time reduction at B is essential to eliminate the bottleneck. Additional processing capability at B or the performance of A and C by the same worker in a U-shaped layout are some of the actions that might make heightened interdependence workable in this instance.[13]

- **A more reliable manufacturing process**. A process in which breakdowns are frequent could very easily jeopardize the achievement of a tightly-knit, value-driven organization since failure of one operation means that all other connected operations would perforce be idled too. Implementing a program of frequent routine maintenance by operators and undertaking cooperative repairs on stopped machines to get the line started again are among the more effective measures to deal with this impediment to interdependence.[14] Service business reliability checks are no less important and useful.

- **An increased emphasis on *self-supervision***. One of the primary areas in which *responsibility* has to be seen to devolve upon the workers themselves is that of quality. In regard to quality, the adoption of statistical process control techniques to detect and nip potential problems in the bud would help. Self-inspection (carried out by the worker) and successive inspection (carried out by the next operation) procedures would also support the assumption of greater responsibility by workers on the floor. The use of "poka-yoke" or error-proofing techniques (whereby dimensions and fits are checked and inclusion of all components ensured), makes interdependence easier to live with since fewer wrongly processed parts will be passed on down the line. In fact, all actions that instill the philosophy that the "next process is the customer" ought to be adopted and promoted. If serving *internal* customers is accepted and practiced as an essential aspect of serving *external* customers, we are surely not far from overcoming the real and imagined pressures exerted by interdependence.[15]

Our normal, culturally based response to increased dependency on other operations is to oppose it. Unless care is taken to explain and implement techniques relating to set up reductions, batch size contraction, and layout modifications, the need for them may not be clearly understood. They may even be misunderstood (as a means to slash wages/employment) or treated with indifference and contempt ("Just another one of management's passing fancies"). An unmistakable emphasis on customers (external and internal) has to be conveyed as being central to the actions adopted.

SERVICE DEPENDENCIES

The notion of tightening interdependence between operations to maximize value is not confined just to the manufacturing process. Service operations as well as other areas of value creation (such as its conceptualization) are also amenable to tightening linkages with the objective of maximizing value created. Service industries like airlines, for instance, also prefer to operate, whenever possible, with large batch sizes through the use of long-range, high-capacity planes, and high-volume passenger/baggage processing systems. However, since there is considerable traffic to intermediate points, smaller and shorter range craft are necessitated, which raises the cost per passenger mile. It also forces a sequence of "small batches" to be scheduled, each of the small batches being interdependent on the other. Delays become cumulative and may even become endemic unless crews feel they are *responsible* for the timely departure of the next crew (unavoidable delays excepted of course). The same applies in terms of safety, and not so obviously, in regard to passenger comfort level. In the case of an office, its layout often determines its internal linkages which reflect the extent of its commitment to value. Take, for example, a contracting firm which submits bids and executes them. It has individuals to undertake the Design, Estimation, Marketing, Construction, and Management of contracts. The more physically near to each other these individuals are located, the better value will be rendered to customers in the form of information, additional services, design modifications to suit site conditions, and lower cost. Locating them in different cities, buildings, or even floors could hinder the instantaneous response of one to the other's, and hence to the customer's, needs.[16]

Figure 4.7
Tight Linkage in Value Conceptualization

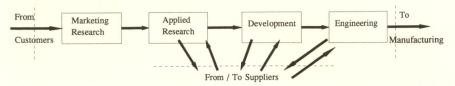

INTERDEPENDENCE IN VALUE CONCEPTUALIZATION

Business activities at other stages of the value creation process besides manufacturing can also benefit from more intense dependencies. The value conceptualization activity is an apt illustration. It may be envisioned comprising Marketing Research, Applied Research, Product Development, and Engineering, as shown in Figure 4.7. Marketing Research and Applied Research are the demand and supply sides of the same coin, the coin of customer needs. One determines what these needs are (and how well they are being met) while the other tries to design a product to fulfill customer needs progressively better. And how does one establish the connection between MR and AR? Direct communication looks like the solution but it often runs into difficulties because of language differences—even if both groups speak English or Japanese or German or whatever the common language might be. The language difference here is one of terminology. The market researchers speak the language of the customer while the designers have an engineering accent. For example, buyers of vacuum cleaners might emphasize noiseless operation, maneuverability and effective cleaning as important product attributes which are translated, from the Applied Research viewpoint into the design characteristics shown in Figure 4.8. The rows represent the Quality Characteristics desired (by customers) while the columns provide the Quality Deployment (designed). A high correlation is shown by ⊡, a moderate correlation by ■, and a blank indicates no correlation at all. A negative sign over the correlation indicator means an inverse relationship. For instance, while size is moderately related to effective cleaning, it is strongly negatively correlated with maneuverability. Similarly, maneuverability is correlated with height adjustment, carpet beating, size, weight, and edge cleaning capability in the degree and direction shown. Refinements such as rating one's products relative to one's competitors' offerings, or multilevel descriptions and categorization of quality characteristics are possible and are among the numerous applications described in Akao's *Quality Function Deployment*,[17] to which we refer the interested reader.

The linkage between Applied Research and Development is basically one of determining feasibility. In other words, while MR and AR together

Figure 4.8
The Customer-Research Connection

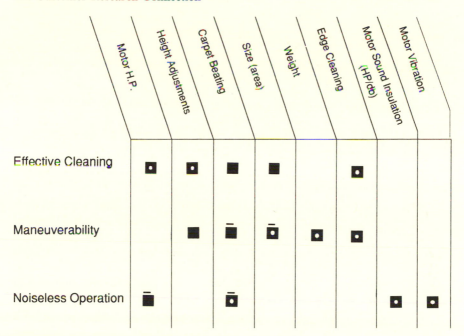

measure the gaps between what *is* and what *should be*, Development has to deal with what *can* be. Development, therefore, uses the filter of cold reality and, based on a document such as Figure 4.8, evaluates which requirements need to be addressed, in what order, and which needs have to be shelved depending on resource availability. A tool such as Computer Aided Design (CAD) could also strengthen the bonds between Research and Development since it helps visualize products as designed and to deal with "What if?" questions. Changes in dimensions, shapes, even materials can be "discussed" on the screen by the two groups, and either adopted, rejected, or modified. The connection between Development and Engineering, on the other hand, is strongly predicated upon the Engineering-Manufacturing nexus. The latter's capabilities and practices are reflected in Engineering's response to Development's needs. If Development specifies an increase in product styles or models from, say, three to ten, Engineering investigates the ability of Manufacturing to produce the increased number of styles, the additional resources, the delays possible, etc. On the other hand, Engineering also suggests design(s) for producibility (using the existing equipment, people, suppliers and other capabilities), the possibility of modularizing the design (product variety through the use of many standardized sub-assemblies), and so on.[18]

Figure 4.9
The Cycle of Value

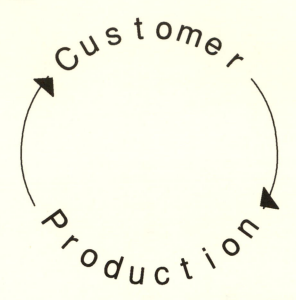

In a formal sense, the process of conceptualizing value starts with Marketing Research, whose source is the customer, and ends with Engineering, whose object is production. In reality, value conceptualization doesn't start and end anywhere. It is everyone's concern. Unless customers' needs are effectively fed into the productive system, the latter will not be able to fulfill them. Tight links among the value conceptualization activities ensure the accuracy of information flow to production, enabling the latter to better serve the firm's customers.

SELF-FULFILLED VALUE CREATION

Just as strong interdependence enhances value in the first two Cs, a similar case can be made for value communication to customers through transportation, storage (if necessary), routing, distribution, sales, advertising/promotion, public relations, and so on. The sequence of activities may be traced pretty much the way we did for conceptualization. While we shall not develop the full linkage here, we do stress that tight linkages within and between the various activities is essential to make for a strong and sustained production-customer connection. The prime mover of the productive system is the customer, whose needs, in turn, are satisfied by it. As Figure 4.9 shows, the relationship could become a circular self-powered one if the two are tuned in to each other (through the other Cs of the value process). We offer the analogy of resonance. Wooden bridges

Figure 4.10
Interdependence—A Look Back

Individualism (and self interest)—valued in society

Interdependence (and coordination)—critical to organizations

Insulation helps reduce dependencies

    —Forecasting, Smoothing, Scheduling, Inventories

The damage done by inventories—costs, complacency, and the *destruction of value*

Thinking Big as an impediment to value—Scheduling, layouts, and line-stops

Making interdependence easier to live with

    —Set up reductions

    —Balanced load

    —Reliable (trouble-free) operations

    —Workers assume more responsibility

    —Self supervision, "poka-yoke"

Interdependencies in Service

Value conceptualization and tight linkages from Marketing through Engineering——the possibilities of QFD

Progressively tighter interdependencies—the key to continuous value creation

have been known to collapse if troops march on them without breaking step. The vibrations are additive and destructive. Most of us have experienced another type of resonance, that of public address systems which suddenly emit a high pitched noise; part of the sound carried by the speakers is fed back into the microphone causing the disturbance. We visualize a similar scenario for product value with one difference—the reinforcing "vibrations" are beneficial not harmful.

Our emphasis in this chapter has been on interdependencies within each of the 3Cs as stepping stones to enhancing value. Figure 4.10 summarizes the ground covered in this chapter. In our view, the creation of value is squarely based in the introduction and acceptance of increased interdependence. However, the story certainly does not end there. Other factors that are indispensable to achieving and sustaining maximum value will now enter the picture. Some of these drivers of value are

- the interfaces *among* the 3Cs as well as with outside entities (such as suppliers and customers);
- internally generated, continuous efforts to enhance value based on employee motivation and enthusiasm;
- an organizational culture that fosters and cements the beliefs and norms that make the edifice of the value-creating firm an unshakable one;
- measures that help find out if the firm is on the right course and provide for corrective actions to be taken where necessary.

We shall address these concerns, in sequence, in the chapters to follow.

NOTES

1. For a sampling of Ayn Rand's views see "What is Capitalism," in Ayn Rand, ed., *Capitalism: The Unknown Ideal* (New York: Signet, 1967), pp. 11–34.

2. The market failure framework was first proposed by Ronald Coase, "The Nature of the Firm," *Economica*, new series, 1938, 4: 386–405. It was subsequently expanded and refined by Oliver Williamson, *Markets and Hierarchies: Analysis and Antitrust Implications* (New York: Free Press, 1975).

3. The group orientation of the Japanese and the effect of this emphasis on organizations, the importance of harmony and of "face" are lucidly analyzed in Edwin Reischauer, *The Japanese Today* (Cambridge, MA: Harvard University Press, 1988), pp. 128–37.

4. James Thompson, *Organizations in Action* (New York: McGraw-Hill, 1967), pp. 54–59.

5. Ibid., pp. 19–23.

6. Ibid., pp. 56–65.

7. See Taiichi Ohno, *Toyota Production System: Beyond Large Scale Production* (Cambridge, MA: Productivity Press, 1988).

8. Ibid.

9. Kiyoshi Suzaki, *The New Manufacturing Challenge* (New York: The Free Press, 1987), pp. 45–68.

10. Ibid., p. 49.

11. Ibid., pp. 146–79.

12. James Thompson, *Organizations in Action*, p. 56.

13. Edward Hay, *The Just-in-Time Breakthrough* (New York: Wiley, 1988) provides a detailed analysis of the centrality of line balance to make a program of inventory reduction and smooth production flow realizable.

14. Seiichi Nakajima, *Introduction to TPM* (Cambridge, MA: Productivity Press, 1988).

15. For an in-depth explanation of "self-check systems" and of the use of "poka-yoke" devices see Shigeo Shingo's *Zero Quality Control: Source Inspection and the Poka-Yoke System* (Cambridge, MA: Productivity Press, 1986), pp. 77–97.

16. Arlyn Melcher, *Structure and Process of Organizations: A Systems Approach* (Englewood Cliffs, NJ: Prentice-Hall, 1975).

17. Yoji Akao, *Quality Function Deployment* (Cambridge, MA: Productivity Press, 1990).

18. Richard Schonberger, in *Building a Chain of Customers* (New York: Free Press, 1990, pp. 217–24), outlines a program for Designing For Operations applicable both to manufacturing as well as service industries. William Davidow and Bro Uttal (*Total Customer Service*, New York: Harper Perennial, 1990) provide an extended and absorbing example of designing for serviceability in the aircraft industry—the McDonnell Douglas DC-10/American Airlines design-service fiasco that led to disaster.

5

INTEGRATION: CREATING
A SHARED VISION
OF VALUE

THE BRAIN AND THE COMMAND-CONTROL MODEL

The human brain, with its capability to carry out tremendously complex functions is indeed an amazing instrument. Contained within our cranial cavities is a versatile, highly specialized device. Among the more important cerebral components and the functions they perform are:

- the cerebrum, consisting of two hemispheres, each similar in appearance to a walnut kernel. Under the surface of the cerebrum is the cerebral cortex, the center of sensory, associative and motor activities. Memory capability is a property of the cortex but one that is dispersed rather than confined to any part of it;

- the cerebellum, found under the rear part of the cerebrum. Like the cerebrum, it, too, is comprised of two hemispheres. It coordinates muscular activity and functions as the motor feedback center;

- the limbic system, or "the mammalian brain," makes an organism warm-blooded, and is the processor of emotional reactions and the aggression urge;

- the brain stem which, coupled with the spinal cord, comprises the central nervous system. It acts as the locus of incoming messages and outgoing commands.[1]

The most popular image of the brain is that it is the central control point for all the actions—be it information processing, physical movement or verbal communication—performed by an individual. The exercise of control is no doubt a critical aspect of the brain's activities. As such it has also served as a powerful metaphor for organizations. The specialization that characterizes the brain is intrinsic to all organizations and the dominant problem that specialization gives rise to—the tendency of the component parts to perform independently of, and even in conflict with, one another—is one that particularly afflicts organizations. For instance, the military's command-control-communication structure and its hierarchic, information-processing-based functioning are roughly fashioned in the cerebral mold. The overall task of preparing for combat with a specific enemy (or set of enemies) is broken down into sub-roles such as intelligence, surveillance, air cover, armored vehicles (light and heavy), artillery, and infantry. While each of these groups is assigned a well-defined set of functions, the entire edifice could quickly degenerate and collapse in the absence of a coordinating mechanism, which typically is a composite of both centralized command and direct communication among the various units. Along the same lines, worldwide organizations seeking to articulate a global vision and to coordinate their dispersed operations have to

• clearly articulate the basis of shared value;
• communicate the value "doctrine" to all the dispersed locations;
• continuously fine-tune the transfer of resources;
• respond to competitors' emergent challenges, and so on.[2]

Such an organization is specialized by location and possibly by product, market (tastes differ across the world), technology (e.g., due to variations in labor costs), and time (R&D thinks long-term while Production may be more concerned about this week). Some way of unifying the organization is essential to prevent it from breaking apart due to internal differences and geographic distances. The hierarchy, or coordination by providing information, advice and instructions, has typically been the method of choice to create a climate of fusion rather than fission. Hierarchic control mirrors cerebral commands.

THE TWO-SIDED BRAIN

While the command model has probably been the most popular analogy between the brain and human organizations, another view based on the two hemispheres comprising the cerebrum, has, in recent years, gained currency. (The two views are not incompatible with each other.) The left hemisphere or left brain is the center of a person's logical and analytical abilities (computation, language, science) while the right hemisphere or right brain is the locus of one's artistic and emotional make-up (music, art, imagination).[3] Left-brain dominant individuals would fit in better in an organization or department where the bulk of the information processing and decision-making tasks require rigorous analysis and/or calculation like the design and manufacture of production machinery or the fabrication of steel support structures for a building. On the other hand, right brain dominance would make one better suited to carrying out interior decoration or the development of advertising plans and copy. As attractive and useful as the right brain-left brain concept might appear to be, in assigning people to specific jobs, it isn't the easiest thing in the world to find out who's a right-brain person and who's left-brain dominant. Few, if any, of us are solely one or the other; moreover, few jobs require only one type of thinking from the person occupying the position. For example, in designing machinery, other factors besides production efficiency need to be considered—operator comfort levels, maintenance and cleaning access, and appearance, to name a few. On the other hand, artists, in order to successfully develop and give full expression to their talents, have to cultivate a knowledge of materials and effective techniques, as well as skills in negotiating and finalizing business arrangements.

In spite of the limitations inherent in trying to broadly classify people and occupations, the left brain-right brain hypothesis retains considerable appeal. It provides a convenient way of describing jobs and employees and, particularly in the case of managerial positions, helps in visualizing the specific skills (analytical ability, language and interpersonal skills, computational talents, and creativity) that an executive should possess.[4] Some organizations have taken the concept one step further and loosely split the organization into right and left brain components. The split-organization separates the "creative" wing, which typically encompasses the first and third Cs of value (conceptualization and communication) on the one hand, from value construction and the other "routine" functions such as finance, accounting and personnel, on the other.[5] The arm's length relationship implied in the split design (as in the left brain-right brain perspective) clearly stresses the different skills in which parts of the organization (or brain) have specialized. But just as clearly, we must steer clear of the insulation (and in the case of the firm, indifference) that such a separation can breed. The temptation to treat the separate components as self-sufficient and independent is no less strong *between* value functions as it is *within* them. While physical inventory and delinking through large batch scheduling are typical sources of insulation within any stage of the value chain, possible separations between product development and market research, and delinking by dissociation (say, designs that do not build upon the firm's manufacturing capabilities) are examples of the types of chasms that often exist *between* rather than *within* the 3Cs.

LIMITATIONS OF THE COMPARTMENTAL ANALOGIES

The command-control and left-right brain views of the brain are illustrative of specialized and hierarchically run organizations. However, these models do not do adequate justice to the capabilities of the brain. Nor do they provide a completely appropriate model when it comes to managing a complex modern firm. In fact, the problems faced by many firms today arise precisely due to horizontal separation (in terms of geographic distances, goals, and attitudes) among groups as well as the vertical separation that often exists among hierarchic levels (in terms of goals, perceived abilities, and needs). Extending the brain's power of specialization and its command-control capability to organizations results in the creation of both horizontal as well as vertical gaps. Attempts to coordinate and motivate employees within such a framework could turn out to be an exercise in futility. At any rate, such a design would certainly be inadequate if we wish to create an organization with an inbuilt, self-regulated value drive rather than one in which the value orientation has to be intermittently, if not constantly, imposed from above.

Redundancy of components and in-functions gives the human brain a flexibility and versatility that few organizations can match.[6] Due to redundant components, removal of even forty or fifty percent of certain portions of the brain do not result in a significant loss in capabilities. Moreover, functions such as memory are so dispersed that damage to one part activates similar functions located elsewhere. (The left brain/right brain division is also, on occasion, known to break down—damage to one hemisphere results in the other one coming to its rescue.) Can firms evolve from a stick to your job, keep your distance style of functioning to a "we're all in this together" mode? Is it possible to even visualize an organization in which management's right to command and control takes second place to the need to consult and to create value irrespective of position or status, and without periodic intervention?

LESSONS FROM SMALL BUSINESSES

Small businesses, whether established to sell ice cream, manufacture low-capacity pumps, organize newspaper delivery or repair sporting equipment, can provide valuable guidance, in addressing these questions, to their larger and presumably more successful business cousins. One of the biggest differences between small firms and most large ones is the easy informality and flexibility that typically governs relationships in the former. Schedules are changed to accommodate commitments made by the salesperson to a customer. Problems in the field are quickly communicated back to Design/Production by the service personnel. Incoming materials are often dispatched, used and paid for on the basis of verbal agreements. A small business is not a big business reduced by a few scales of magnitude. It is a completely different *species* of organization.[7] The urgency of survival is much greater, which contributes somewhat to the increased willingness to cooperate. When a firm's next mistake could be its last one, it helps to, as was once said of the possibility of death by hanging, "focus the mind." Employees in a small business are generally more sensitive to the potential for imminent disaster because they typically do not have the luxury of a "fall back" position in case things go wrong or if special needs cannot be catered to. If a machine is being used for regularly scheduled production, disruptions can be avoided if similar machines are available either at the same plant or at a different location. Yet, resource stringency often dictates otherwise. When the employees of the firm realize (and they must) the firm's total dependence on its customers, cooperation and understanding of the roles others play in fulfilling customers' needs are relatively easier to generate. In effect, small businesses achieve connections *among* the value activities not by constantly exhorting or coercing them to coordinate their efforts and to be adaptive to emerging needs but by creating a common vision in all of them, the vision of value delivered. When survival is at stake, a sense of missionary zeal is indispensable.

In earlier diagrams we have shown the 3Cs *sequentially* leading to the customer, with Communication playing the anchor role, so to speak, in this "relay race." That, however, is only a depiction of the physical flow of the product or service. For value to be successfully and continuously accumulated, a unifying vision of what value consists of and how it is to be achieved are indispensable prerequisites. In other words, it is not enough to improve the 3Cs individually. They have to be brought into step with one another. Equally important, the communication of the vision has to be complemented by a *willingness* to pull together. Why do most small businesses find it easier to arrive at the integrating vision that their larger (and presumably successful) counterparts find so elusive? One big reason is the partiality that growing firms have for adding department and job titles. As Joe, employed by a start-up, struggles along, making a living by trying to sell medical supplies to area hospitals or tools to local factories, making the next sale and keeping customers satisfied is far more important to him than his position within the firm or his departmental affiliation. Once the product and the firm gain acceptance in the marketplace, Joe, along with his recently acquired colleagues Jim and Jane, will probably be designated the Sales Department. More success will bring with it the perceived (and presumably urgent) need to induct into the firm specialists in feeling the pulse of the customer, in devising means to increase demand or in providing wider availability of the product. As the Marketing Research, Promotion, and Channel Management functions are added, the creation of an all-inclusive group such as the Marketing Department becomes a pressing need. Our three Js may continue in Sales or may have opted to join one of the new entities. It hardly matters. Their primary allegiance is now likely to be with the "specialist" function of which they are a part, rather than to the firm in whose shade they have flourished. (It is entirely possible that their secondary loyalty would be to the department and/or its manager; the company may come in a poor third.)

As new functional groups are created, the potential for disagreement and conflict goes up. Uniting in the common cause of value becomes almost impossible when apparently incompatible goals, work methods, and philosophies keep groups apart.[8] What makes things worse is that the Owner's (or CEO's) vision may not be enough to pull divergent perspectives together. Typically, the CEO's time and energy are mostly expended in studying and dealing with the external environment and what most employees get is a second- or third-hand vision. The excitement of being in on a risky, pioneering, potentially lucrative venture gives way to doing something because "it's my job." What can we do so we can have our cake—retain the flexibility and passion that pervades many small businesses—and eat it too by enjoying the fruits of growth?

FIRMS OF ALL SIZES AND HOLOGRAPHY

Much can be done to achieve this culinary miracle. But to begin with, we have to reconcile ourselves to the fact that time is irreversible. That is, no person or firm can ever return to a past state. While in the case of humans and other living creatures, physiological reasons explain this "arrow of time," the process of learning through collective experience often leaves an indelible stamp on organizations. A product or service that "bombs," customers who do not pay up, pilferage by employees, and unethical advertising practices adopted by competitors are but a sprinkling of the situations against which firms develop defense mechanisms (such as refusing to sell to previously delinquent customers) and even preemptive tactics (e.g., provide ethics education to employees), none of which can or should be unlearned. These experiences are all a part of the process of growing up. Ideally, the various components of the firm should grow up together with a similar outlook on the firm, its product(s) and the basis of customer value.

Sharing events and experiences as an organization grows in age, size and capability, is an important way of locking different value activities into a common vision. We offer the *hologram* as a model.[9] In holography, a ray of light is split in two, one half striking the object (O) to be reproduced and the other half impinging on a sensitive holographic plate (P) (Figure 5.1). Light from S reflected off the object also travels to P and through the phenomenon of interference, an image is formed on the plate. Not

Figure 5.1
Holography

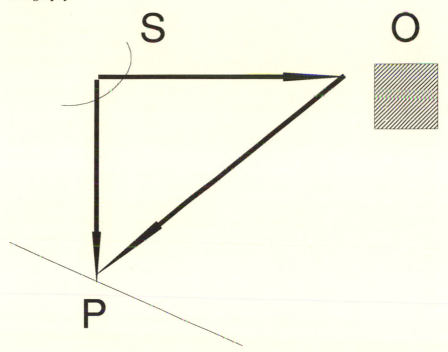

only is the image a faithful reproduction of the object with an appearance of three dimensionality, the absence of a lens (as in photography) reduces distortion and increases clarity. Moreover, the image of the entire object can be recreated from *parts* of the hologram. The whole is *in* the parts!

The organizational equivalent of a hologram is one where *every* employee, regardless of departmental affiliation (or hierarchic level), is a microcosm of the entire organization. Not that we expect each employee to be capable of performing any task that needs to be performed. Rather, the intent is to equip as many people as possible with *information* about what everyone else does, why and how they do it, and how they fit in with the grand scheme of things in the firm. Gareth Morgan[10] suggests that, to be considered holographic, an organization must also create (a) connectivity and redundancy, (b) both specialization and generalization and (c) the ability to self-organize. Such a holistic, empathic attitude is based upon spreading the message of value clearly and effectively. SAS (Scandinavian Airline System) Chief Executive Carlzon,[11] in emphasizing the need for courtesy, accuracy and timeliness in dealings with customers was, in effect, giving all SAS employees a single vision to guide them during their numerous "moments of truth" (interactions with customers) everyday. He realized that, particularly in dealing with customers, every employee *is* the entire firm and must convey to the customer, everything that the firm stands for. For every employee to be familiar with the firm's value thrust, the latter has to be clearly enunciated and conveyed, preferably through face-to-face meetings arranged between the top functional executive and the employees in that activity area. For example, the Vice President for Marketing should make it a point to periodically meet with groups of Marketing people. At a minimum, each group should have direct contact with this executive once every year in order to renew the message of value.[12] Essentially, the meetings should be used to articulate and prioritize the firm's sources of value (responsiveness, post-sale service, quality, and flexibility) explaining the group's specific role in delivering the value envisioned. Even a hint of rivalry with other (supporting) value activities is to be avoided. How the function or department fits into the interdependent "value system" is to be emphasized. Ideally, of course, the Chief Executive should communicate the firm's value emphasis directly to all the employees, since he or she is less likely to be linked with any departmental affiliation. However, as an organization grows, this quickly becomes infeasible due to the sheer numbers involved and the need to keep the group sizes manageable. (In a company with 5000 employees, at least 200 such direct access meetings would be required if the number present at each gathering were to be limited to 25.) Except in the case of smaller and medium-sized firms, therefore, the head of the (functional) value activity is probably the best person for the job provided he or she can rise above the narrower interests of the group and persuade others to do likewise.

THE MULTIPLE PERSPECTIVES OF JOB ROTATION

Regardless of the industry or type of firm, disseminating the nature and roots of value across the organization is an excellent way of laying the foundation for the holographic organization. Once unanimity of vision, or as near it as possible, becomes a reality, *redundancy of function* can be attempted. Job rotation makes the latter more attainable. Rotating people from one job to another not only gives them a greater variety of experience, it recharges workers with a sense of purpose. Having been in someone else's shoes makes it easier to step into them when the need arises. The ultimate objective of job rotation, however, is not the interchangeability of employees nor the prevention of boredom. Rather, job rotation should help individuals leave their individual and departmental baggage behind and see their department and organization from as many different angles as possible. Empathy and understanding develop among the various positions regardless of whether the jobs being rotated are supervisory or skilled in nature.[13]

If job rotation is to be beneficial to employee and organization, successive moves should occur between jobs in *related* value activities since the underlying purpose is the development of a holistic view of value. Stints in Sales, Production Planning, and Marketing Research would make for a better awareness among managerial personnel of customer needs and the firm's ability to fulfill them—across the board and not just within the confines of one department or activity. For skilled workers, however, rotation *within* departmental limits would be more meaningful to the employee and of direct impact to the firm.[14] Making highly disparate job assignments could be counterproductive if the individual does not clearly see the value linkage among the value activities. If, for instance, someone were to be rotated through Engineering, Advertising, and Inventory Management, he or she might not readily grasp the interwoven character of the value creation process. Neither the firm nor the individual is likely to benefit from such an experience.

The duration of rotation should be sufficient for adequate learning to take place. In most jobs this time period is of the order of two to five years. (It should be at least equal to the product lead time, which in the case of products such as steam turbines, missile systems and the like would be near the upper end of this scale.) Short stays in any department tend to devalue the importance of learning and encourage some to treat the interval as a chance for some much needed R&R. Also, product value is likely to be an early casualty—employees are likely to contribute little and gain even less—as would the level of commitment, enthusiasm and morale.

A value-integrative focus can be extended to human resource systems as well. For example, selection techniques (screening, testing, interviewing) should assess the complete person—how well he or she meshes with the company's value creation process, and their ability to absorb and see many points of view.[15] In addition to productivity, quality, and responsiveness, an important method of evaluating people would be based on their ability to take a holographic view of the firm. Rewards may be based, therefore, partly on the variety of skills learned or number of jobs performed satisfactorily. Training programs, in addition to targeting and teaching specific skills and techniques, could also help supplement selection and appraisal strategies by building awareness and support of the holistic nature of the firm's value mission.[16]

The objective of job rotation is not to manufacture interchangeable people, who can, like standardized parts or modules in the case of mass-produced products, be easily replaced or substituted. While such redundancy of function certainly does provide backup support and flexibility, the deepest, most durable outcome of a successful rotation system is the total commitment of each employee to the firm's value base. The products and the value it delivers then become a centripetal force binding the

Figure 5.2
Functional Framework for Organization

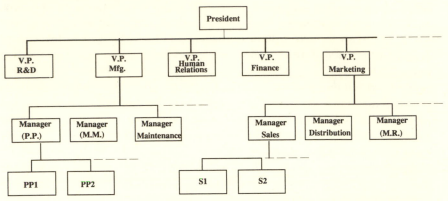

PP: Production Planning
MM: Materials Management
MR: Marketing Research

diverse activities performed within the firm together. The fusion of different value perspectives—their implosion, so to speak, in one person and the pursuit of customer value through internal synchronization can be undertaken in other ways as well. One such implosion device is triggered by changes in the structure.

STRUCTURE BUSTING

Mention "organization structure" to managers, salespersons, machine operators and almost anyone else and the odds are they'll shudder involuntarily. Structure typically evokes images of restrictions and prohibitions, of whom to report to and whom to communicate with, of departments, power and dry, unimaginative rules. We have little argument with this perception. For structures often become sterile, inert things that succeed only too well in creating barriers with far greater efficiency than they can integrate. Consider the functional (or process-based) structure, shown in Figure 5.2. The functional design emphasizes specialist skills in the performance of activities to create value *separately* from one another. Typically, vertical coordination is performed by hierarchic authority (or the handing down of procedures, rules and regulations derived from such authority) while horizontal coordination is, according to the chart, performed by the common boss. (While we shall tackle vertical linkage in the next chapter, we cannot resist the temptation to point out that the command-control model suggested by early brain research is the operative model here—and it is an inadequate one.) Referring to Figure 5.2, horizontal coordination and communication between, say, salesperson S1 and Production Planner PP1, can only be achieved, technically by climbing up the ladder to the common managerial level, which could be time consuming and frustrating due to interdepartmental differences. It could even get worse. Managers may not understand what they're supposed to be coordinating. After all, managers, too, have pet disciplines and the mill manager of a paper mill may not have the expertise to mediate between the Maintenance and Quality Control departments. Individuals and groups, as we stressed earlier, have a tendency to grow away from each other and, much in the same way as sibling rivalry is impervious to parental authority, managers find that mutual understanding and compromise cannot be imposed.

One way to encourage movement toward such an understanding is through the formation of "Structure-Busting Teams" (SBTs). The purpose of these teams is to overcome the compartmental, territorial instincts that many structural arrangements breed. Diversified firms deal with the complexity associated with many products and many functions by creating product divisions or units. These are essentially autonomous or semi-autonomous groups. They start as SBTs, since functional separation is reduced by focusing attention on the product—a return to the days of the firm's youth when in all probability a dedicated core of employees single -mindedly pursued customers and customer value.[17] Divisions also, unfortunately, develop the pathological traits of their predecessors. For one thing, if they are successful, they start erecting the same differences they were supposed to demolish. Worse still, they operate in splendid isolation from the rest of the organization since they are generally held separately accountable for results. Not only do horizontal communication problems persist, impeding value enhancement *within* each product division, they are further compounded by interproduct barriers which reduce the degree of value-sharing among them. Both the *intensive* as well as *extensive* dimensions of value suffer.

A variation on the divisional grouping is the hub and spoke system adopted by most major airlines. The hub and spoke arrangement is an attempt to back off from (regional) autonomy. If the trunk national airlines were to divide the country up into regions and give each region the freedom to decide routing, scheduling and number of flights, wasteful overlapping of flight patterns and a low utilization of plane capacity would result. The larger airlines have therefore struck a compromise between total centralization of all flights emanating from and terminating at any point, on the one hand, and total autonomy of each region to manage its own affairs independently. Delta, for instance, has its primary hub at Atlanta and many Delta flights between the larger U.S. cities are routed through Atlanta.[18] If you needed to get to Dallas from New York, chances are you would first go to Atlanta and take another flight onward to Dallas.

If you needed to go on to a small town near Dallas by plane, you are likely to be routed through a commuter airline, an extension of the Atlanta-Dallas spoke. It might appear that this is a staggeringly centralized structure in which all the routes, planes, equipment, personnel, and decision making are centralized at the hub. This is undoubtedly true where national routes are concerned. The "non-hub" operations, however, have considerable discretion in arrangements made to service customer needs at their location, both in terms of airport operations as well as linkages with satellite towns and cities served. Moreover, the successful airlines that have expanded explosively since deregulation have established additional hubs. Delta operates secondary hubs at Cincinnati and Seattle. A single hub can take an airline only so far before the communication and cooperation needed acquire a negative force large enough to outweigh the positive forces generated by better control and coordination. A large airline with one hub must learn to deal with the drag and turbulence, so to speak, of geographic dispersion or possibly divergent views of the firm's interests and mission. On the other hand, airlines with two or more hubs face problems of coordination every bit as gargantuan and complex as the wide-body jets they employ on most transcontinental flights. The problems are miniscule, however, when compared to the resource and value-possessiveness they replace.

The hub and spoke system, incidentally, can be used in other industries as well. DVC Industries, which manufactures a range of vinyl binders, folders and other stationery (for corporate, commercial and personal use) operates out of five facilities nationally. Orders are centralized at the main office (hub) in Long Island and, based on the capability, capacity and materials available at each of the plants (spokes) the orders are farmed out. Even though the customer isn't in the system continuously (as in the instance of an airline), the same problems of separation, disunity and narrowness of focus arise and must be addressed. Why adopt a hub and spoke manufacturing (or its equivalent in the worldwide sense, globally coordinated manufacturing) system at all? Why not allow each plant to book its own orders and service its own customers? A firm with a closely related array of products can ill afford the barriers that will inevitably be erected between product divisions. The reluctance to share information on value and the costs caused by duplicated resources will be intolerably heavy, especially for the small- or medium-sized firm.

Autonomous product divisions are not always guilty of dissipating value, even if the divisions are in highly related fields. Sometimes corporate divisions help coordinate the value capabilities (3Cs) of the divisions, if similar components of value (flexibility in time or volume, pre- and post-sales service, etc.) apply to them. However, since corporate coordination, once initiated, often grows to monstrously expensive proportions—and takes on a life and meaning of its own—this option should, in our judgement, be considered as a last resort.

Another approach to partly neutralizing the fissures created by divisionalizing is the Strategic Business Unit (SBU). Obviously, for a firm that in separate divisions makes many highly related products, attempts at developing a *common value focus* toward these products (e.g., washers, dryers, ovens, microwaves, refrigerators, and air conditioners) could only be for the good of the firm. In this instance a large appliance SBU would, therefore, be invaluable in articulating a common design philosophy (particularly helpful when these appliances are sold through bidding to builders of homes and apartments), in sharing production facilities to improve quality and lead times and reduce costs, and in conveying a uniform image and message to customers.[19] SBUs, in the sense that they help share value (even if imperfectly), are most certainly SBTs as well. They occupy the middle ground between the value-concentration of the functional form and the value-dispersion of the divisional organization. In hub and spoke non-airline firms, SBUs are invaluable because they help the adoption of a single value focus within a product or product family across geographic locations. If such coordination did not exist, the hub and spoke arrangement would fall victim to the malady that affects most regionally organized firms in which product attention and a value focus tend to take a back seat to regional performance.

CUTTING ACROSS THE 3Cs

Product divisions and SBUs demonstrate their structure-busting properties in diversified firms by spreading the bases of value around. However, the problem of unifying a firm laterally, by cutting across functional boundaries, still remains. Job rotation and other human resource strategies help turn employees into Corporate Citizens (not just Departmental Loyalists) with a broad, unifying perspective on delivering value, and are extremely effective at the *individual* level. Teams that cut across functional groupings are an excellent structural (or structure-busting) complement to holographic individuals and the firm's value orientation provides a solid basis for the formation of this type of SBT. For example, if response time and flexibility in being able to supply in varying quantities and styles are dominant criteria, a team may be constituted consisting of one or more people from each of the 3Cs (Development, Production Planning, Manufacturing, Quality Assurance, Sales, and Marketing Research being a fairly representative team) and from other areas such as Finance/ Accounting and Human Resource Management, if necessary. Team members should preferably have been exposed through training, job rotation, or otherwise, to at least two functional specialisms, so that they bring to the team a broad view of the product, the firm, its customers and the rest of the external environment. When, for instance, two or more individuals in a team have sales experience they would bring a greater wealth of ideas to a discussion of how the sales function could enhance flexibility and response time than if there were only one person to provide the "sales point of view." While such value-maximizing teams should have wide ranging membership, they typically will play only an advisory role.[20] Authority to make decisions must continue to rest with the functional manager, otherwise the organization will begin to resemble a commune or cooperative society. We don't have anything against these admirable organizational forms, but they best exist in the right places and under the right conditions. Both types often fulfill the dominant concerns of their members (survival in a harsh natural environment, producing and distributing a limited range of products solely for their members' consumption.) However, giving peer groups line authority in customer value-driven organizations would severely undercut the standing of managers designated to make such decisions. Organizing an entire firm on the basis of peer groups is of course, a possibility, albeit an expensive one. Since, as Michel's Iron Law of Oligarchy rather pessimistically suggests, all peer group systems will inevitably tend to become hierarchic, collegiality is unlikely in a corporate setting.[21] True, firms have successfully deployed autonomous or nearly autonomous groups, as we indicated in the previous chapter, which have taken on considerable decision-making responsibility. Volvo's and Nissan's teams (in Smyrna, Tennessee) are well-known instances. However, such peer groups cannot both perform a wide range of manufacturing tasks and produce in high volumes nor are they designed to cut across functional or activity barriers. Rather, they try to link sequentially interdependent activities by encompassing them within one comprehensive group.[22]

Our interdepartmental team, we have argued at some length, should have persuasive and not binding authority on line managers. Its membership should be rotated among individuals within each functional activity so as to provide more individuals exposure to holistic thinking as well as to broaden the range of experience commanded by these value-maximizing teams. Ideally, the suggestions and ideas generated by such SBTs should be disseminated to the rank and file by the departmental team member. However, given the realities of organizational life, communication provided by the manager will do almost as well—better, perhaps, given the greater credence many of us attach to information flowing downward.

Apart from the value-focused team or teams—there may be many, each concerned with one face of value (conflict and overlap would have to be carefully tracked)—other types of cross-functional teams such as product development teams should be established to further expand the web of horizontal connections.[23] (Again, the teams' focus must be clear and the membership eclectic.) Another instance of a cross-functional team is the benchmarking team. Its primary mission is to keep track of and accurately measure competitors' positions and achievements relative to those of the firm. The benchmarking team may draw its members from the same or different departments as the value-team(s). Competitor intelligence useful to other teams would be passed on through the team leader. Departmental managers and team members belonging to the same department would be supplemental interface points for transfer of information. Benchmarking teams assume greater importance when markets turn nasty of their own volition (as in an economic downturn) or are forced into nastiness. Some examples are

- the sudden influx of new competitors as happened in the microcomputer industry in the early 1980s and, more recently, in the commercial aircraft industry;

- the numerous alliances that have reshaped the book publishing industry in less than a decade, making it imperative not only to keep tabs on competitors' product line strategies but also the components and capabilities for value delivery intrinsic to each of them;

- and the articulation of value through distinctive service strategies by firms such as Weyerhauser in order to gain a competitive edge over their rivals in the lumber industry.

THE VALUE OF INFORMATION

Another way in which information can contribute, albeit indirectly, to the enhancement of value is by its being made available where and when needed within the firm. Obviously, the needs of decision makers at higher levels of the firm must be catered to and various alternative designs of Management Information Systems can be evaluated and deployed depending on the nature of the industry, the details of information needed, and the frameworks or models chosen for decision making. In addition to the decision-making needs that information fills, it also helps movement toward the holographic organization and supports measures like job rotation, SBTs, and training. Information systems that facilitate the sharing of information *across value areas* in addition to providing information specific to each value area are necessary. The use of comprehensive data bases (perhaps with restricted access to sensitive information) would be one approach to wider sharing of information. The wider use of real time data-sharing systems has undoubtedly helped strengthen the linkages among disparate activity areas and dispersed locations.

SUPPLIER LINKAGES

Not all types of teams will consist of members drawn only from within the firm. Where the purpose, for instance, is to establish effective connections with parts of the external environment—suppliers and customers being two of the more important elements to attract this sort of effort—the teams will perforce be not just on an inter-activity and interdepartmental basis but also intercompany. That is, the value vision has to transcend both internal and external barriers. Internal barriers to horizontal value exchanges can be reduced through the use of value teams, job rotation, broader training, etc. External barriers need to be separately tackled. It is not uncommon for firms to assume a stance of confrontation or hostility, particularly toward suppliers. The argument is typically made that competition among suppliers will, as in any free market context, bring out the best in them, and hence the best for the firm. The following aggressive (and cliché-ridden) sentiments have tended to characterize the approach selected by many firms for dealing with their suppliers: The more suppliers we have the better it is for us since we have more fall back positions. Never paint yourself into a "single-supplier corner" for any material. The squeeze won't be long in coming. Lay down the law (specification-wise), and keep an eye on them constantly to make sure they don't deviate. They'll quickly learn who's boss!

This is understandable. Many of us as price-conscious consumers would willingly switch from a brand of soap, tire, or copier paper we've been using regularly to a newly introduced product, particularly if it's priced, packaged and promoted attractively. Shouldn't buyers of raw materials, components, assemblies, and intermediate products do likewise in order to benefit the buying firm? Buyers do indeed have the *right* to assert their dominance, though they should beware of the economic equivalent of killing the goose that laid the golden egg. That is, impose such a nest of restrictions and caveats that the supplier is either forced to find more understanding buyers or slip slowly toward financial disaster.

Again, "playing the field" with suppliers, while it induces a sense of independence and freedom of choice, certainly does little to foster a sense of commitment, and of mutual resolve to tackle jointly the problems and possibilities of delivering value to the ultimate user of the product. The type of relationship evolving between certain suppliers and customers in the paper industry may, however, be a sign of the times. Engelhard's Pigments and Additives Division mines, processes, and delivers products (derived from minerals such as kaolin) to a range of customers, one of which is the giant International Paper Corporation. One might expect that the relationship between firms of such magnitude would be characterized by impersonality and mere economics. Not on your life. The divisions of

Englehard and International Paper that do business with each other are engaged in developing the long-term aspects of the linkage by

- helping the supplier find ways of meeting specifications;
- providing information (from supplier to customer or vice-versa) that will lead to quality and/or productivity improvements;
- the supplier collecting information about the ultimate consumer (concerning, say, preferences for a specific type of coated paper for magazine printing) in order to benefit the intermediate buyer—in this case International Paper.[24]

The customer (say, IP) commits to buying a certain minimum amount of the material every quarter, establishing a certain level of commitment on its part to the supplier (Englehard). The supplier in return will devote more time and attention to dealing with any problems the customer might face, even to the extent of studying and filling the needs of subsequent buyers along the chain.

Black-Clawson, one of the most highly-regarded producers of paper-making machinery in the world has, in its Shartle Division (where its focus is primarily on the recycling process) gone one step further. Perceiving that its major competency lay in the conceptualization of value, the firm has considerably strengthened its Research, Development, Engineering, and related capabilities, while increasingly outsourcing its equipment needs. In certain instances, products are completely assembled by suppliers to Black-Clawson's detailed specs.[25]

SUPPLIER-CUSTOMER TEAMS

In building on its design expertise and seeking to coopt its upstream vendors (by sharing know-how with them) Black-Clawson's Shartle Division has demonstrated a willingness to maximize value through external dependence. It becomes critical in situations like this to link the mutually dependent parties together effectively. The traditional boundaries and barriers between vendor and buyer have to be moderated and even erased. As the two become increasingly interdependent they have to develop more openness of access to each other's people, information and materials. The development of greater openness, understanding and dependence with suppliers is part of a larger process of establishing partnership and cooperative arrangements with vendors. Vendors are regarded not merely as providers of materials but also as worthy recipients of information which can be *leveraged* and returned to the buyer with increasing returns.[26] Helping vendors can help the buyer many times over. Opening up access to more activities in each others' firms is one way to accomplish this. That is, rather than confining contact to preassigned departments

Figure 5.3
Porous Value Chains

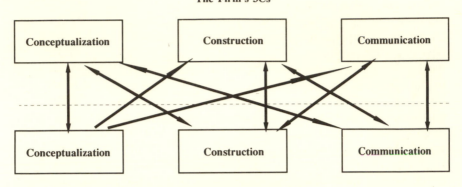

(Purchasing, Materials Management, Sales, Shipping, etc.) employees are granted authorization, even encouraged, to call, write or meet the activity person they deem most relevant to the job at hand. For example, if production (and shipment) are being delayed by a bottleneck in the Heat-treatment department, the buying firm's representative should feel no qualms in getting in touch with someone in this department to ascertain the status of orders. Similarly, when design and/or manufacturing-related problems occur, communication should be as unrestricted between the R&D of the vendor and the manufacturing department of the buyer, or vice-versa, as necessary. In other words, the value chains of the firm and its vendors should become *porous* to each other as shown in Figure 5.3. No activity should remain a black box, accessible only through the intervention of a "contact" activity or department. A way of enhancing customer value through an optimal sharing of information between customer and vendor is through the increasingly popular technique of Electronic Data Interchange (EDI). EDI, in essence, is an information system which renders the firm and its vendors progressively transparent to each other. The information needed (status of orders, design modifications being attempted, material substitution results) is provided both ways on-line. Obviously, the more value areas in each firm that come under the realm of EDI, the greater will be the linkage between them. EDI could also prove helpful in rethinking the nature of linkages among activities, and serve to reengineer them, in order to facilitate the flow of information within the firm as well as outside the firm to its suppliers and customers.[27] However, we would urge that before direct computer linkages are attempted, teams be employed to deal with some of the problems arising from differences in procedures, management styles, and culture that are almost sure to crop up and stymie the functioning of the information system. Initiating greater permeability, so to speak, between firms and their vendors is difficult to achieve because old ideas die hard. Whoever heard of treating suppliers as equal partners? In the natural order of things, suppliers are supplicants, orders are favors, and passive agreement is the best type of communication. However, this seemingly best of all possible worlds (from the buyer's point of view) is not necessarily beneficial even in the short run to the ultimate consumer. In the long run it benefits no one. Imposing one's will on suppliers often results in their being unwilling partners, in a drying up of mutually useful ideas, and perhaps in short-lived vendor relationships leading to quality, delivery and, later, cost-related problems. Locating the best vendor, from time to time, as a particular product/component need arises *might* work for commodity-like, off the shelf items such as fasteners, enamel paints or lubricants, for which many suppliers, each capable of similar levels of service, exist. (Even for such products, supply improvements based on an intimate knowledge of buyers' emergent needs are always possible.) Specific-purpose components (tailored to a particular application to suit a firm's needs) whose design and manufacturing process are being constantly improved, however, call for significant interaction between a firm and its vendor.

The initiative for rising above the inertial tendency to slip into the customary vendor/buyer stereotype has to be exercised by the party with the greater leverage. This could be the larger firm, the firm with concentrated buying/selling power, or the one with the distinctive product. Xerox, for example, has been able to establish exceptionally close links with many of its suppliers, resulting in the receipt of daily shipments in the quantities and to the quality needed, due to its ability to purchase the entire outputs of most of these suppliers.[28] The suppliers, on the other hand, are able to provide components tailored to Xerox's needs. At its best, the relationship is transformed from a manipulative to a symbiotic one. Rather than seeking to get the most out of the other, the objective becomes one of maximizing mutual gains by concentrating on the product and *its* users.

Not only is it imperative to achieve greater permeability to adjacent value chains, contact with value chains even further removed should not be taboo. Access to information about our customer's customers should not be granted as a special favor but as a matter of course, particularly if it will improve our vendor's service to us. Knowing the present and projected quality, quantity and response-time needs of magazine or newspaper publishers enables Black-Clawson to design better equipment for its papermaking customers. Similarly, Engelhard's quality concerns should not (and are not) limited to its *immediate* customers such as International Paper but range far wider to the ultimate user. The next process

Figure 5.4
Integration—A Look Back

The brain as an organizational analogy

    — The Command Control model
    — The left brain-right brain view

Limitations of compartmental views

Multifunctional capabilities of the brain

The essence of small business

Holography and the development of multiple views

Empathy and cooperation

Job-rotation—concepts and actions

Structures and structure busting

    SBTs: Hub and Spoke, value teams, training

    SBUs: Coordinated action on value

    Suppliers as partners; trust and cooperation
        — the use of EDI, providing mutual access to each other's
           3Cs

is indeed the customer, and this statement undoubtedly exemplifies the need to tighten interdependencies among successive operations and processes (as discussed in the preceding chapter). However, customers are not to be found at the *next process alone*. **Every downstream process is a customer and every parallel process is a partner.** Anything that enhances downstream and parallel value will, in the end, enhance value delivered.

The paper industry is a particularly apt vehicle to use in illustrating the changing nature of supplier-customer relationships. The industry is becoming increasingly global in terms of market needs, competition, and manufacturing base. Consolidation through acquisition of smaller firms is an ongoing phenomenon. Firms, in honing their skills and ability to compete with firms from across the world are looking for allies wherever they can find them. One of the first such allegiances seems to be between the supplier and customer. Exploitative tendencies are giving way to cooperation, synergy and mutually reinforcing value-creation processes. The paper industry, in our perspective, is bestirring itself in its mission of value and is unlikely to go the way of the steel, automobile, and consumer electronics industries, which succumbed to the onslaught of foreign competitors. Of course, not only are paper firms embarked on a revolution in the management of supplier-customer dependencies, they are attempting to come to grips with other problems impeding value creation and delivery. One such problem is that of not utilizing the human resource to the fullest extent possible, of not realizing the entire potential of the firm's employees. In taking up this issue next, we shall explore what can be done to more fully elicit commitment and to breathe new life into the firm's strategies, perhaps even generate more effective ones.

NOTES

1. See, for instance, *Collier's Encyclopedia* (New York: Macmillan, 1991), pp. 463–67.

2. See, for example, Arlyn Melcher and Bernard Arogyaswamy, "The Shifting Playing Field in Global Competition," in William Wallace, ed., *Global Manufacturing: Technological and Economic Opportunities and Research Issues* (Greenwich, CT: Jai Press, 1992).

3. For a detailed discussion of asymmetry in brain functions see Michael Corballis, *Human Laterality* (New York: Academic Press, 1983), pp. 29–64.

4. For a look at the managerial implications of such asymmetry, see Henry Mintzberg, "Planning on the Left Side and Managing on the Right," *Harvard Business Review*, 1976, 54: 49–58.

5. Raymond Radosevich, "Strategic Implications for Organizational Design," in Igor Ansoff, Roger Declerck and Robert Hayes, eds., *From Strategic Planning to Strategic Management* (New York: Wiley, 1976), pp. 161–77.

6. Gareth Morgan's *Images of Organization* (Beverly Hills: Sage, 1986) includes an excellent treatment of redundancy of both parts and functions (pp. 98–9). In fact, the work offers a detailed analysis of the brain as a metaphor for organizations (pp. 79–109).

7. Peter Drucker's *Innovation and Entrepreneurship* suggests that small businesses could be managed by attending to or modifying the success employed in running large organizations. We tend to agree with Hawken's (*Growing a Business,* pp. 12, 15) experience and argument which assert that a completely different attitude is required to manage a small business.

8. Paul Lawrence and Jay Lorsch, *Organization and Environment*, (Cambridge: Harvard University Press, 1967).

9. W. T. Welford's *Optics* (Oxford: Oxford University Press, 1980, pp. 106–20) provides a detailed technical view while S. Tolousky's *Revolution in Optics* (Harmondsworth, UK: Penguin, 1968, pp. 207–11) tackles the subject in a more general manner.

10. Gareth Morgan, *Images of Organization*, pp. 97–105.

11. Jan Carlzon, *Moments of Truth* (New York: Ballinger, 1987), pp. 21–29.

12. Buck Rogers (*The IBM Way*, New York: Harper & Row, 1987), who was IBM's top marketing executive for many years, asserts that all levels of management need to meet periodically with the groups reporting to them. In fact, he used to bring a group once every three months to headquarters to meet with him.

13. Kiyoshi Suzaki, *The New Manufacturing Challenge* (New York: The Free Press, 1987), pp. 65–67.

14. Ibid.

15. Not only should selection consider the compatibility of firm and individual (Tony Hein, "Japanese Management in the United States," in Sang Lee and Gary Schwendiman, eds., *Management by Japanese Systems*, New York: Praeger, 1982, pp. 446–47), the level of education sought would be typically higher since a wider-angle view of the firm has to be brought to bear. See Arlyn Melcher, William Acar, Peter DuMont and Moutaz Khouja, "Standard-Maintaining and Continuous-Improvement Systems: Experiences and Comparisons," *Interfaces*, 20:3 May-June 1990, pp. 24–40.

16. The training is extensive and analytical as Melcher, Acar, DuMont and Khouya (Ibid.) point out.

17. The reduced need for coordination and the resulting possibilities for almost unlimited increases in size are undoubtedly what led Peters and Waterman (*In Search of Excellence*, New York: Harper & Row, 1982, p. 315) to extol the virtues of this form of organization.

18. Patricia McDougall, "Delta Airlines, Inc.," in John Montanari, Cyril Morgan and Jeffrey Bracker, eds., *Strategic Management* (Chicago: Dryden, 1990), pp. 657–70.

19. George S. Day, "Strategic Perspective on Product Planning," in Philip Kotler and Keith Cox, eds., *Marketing Management and Strategy: a Reader* (Englewood Cliffs, NJ: Prentice-Hall, 1980).

20. Having established a formal authority structure, organizations should obviously not do anything to undercut it. The manager should, however, be encouraged to be an empowering and true motivating leader. See Warren Bennis and Burt Nanus, *Leaders* (New York: Harper & Row, 1985), p. 217.

21. Henry Mintzberg, "Who Should Control the Corporation," (*California Management Review*, Fall 1986, pp. 90–115) discusses organizational democracy and suggests that, in spite of its unwieldy nature, some form of participatory democracy may need to be developed in organizations to mirror the world outside.

22. Neal Herrick, *Joint Management and Employee Participation* (San Francisco: Jossey-Bass, 1990, pp. 242–47) analyzes some of the principles underlying the formation and functioning of semi-autonomous teams. John Adair's *Effective Teambuilding* (London: Pan Books, 1987, pp. 102–3) describes the Nissan teams and also GM's unsatisfactory experience with teams.

23. Masaaki Imai, *Kaizen* (New York: Random House Business Division, 1986), pp. 125–42. Imai's cross-functional teams correspond to our value teams. Quality, Cost and Scheduling are their concern. The three criteria together roughly parallel our concept of value.

24. Based on a lecture given by a senior executive of Engelhard's Paints and Additives Division at the Paper Science Department of the State of University of New York, Syracuse in March 1991.

25. Based on a lecture given by a senior executive from Black-Clawson at the Paper Science Department of the State University of New York, Syracuse in April 1991.

26. For a detailed exploration of supplier linkages see Georgio Merli's *Total Manufacturing Management: Production Organization for the 1990s* (Cambridge, MA: Productivity Press, 1990), pp. 251–72. Merli describes different levels of the relationship as well as approaches to evaluation and certification.

27. For an ongoing discussion and evaluation of EDI see recent issues of *Production and Inventory Management*, particularly August 1991, p. 20.

28. Gary Jacobson and John Hillkirk, *Xerox: American Samurai* (New York: Collier Books, 1986), p. 254.

6

INVOLVEMENT: POWER OUT, VALUE IN

COMMUNISM AND THE CORPORATION

One of the most dramatic and cataclysmic events of the late-twentieth century has been the total rejection of and disgust shown toward Communism as a doctrine and as a philosophy of government. While the feeling of revulsion has run strongest in Eastern Europe, the likelihood of Communism emerging again on a worldwide scale as an economic and political counterpoint to free enterprise and democracy must be rated somewhere between remote and nonexistent. The domino effect, which was a dreaded possibility in Southeast Asia in the 1960s and 1970s, seems to have played itself out in a quite different context. Political pundits were stunned by the suddenness, speed, and in some cases, violence with which the Warsaw Pact disintegrated. The parting of the ways among the Republics of the Soviet Union was no less shocking even if, in hindsight, it appears to have been a logical conclusion to the anger felt and expressed in the rest of the Eastern Bloc. The transformation of the face of most of the erstwhile Communist countries has, by and large, been a bracing experience for democratic countries everywhere. Though the tensions caused by the splitting apart of nations could complicate international relations, the dilemma of MAD (Mutually Assured Destruction) and the threat of "instant" world wars have receded somewhat.

Before the alert reader gets the impression that our minds have been afflicted by a case of terminal wandering we hasten to point out the connection between Marxism's misery and our mission of value. In one word: power. If there's any lesson we should and must learn from the death throes of the "Evil Empire" it's about how to use and manage power. Or, to be more precise, how *not* to use and manage power.

In theory, under Communism, the people have all the power—the dictatorship of the proletariat, in Marx's immortal and ironic terminology—and the rulers merely do the common man and woman a favor by exercising power on their behalf. With the gradually increasing isolation between the powers-that-be and the "powers-that-do," something had to snap. If Gorbachev and glasnost hadn't happened along, the downward drift in the economy and the alienation of the rulers from the ruled would most likely have accelerated, resulting in an even worse explosion and fallout.

The estrangement of the rank and file from the upper echelons is not peculiar to dictatorships. It happens all the time in democracies, except that leaders pay the price for voter disillusionment. Churchill's defeat in the British elections soon after the Second World War and Lyndon Johnson's foundering candidacy in the wake of the Vietnam War are just two of the more prominent examples. It happens all the time in organizations and has, in fact, often worked to the benefit of the organization, the leader and the employees. Henry Ford, Carnegie, and J. P. Morgan, each of whom strode the early American business scene like a colossus, were not overly concerned about being popular with their employees or about eliciting worker ideas on improving job performance.[1] These and most other business leaders of the time laid down the law to their workers. There was no question who had the power, the absolute power within the firm. Along came Taylor's Scientific Management and it fit right in with the authoritarian style of the times. Not that these or the other movers and shakers of industry didn't care about their workers. Ford, for example, paid his workers more than the average market wage.[2] But when it came to power, executives and lower-level employees alike had little to none. They were expected to listen carefully and faithfully carry out instructions. The attitude toward workers was typically paternal, even patronizing. More recently, ITT's Harold Geneen and Occidental Petroleum's Armand Hammer have also wielded considerable power over their firms and the firms they directed were held up as shining examples of well-managed firms while these executives were in charge. Though concentration of power in the hands of one sovereign executive was not necessarily detrimental to the firm up until the 1930s, gradual changes have occurred. Society has become steadily more pluralistic, governments have become more active in designing and enforcing regulation, age and income patterns and gender roles keep changing almost from generation to generation, (domestic and international) competition has become more sophisticated and intensive, and customers expect products to deliver value in all its dimensions and to do so on a continuing basis. Good luck to the Chief Executive who thinks he or she can understand in detail and satisfy the needs of these and other important stakeholders. The word stake-holders is used to denote anyone who has a stake in the firm's actions and future. We prefer to view them as organizations or individuals who literally hold, in each hand, a stake which could be driven through the firm's heart.

POWER: COORDINATIVE AND ADDICTIVE

The principle of horizontal differentiation has been with us ever since the earliest hunter-gatherers decided to divide up the work so that some foraged for food, some cared for the young, while others gathered fuel, and so on. Unquestionably, managing a modern firm (even a small one) calls for dealing with a range of factors far wider than those that confronted any primitive tribe, and organizations have become accordingly more and more complex (an increased number of activities, linked to one another) in order to deal with increasing environmental complexity (increase in the number of stakeholders, also linked to one another) in the environment. As we saw in the preceding chapter, the resulting tendency for the firm to rush off madly in all directions, so to speak, has to be actively (and constantly) controlled. Under the regimen of interdependence we have prescribed for the firm's fitness and health (that is, delivering ever-increasing value), coordinating the activities of various departments is a key requirement to prevent value from disappearing into the cracks between the groups concerned. In addition to bridging the gaps between groups and linking them together more tightly, thus nudging the firm in the high-value direction, integration is equally critical to ensuring that where cooperative action among two or more parts of the firm is needed it happens as a matter of course or is mediated through a third party. The development of a protocol working toward the mutual benefit of the parties concerned requires considerable expertise and awareness of the firm's workings. The most convenient and time-tested alternative to self-coordination is the installation of a hierarchy to internally integrate the 3Cs of value and, externally, to point the firm in the right direction.

Without some form of hierarchy, most firms would quickly descend to a chaotic state for lack of both a focus for their actions and a glue to hold them together. Anyone who has been in collegial groups where everyone enjoys about equal levels of power will not question this statement—nor forget the agonizing experience! Our distaste for the use of power in authoritarian nations and firms is not directed against the *existence* of a hierarchy but of total *dependence* on it for control. Imagine a firm with, say, sixteen departments, each designed to perform distinct activities, some of which need to be more closely coordinated with each other. If the coordination is to be undertaken in groups of four departments, as shown in Figure 6.1, it is not unusual to find the hierarchy shown. (That

Figure 6.1
Typical Organizational Hierarchy

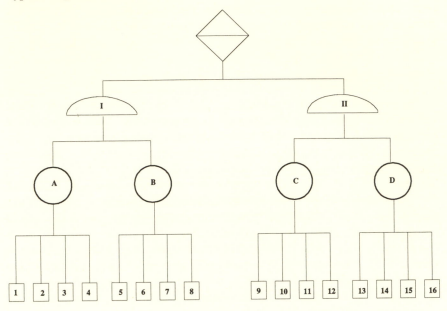

is, with three levels above that of department head or manager.) The stratification of course repeats itself within departments as well and one shouldn't be surprised to find four or five levels below that of the manager. In some firms, such multitiering (seven to eight levels) is common, starting with the corporate headquarters. The extent of the hierarchic "fix" adopted by divisions and branches, given the tendency to imitate the corporate example, can best be left to the imaginative reader. We use the word "fix" advisedly. The initial increases in cohesion (through supervision) tend to create the impression that more is better. Unfortunately, there are some things which are very difficult, if not impossible, to reverse. Along with time and government regulations, we include the wielding of power over one's subordinates in the category of irreversibles. If I have authority (the right to power), it is often assumed that I must exercise it by issuing instructions instead of encouraging cooperation among lower levels. Soon power addiction takes over. The power addicted manager views his or her subordinates as underlings to be ordered around because the poor, misguided things have no idea what they ought to be doing. The power addicted manager suffers from the malady of "means-ends inversion" or the treatment of power as an end in itself rather than as a means of coordination.[3] Persistently employing the same means (pulling rank) results in replacing the goal of cooperation and harmony among inter-dependent or complementary activities by the means (issuing orders), in part because the latter are obvious, tangible, and convenient. One of the most quoted statements about power is that it corrupts. Unfortunately, it does worse. It deludes those who have it into believing that their de-cisions and interventions are the fulcrum on which the firm rests. In a sense power becomes like a virus invading the human body. At the first sign of a virus' entry, antibodies rush to attack the intruder. This action by the immune system generally ends in a successful repulsion of the virus assault force. When, in the rare cases the antibodies themselves are disarmed and the immune system fails, the virus is free to enter un-checked. Addictive power is a virus, one which, in addition, renders the firm's defenses futile. The more managers accumulate and exercise power, the less sensitive they become to the needs of their subordinates and to the ways in which flexible, mutual adjustments could unite the firm in pursuing an *overriding cause*.[4] The cooperation among groups that could serve as counterpoint to the point of power is stifled and subordinated to the exercise of authority by the boss(es). Kipnis[5] provides a fascinating picture of the evolution of power addiction. He concludes that the arrog-ance of power warps not only its possessor but those who do not possess it. The have-nots tend to devalue themselves.

By now, it must be obvious that we have, to put it mildly, serious misgivings about the ability of the hierarchy and the resulting entrench-ment of power centers to bring value activities into step with one another. It doesn't matter whether the value activities are contained within one department or encompass many departments. The limits of the exercise of power in delivering value must be recognized and observed. The ques-tion of value has its *origins* in the sensitivity the firm displays to the components of customer needs and in its ability to tightly link, with little or no side effects, the value activities into an Interdependent and Inte-grated whole. However, the fire of value will die out all too easily if left untended, if the effort to deliver and to improve upon value delivered are not continuous and ambitious. There can be no slackening in the search for value enhancement possibilities (which, theoretically at least, are in-finite) nor should the firm become just a follower or initiator. Bench-marking is certainly healthy and informative, and even sobering, since it quickly dissolves all the illusions that firms might have of their product's superior value. However, benchmarking should be used more as a means to evaluate the firm's value outcomes relative to its competitors rather than as the prime mover of the value drive. Without a clear view of what customers need and a commitment to the creation of value, benchmarking, even in companies like Xerox[6] which swear by it, can degenerate into mindless imitation.

POWER TO THE PEOPLE

If neither competitors nor bosses can or should serve as the sole inspiration for a firm's value ethic, where does the spark, or indeed the fuel come from? A glimpse at the "how" and "where" is provided by successful sports teams. Baseball teams during the heat of a pennant race (particularly during the last month or so of the regular season), and during the playoffs are a case in point. The Cincinnati Reds, during the 1990 National League Championship Series and World Series, showed us how value can be generated and where its source lies. Having led their division right from day one of the season, they had ended the season with a whimper, almost backing into postseason play. Imagine the surprise of the Pittsburgh Pirates (whom they beat in the National League Championship Series) and even more so that of the Oakland Athletics (who were clear favorites in the World Series) when they found out they were facing a totally transformed Reds team. *This* team's pitching was aggressive and tenacious, its hitting crisp, its running almost cheeky, and its fielding nothing short of brilliant. Manager Lou Pinella, moreover, did not attempt to steal any of the limelight and played a low-profile role throughout the playoffs. It became obvious that this was truly a *team*, a group in which the interdependence among supervisors and players was fully acknowledged and the need for a persistent, rising level of effort was *internalized*. Except for the strategizing, histrionics, and line-up shuffling that normally occurs in baseball, the players did not need to be told what they *had* to do. Vince Lombardi's Green Bay Packers were a force to be reckoned with, perhaps due as much to their performance as to the coach's dominating personality. Now this was no collection of equals. Lombardi was, so to speak, far more equal than his players. But, his players, almost to a man, aver that the quality and intensity of their play stemmed only in part from their desire to avoid their coach's censure and deserve his praise. Players like Bart Starr, in reflecting on their halcyon days, are quite positive that, more than the opinion of their leader, what drove them to untiring, unceasing effort was their *desire to excel*. Doubtless, Coach Lombardi's philosophy was catching.

As we have pointed out earlier, extending sports analogies to business organizations is instructive since we can more easily relate to people and teams that are constantly in the news. However, we have to be careful not to extend the analogy beyond its limits. While the cooperative spirit is worth emulating, the fact remains that, in professional sports, competition often *is* the product, the employees are sometimes millionaires who bask in the glow of the spotlight and are aware they have to perform individually as well as a team, and the fans are, in the main, captive consumers. All of which often makes for a sharp divergence between sports and business. In spite of these and other differences, the success enjoyed by the best sports teams in *self-motivation* toward a common purpose, in the presence of frequently frustrating interdependence, is worth working toward.

We do not mean to imply that a self-generated striving toward customer value is exclusive to sports teams. Delta Airlines has for long been viewed as the leader among domestic airlines in infusing its employees with the customer service philosophy. In an industry in which price and routing differences among competitors were negligible, and where leading firms (such as United or American) enjoyed an edge due to their popular reservation system, Delta zeroed in on an important source of value to customers—how they are treated during their actual presence in the system, starting with their arrival at the airport and ending with the completion of their travel. Customer service agents at the counters do not have their hands tied by their job descriptions but are encouraged to pitch in wherever their help is needed. It is not uncommon for flight attendants, on their own time and initiative, to come to the assistance of ticketing staff if customer delays in line appear excessive. Actions that go far beyond the call-of-duty or enhancement of value have become the stuff of legend in Delta. A Delta employee accompanied a passenger (who was traveling with small children) needing medical attention to the hospital, waited for the treatment to be completed, and on the following day, escorted the family (none of whom spoke English) to the airport and helped them check in before getting back to her regular assignment.[7] Stories such as this, some apocryphal but mostly true or based in reality, abound in firms that have, or wish to, set their sights on superior customer service as the crowning achievement of their quest for continuously improving value. The Federal Expresses and UPSs,[8] whose personnel are reputed to go to almost any lengths to effect timely deliveries, and the Nordstroms,[9] whose sales associates display an almost obsessive drive to cater to and anticipate their customers' needs, have also successfully demonstrated the importance of prompt and tireless service. Dana Corporation's chairman, Rene McPherson used to advise his people to "talk back to the boss" in an attempt to mitigate the effect of bureaucracy and authoritarianism. "We instilled trust," he recalls.[10]

Since so many firms enjoy a reputation for service because their employees have been empowered to make decisions and to act as the situation warrants, every firm should empower its employees similarly. Right? Not quite. It's one thing to talk about employees who go the extra mile but it's quite another to hand the reins over completely. While we had some difficulty earlier disguising our distaste for the frequent use of supervisory power to coordinate and enforce cooperation among subordinates, we are equally uneasy about making everyone a self-contained center of power. In shifting from one to the other extreme the firm likely will go from a state of discontent and stagnation to one of stimulation and chaos.

To digress briefly: Why do firms typically tend to perform far more than the minimum level of production/operations in-house? Logically, every firm would, in a free enterprise system, prefer to conclude all its transactions through the market. This ensures the best price and optimizes the other terms of exchange. For instance, the argument goes, automotive firms would find it most profitable to buy all the necessary components from various suppliers and be pure assemblers of cars and trucks. However, as markets develop, imperfections often creep into this apparently best of all possible competitive worlds.[11] Certain buyers could start cornering the bulk of the supplies, and suppliers could also gain a stranglehold over the industry due to a monopolistic access to raw materials, economies of scale, and so on. Catering to the specific technological needs of buyers and the signing of long-term contracts only contribute to making market-based transactions even more costly. As these so-called transaction costs mount, the firm at some point comes to the conclusion that vertical integration, or incorporating the (external) value activities into the firm, would be advantageous. Vertical integration could be backward or forward depending upon the direction of absorption along the value chain. A firm that started as an assembler of microcomputers and later added company-owned retail stores would be an example of forward integration while the addition of manufacturing capacity is an instance of backward integration. Vertical integration results in the replacement of the market, however imperfect, by an organization. And what takes the place of the discipline instilled by competition in the marketplace? Either total understanding among all the employees or the hierarchy. In the absence of considerable empathy among employees *and* a clear vision of what the firm seeks to become, hierarchic control is imperative, particularly if the forces of supply and demand are not dominant.

THE PARADOX OF HIERARCHY

We seem, by bringing to bear a mixture of common sense and logic, to have painted ourselves into a corner! The use of the hierarchy to coordinate value activities is detrimental to the cause of value because it relies on power differentials to impose actions on subordinates. It results in creating permanent *power* relationships rather than permanent *value-building* linkages. On the other hand, in the absence of the market's insistent and unrelenting demands to mediate internal exchanges, firms will most likely reach an advanced state of pandemonium unless they have a firm hierarchy in place *or* have carefully prepared the ground for the withering away of a power-based organization. So, the answer to the apparent paradox ("Hierarchy: You can't live with it and you can't live without it") is simple—and yet not quite simple. Lest the reader imagines he or she has strayed into a Greek paradox competition, we hasten to

Figure 6.2
"Horizontal" and "Vertical" Chains

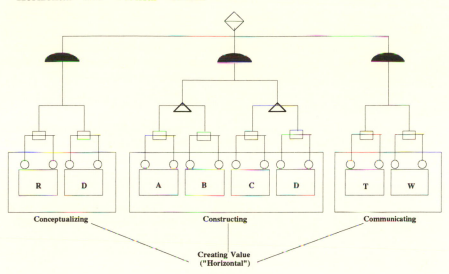

explain. The solution is easy to state but not so easy to formulate or implement.

The paradox of hierarchy is best understood by going back to an earlier graphic (Figure 2.2) and superimposing a hierarchy on it as in Figure 6.2. Conceptualizing broadly covers *R*esearch and *D*evelopment while Construction includes Material Handling, Cutting/Welding, Machining, and Painting represented by *A*, *B*, *C*, and *D* respectively. *T* and *W* stand for the Value Communication activities of Transportation and Warehousing. Three layers of supervision above the department level are shown in the Conceptualizing and Communication phases and four layers in the Construction phase; levels lower than the departmental are not shown to help reduce clutter in the chart. The tight linkage of activities *within* each of the 3Cs and *among* them are what enhance and sustain customer value. The hierarchy also forms a *chain*, one that spans the organization in a vertical direction rather than horizontally. Strictly speaking, the vertical chain does not create any value for the firm. At best, it is meant to *facilitate* the creation and prevent the destruction of value. The hierarchy is, in its ideal form, a guardian of value. It should serve as a watchdog to make sure that all value creation activities work in tandem with one another. However, as the number of levels in the hierarchy rises, its value mission gets lost in the power transfer. Tight linkages in the horizontal (and true) chain of value, therefore, must be paralleled by tight linkages in the vertical (and virtual) chain. Furthermore, as Bennis and Nanus[12] forcefully argue, the style of leadership should *pull* employees' efforts through rather than *push* them to higher levels of achievement. Empowering employees is seen as the pull mechanism. In a sense, therefore, hierarchic pull should parallel the pull, based on tight connections, along the chain of value creation advocated in chapter 4.

Just as there are transaction costs associated with the market mechanism due to imperfections in competition, transaction costs arise in multilevel organizations. Following are some of the more prominent of these transaction costs.

- There are delays and distortions in the transfer of information both downward and upward. Subordinates who say what the boss wants to hear, managers who interpret their supervisors' vision before transmitting it to their subordinates ("enhancing value" becomes "cutting costs" or "increasing sales"), and the often irresistible need to preserve a written record of actions and decisions exemplify the lags in information transfer.

- There can be the conscious blocking of information flow downward ("Why should *they* know?", "The more you tell them, the bigger they'll get for their boots!" or even "They wouldn't know what it means or how to use it") and upward ("Let them find out for themselves!" "They'll either pretend to listen or won't pay any attention," or even "What have they ever done for me?") Information *is* power and the jealous defense of power through the denial of information to another level is a drama that plays itself out in all power-coordinated organizations.

- There is the alienation that accompanies any power differential. A quick comparison to electric energy will illustrate this point. A potential difference has to exist between two points for an electric current to flow, and for energy to be available to work a hair dryer, washer or TV. As the difference in potential or voltage rises, the current flow increases assuming no changes in the electrical resistance. Due to the increase in current more heat is generated and energy wasted in the resistance. Anyone who is even moderately familiar with the ways of "high voltage" organizations will recognize how easily resistance to the flow of instructions results in the generation of heat! Moreover, no current flow can take place from points at a lower voltage to those at a higher voltage. The flow of ideas from one level to a higher one is often as unlikely.

How can we create the low-voltage, high-value seeking organization? Is there any way we can reduce and minimize differences in power among employees, irrespective of their "level" in the firm, without in any way compromising the coordination exercised by supervisors and yet create and retain the unified focus of the value-seeking and value-improving organization? There undoubtedly is, but before we can address the issue of neutralizing the unhealthy main and side effects of a power-orientation (as opposed to a value orientation), much of the preparatory work we have alluded to earlier needs to be undertaken.

REALIZING THE HIGH-VALUE,
LOW-VOLTAGE ORGANIZATION

At the risk of testing our readers' patience, we recapitulate, at some length, the goundwork necessary. It is necessary to articulate and pursue a vision, a long term purpose which gives shape to a strategy of value. Value-intensive and value-extensive strategies, while not necessarily mutually contradictory, must be weighed carefully with respect to the bases of value, the relative intensity to be brought to bear on them, and the components of value which are worth sharing with other parts of the firm. Farsightedness and a firm belief in the vision must also be accompanied by an unwavering commitment to the sources of value identified. A firm that seeks to deliver value by zealously supporting products that do not harm the environment exemplifies the qualities of mind and will needed. Firms that believe their competitive edge is generated by the knowledge-based services their employees provide to customers will have to persist in cementing this value source, come recession or boom, year in and year out. For firms that have expanded their horizons (internationally, into other products and services, through joint ventures or vertical integration) the intermeshing and magnification of value across nations, products, and companies makes the pursuit of value a positive-sum game. As the value transferred is enhanced the store of value held by the firm, in a manner of speaking, rises. For example, competence in environmental preservation can facilitate an increased service level to customers. Value doesn't abide by a law of conservation. It is, on the other hand, similar to an organism. It can reproduce and propagate itself.

Instill in the organization not merely a tolerance of, but even a desire for a higher level of mutual dependence. Overcoming the inherent urge to be independent and insulated calls for top executives who can be diplomats, straight shooters and firefighters all rolled into one. Whether the organization be for manufacturing or service, and irrespective of which part of the value chain is under consideration, the instinctive human tendency to provide margins of safety must be tackled and overcome. Initially, firm recommendation if not outright imposition of tight linkage may be the best medicine to prescribe. Changing layouts in manufacturing, eliminating inventory "cushions" in finished goods, raw material or work-in-process (which could affect distribution, suppliers, and internal operations, respectively), linking Marketing Research and Applied Research using Quality Function Deployment, and so forth, are some of the possible steps. A transition has to be effected from a relatively cozy existence in which individual and group efforts are exerted in isolated splendor to a state of possible turmoil, at least initially, where finger-pointing, feelings of guilt and a generally increased sense of responsibility could be accompanied by spasms of frustration. This transition obviously could and should be eased to prevent the shock waves of resentment from rocking the organization's stability. This might include steps to improve equipment reliability through Total Productive Maintenance or implementing Statistical Process Control, balancing the chain of operations, the use of equipment of lower capacity to increase flexibility, and the encouragement of self-supervision to get employees acquainted with, even drawn to, the notion of taking responsibility for one's tasks and activity performance.

Transfer the holographic organization from the realms of science fiction to the world of everyday experience and effort. The numerous, whole images created of value as delivered to customers cannot be generated by preaching or hoping alone, although talking up a storm of value and a dose of optimism can certainly help systematic actions aimed at diffusing value throughout the organization. Job rotation helps achieve the dispersion of value through progressive empathy and a willingness to accommodate others' demands in the interest of the firm, the product, and the customer. The deployment of Structure Busting Teams serves as a counterpoint to the conventional organization. SBTs are conscious, active and obvious weapons—safeguards against organizations becoming fossils in their own lifetime. If Structure-Busting Teams are value-friendly, Strategic Business Units are value-focused, bringing order and cohesion to a mixture of products and services. Vendor partnerships, preceded where possible by vendor certification, are also excellent stage setters to lowering power differences. Such partnerships seek to combine structure busting and strategy since they break with existing practices and are directed toward better serving the ultimate customer.

Defusing the power-happy organization therefore, does not start with power at all. Switching off the power and pushing all decision making down the hierarchy could result in errors, confusion, and demoralization. Low-voltage organizations should not become synonymous with inactivity or indirection but, paradoxically perhaps, will be characterized by an electric passion for value. Chief Executive Dennis Weatherstone, for instance, has brought about a revolutionary change in management style at J. P. Morgan & Co.[13] Since he prefers consensual decision making, he involves a wider array of executives in discussing the decisions to be made. A team-based approach to tackling problems and opportunities is no longer something to avoid or scoff at, and is making high finance less mystical and more accessible to employees at lower levels. Further lowering the power differential is Weatherstone's personality. He is warm and accessible, frequently stopping to chat with all grades of employees about their work as well as themselves and their families. However, without the acceptance of Interdependence and Integration as essential to value (that is, voluntary linkages along and across the flow of value activities), neutralizing the hierarchic exercise of power in this manner would be nothing short of a prescription for anarchy.

One of the commonly employed methods to lower the power differential is that of shaving off hierarchic levels, making for a "flatter" organization. For example, in Figure 6.1, lopping off one of the intermediate levels results in I and II (now bereft of A, B and C, D respectively) having double the number of employees to supervise. Eliminating levels of supervision does not, as such, make managers more willing to allow their subordinates greater leeway and flexibility in dealing with customers, suppliers, or, for that matter, with other departments, even if their subordinates have rotated jobs, undergone task and decision training, or been a part of SBTs (or SBUs) in the value dispersion process prescribed. Most of us would have to be dragged, kicking and screaming, to the altar of Empowerment and, even then would be reluctant worshippers! When layers of hierarchy are finally, painfully removed, the message has to be clear that persistence and closeness of supervision are things of the past. Managers will (or should, if they know what's good for them) quickly realize that they have too many employees reporting to them now for them to continue peering over their subordinates' shoulders. Conversely, unless subordinates grasp the opportunity to think and act for themselves, they could find themselves depending for direction upon managers who will not or cannot (because of time and information limitations) give as much attention to the high value track as they used to. While Interdependence and Integration are indeed the harbingers of Empowerment (and through it, Involvement), simultaneous action on other fronts needs to be undertaken. Prior intimation of the proposed changes should be given to *all* the employees, irrespective of their level. Ideally, the information should be shared at the CEO/top executive information sessions to impress upon everyone the importance of the changes envisioned in delivering customer value. These high-level communications need to be followed by written and oral communications from the new immediate supervisor. Of course, if some of the displaced supervisors are to be let go, the extent of advance notice has to be weighed against the possibility of organizational disruption caused by discontentment and perhaps disinformation. At any rate, the manager/subordinates sessions should at the very least closely follow the announcement of the changes in reporting relationships to minimize the damage caused by the ever-active grapevine.

In fact, these sessions should become a regular feature and an essential part of the empowerment process. Since managers typically will have less time to spend with employees individually, they must try to compensate for this deficiency by meeting with them in groups, primarily to keep them current about the group, department, and firm's achievements and shortfalls. Customer complaints and compliments, domestic and foreign competitors' conquests and retreats, corporate strategic shifts and even financial performance can be conveyed at these meetings. If empowerment is to be a reality, not only is a low-voltage organization a must, the very possibility of a power differential building up in the future must be obviated. Knowledge, it is worth repeating, is power and the denial of knowledge is the very antithesis of empowerment (it often also results in delusions of grandeur—but that is another story). Flattening the organization without lubricating the flow of communication *downward* is only likely to result in confused, leaderless, and probably resentful employees. Nucor has been one of the most successful firms in the steel minimill business,[14] an industry that has successfully withstood the Japanese onslaught. No small part of Nucor's success is attributed to its flat (five-level) organization and the ability of its top executives, notably Ken Iverson, its Chief Executive, to communicate a unifying vision of the firm's value orientation to the entire workforce. The use of tightly-knit small teams certainly furthers the cause of value. Decentralized divisions with a high level of autonomy conduct their own marketing, purchasing and engineering without interference from the corporate level. There are few distinctions made between hierarchic levels. There are no executive dining or rest rooms, no reserved parking spots or company airplanes. Everyone participates in the same benefits packages as well. As can well be imagined, the firm has been characterized by an openness of communication, even in talking about management mistakes, that is legendary. For those among us who are leery of sharing "sensitive" information with subordinates, we might as well face reality and concede that there is very little information about our competitors' and our own strategies and performance which is inaccessible to anyone who wants to find out. At any rate, it is far better that our employees get their information from us, rather than from the newspapers, local taverns and eateries, or even worse the rumor factory. It would be even worse if a value-conscious firm should ever be reluctant to share *customer* information with its employees. That truly would deliver a body blow to the cause of value.

Manager-subordinate confabs in a newly flat organization should not become arenas for one-way (downward) communication, with predesignated speakers and listeners. If the move toward power equalization is to be taken seriously, listening will have to become a managerial trait.[15] Responses to questions and concerns expressed by subordinates need to be addressed clearly and quickly. Pulling rank at these meetings can only succeed in eroding the credibility of the empowerment initiative. To prevent these information-sharing meetings from becoming gripe sessions, task-guidance centers, or hotbeds of conflict, ground-rules specifying the extent of territory to be covered should be agreed upon in advance.

During the early phase of the power transfer process, supervisors may have to spread themselves slightly thinner than they might want to. Employees might need help in adjusting to new responsibilities. As recently suggested, we seem to have, particularly in the United States, encouraged workers to be content with following instructions.[16] Exercising initiative and assuming responsibility for one's decisions and actions are exceptions to the rule of passivity. The fact that there are diverse underlying causes (management, unions, government, the media) for this "teening" of America in the midst of a greying population is neither here nor there and not of direct interest to us. The result of this carefully nurtured "immaturity" among lower-level employees is that in correcting the skewed division of labor and power, initial setbacks are likely. "It's another of management's fads!", "They want to get more work out of us," "Why should I consult a bunch of ignoramuses?", and "They want me to screw up so they can fire me!" are likely to be among the more common reactions. However, persisting with efforts to shorten and tighten the *vertical* chain is essential if the *true* (activity) value chain is to be increasingly effective in satisfying customer needs.

In order to ease people into roles of higher responsibility, general guidelines, including goals, could be stipulated. The means adopted are left to the discretion of the employee provided he or she stays within the specified boundaries. Waterman describes this sort of decision making within constraints as "solution spaces."[17] For example, "if the part's dimensions do not seem right, stop the entire line immediately." Or, "if a customer without a receipt asks for a refund, issue one if you're sure it was bought at the store. If possible, persuade them to take an exchange for an identical or similar item." As employees get used to gradually rising levels of discretion, particularly if the exhortations to deliver customer value have borne fruit, customer experiences like those at Delta, Nordstrom's and Federal Express will not be rare and isolated occurrences but will tend to become the norm. And in manufacturing firms, soliciting employees' ideas for activities like reducing set-up times (even entrusting the task to a team) and improving layout could give meaning to empowerment while providing valuable inputs for value enhancement. Scott Paper Company has incorporated the empowerment aspect of value into its mission statement. Scott wants its employees to not only perform their jobs but to grow in them, not to carry out instructions but to be empowered to *make* them, and not to think of themselves as employees but as owners.[18] Introducing practices such as self-inspection (inspecting one's own work), successive inspection (checking conformance of all material received from other work centers), and Statistical Process Control, whereby, as described in chapter 4, the process is constantly monitored for being within specified limits, will steadily ratchet up the discretion exerted by workers. Other ways of empowerment through knowledge include the use of techniques such as

- the Ishikawa fish-bone diagram (named after one of the pioneers in the Total Quality Control or TQC movement) to help trace the true source of problems.

- Pareto analysis employed to identify important factors in value failure and to help avoid spending time, energy, and money tracking insignificant problems.
- the so-called "5 Why" approach, in which a succession of questions probing the roots of problems that have arisen in delivering product value are raised, with the successive answers shedding progressively more light on the issue of concern. For example, a sequence of why's starting with "Why does this machine have a higher frequency of failure than all the others?" could provide excellent insights to the repeated breakdowns. In essence, the 5 Why methodology takes workers to a higher level of involvement. *Know-why* provides a deeper understanding of the value process and the ability to get it back on track than *know-how* alone could.[19]

For engineers and managers interested in more advanced problem-solving techniques, the "New Seven" methods provide approaches to analyze interconnections among problems, among goals, and among criteria such as quality parameters.[20]

These, and similar techniques, have typically been employed in Japanese manufacturing firms, particularly in the middle or C2 stage of value creation. There is absolutely no reason why they should not be used in service firms. Hotel employees diagnosing the causes of customer complaints about check-in delays and airline operations personnel coming to grips with the major impediments to customer value in their region are two examples that come to mind. Nor is there any reason to confine such methodologies to any specific stage of value creation. For example, Pareto analysis and the 5 Why method would be equally powerful in Value Conceptualization ("Why does it take us so much time to take a product idea from Research and translate it into a workable product through Development?") as well as in Value Communication ("What does the fish-bone diagram say about our image deficiency?").

In short, exorcising power addiction from an organization means that dependence has to be replaced by interdependence, diffidence by confidence, and incapability by competence. The change will be gradual, not instant. As Neilson[21] suggests, managers will need to progress through several stages of leadership evolution themselves. Starting from a directive mode, Neilson proposes that managers should progressively become, in turn, coaching, participative, appreciative and inspirational leaders to complete the power transfer process. If the prevalent leadership style does not change, empowerment and involvement are likely to remain pipe dreams.

BEYOND CITIZENSHIP—THE PRODUCT-CUSTOMER-ORGANIZATION NEXUS

Knowledge is power, which applies equally to knowledge gained as to knowledge withheld. Knowledge is also value-ability and when employees acquire power and ability, they truly can become one with the organization's mission. They belong to the organization and it belongs to them. Just as the intent of Integration may be compared to views of value being completely shared and dispersed as is the solute in a solvent, involvement seeks to wholly absorb the actions of individuals and groups into crafting the organization's value package. A sense of *ownership* ("This is my company, and its well-being comes first") among all the workers, *loyalty*, *initiatives* to actively pursue value, and unflagging *cooperation* even under stress, each capture pieces of involvement. The concept of Organizational Citizenship[22] (OC) encompasses some of the more important dimensions of involvement. OC describes behavior which occurs when there is little chance of recognition or reward. The convenience store clerk who helps elderly customers with their bags, the retail store salesperson who gift wraps clothing bought elsewhere, the airline attendant who helps passengers who have missed an infrequent connecting flight, and the salesperson or production supervisor who calls his or her counterpart in a sister division to pass on helpful lessons gained from recent experience are exhibiting OC because it has become almost instinctive to them to vest the betterment of the firm (through a dedication to value improvement) with a higher priority than their own individual betterment. In OC the *quid pro quo* of employment (inducements must be provided to workers for them to contribute their best effort) becomes irrelevant since employees obviously have taken the interests of the firm to heart.

While OC is undoubtedly worth striving for, involvement goes even further since it includes the devolution of power, the sharing of information, the cooptation of individuals into the value strategy of the firm and the harnessing of energies otherwise frittered away. The misconception that involvement is desirable because it keeps workers happy cannot be disowned quickly enough. If you seek the type of involvement where employees feel good about their inputs being accepted or even just considered, you are pursuing a mist that will disappear in the heat of reality. If people are not given the tools, the power and the opportunity to participate in making decisions, to act and revel in their successes (or brood over their failures) "involvement" will be a nine days' wonder. The steps that we have taken you through in devising a plan for institutionalizing involvement may seem tortuous and complicated. But their seeming complexity is worth confronting and coping with if value delivery is to flow naturally through the organization, and not be the result of constant pressure from above. Employees who are empowered and are totally absorbed in their mission of value creation can give life and meaning to a strategy of value. The source of value may lie in warranties and after-sales services, safety and environmental neutrality, or in something as prosaic as maintenance and operating costs. The building of value may take place predominately in one, two, or all three of the Cs. No matter *what* value

Figure 6.3
Involvement and the Organization-Product-Customer Nexus of Value

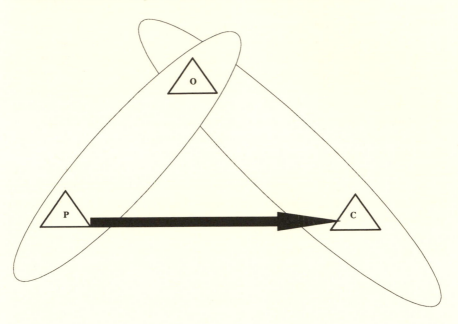

comprises or *how* it is installed, involvement at its best will result in
excellence on both counts. Managers and chroniclers of managerial actions often use terms like "commitment," "excitement," and "passion"
to describe organizations high on involvement. The belief that a high
involvement organization generates these positive, emotional responses
is widely held and well known. We aren't staking any claims to stunning
originality on that score. We hope, however, that we have succeeded in
emphasizing that continuous value enhancement requires total (or ab-
sorptive) involvement. The Product-Organization-Customer nexus mod-
eled in Figure 6.3 might help illustrate this further. The product (P) and
organization (O) are tied together by the organization's *internal* value
focus or its value capabilities (identified in the chain of value creation)
while the organization and the customer (C) are connected by the *external*
value focus or the components of value (costs, flexibility, quality, etc.).
In delivering a product of increasing value to customers, the strength of
the PO and CO bonds determine the PC linkage (where the internal and
external value concerns meet), which is the ultimate target for continuous
improvement, in addition to being the organization's *raison d'être*. The
PO and CO connections are best built and reinforced through an organization-wide and organization-deep effort. A greater commitment to

Figure 6.4
Involvement—A Look Back

Lessons from the fall of Communism
   —how not to use power

Authoritarianism/Paternalism
   —not uncommon in organizations in capitalistic societies

Changing times and a pressing demand
   —the need for involvement

The genesis of power—coordination and direction—and the need for a hierarchy

Of power addiction and viruses

Internalizing value needs
   —successful sports teams and business firms

The paradox of hierarchy:
   "You can't live with it, and you can't live without it."

Tight linkages in the vertical and horizontal chains
   —vertical transaction costs

The low voltage-high value organization

Prerequisites for Involvement: Interdependence and Integration

Moving slowly but surely
   —Fewer levels, more subordinates
   —Share strategic, operational information (the end of secrecy)
   —Importance of downward communication
   —Reversing the "greening" process
   —Guided decisions
   —Techniques for increasing capabilities
   —Organizational citizenship
The Product-Organization-Customer/Involvement Nexus

strengthening the product's and customer's interfaces with the organization is essential to unceasing value enhancement.

Building a value-maximizing organization is not only particularly instrumental in executing the strategy formulated and articulated, it could provide the energy for future strategy. This is possible not only in the sense of providing a distinctive competence for the firm in the value dimensions in which it excels, but also in terms of creating an employee base that is more receptive to new ideas, to value shifts matching customer preference changes, and to value sharing between divisions of the same firm.

Regardless of whether the organization be in the steel, electronics, airlines, recreation or any other industry, if the employees are to be totally wrapped up in the welfare of the firm through the medium of its PC linkage, power relationships must be addressed first. As displayed in Figure 6.4, the realization that power dependence eats away at the very fiber of initiative and enthusiasm is an essential starting point. Any value attained, without involvement, therefore, will not be self-sustaining. Steps to switch off the power orientation by establishing the low-voltage or even no-voltage firm include the elimination of multilayering, encouragement of communication downward (including "sensitive" information) and the dissemination of techniques for better task analysis and performance. Strategies of value can originate from totally involved employees in a bottom-up reversal of the typical strategy process. However, to make the enhancement of value an intimate mingling of voluntary, internal efforts and external needs, a culture of value has to arise. We turn our attention next to the nature and building of such a culture.

NOTES

1. Jonathan Hughes, *The Vital Few* (New York: Oxford University Press, 1986). The book offers a fascinating portrait of the evolution of American entrepreneurship. Carnegie's handling of the Homestead strike, Ford's paternalism, and Morgan's impersonal restructuring of various businesses are striking illustrations of profits being far and away more important than people.

2. Ford's Five Dollar Day was a radical shift in wage policy and levels. While his motives may not have been altruistic, since productivity and purchasing power rose, workers were better off than before (Ibid. pp. 302–4).

3. Richard Cyert and Kenneth Moe Grimmon, "Organizations," in Gardner Lindzey and Elliot Aronson, eds., *Handbook of Social Psychology* (Reading, MA: Addison-Wesley, 1968, 2nd ed., Vol. 1), p. 575.

4. Warren Bennis and Burt Nanus, *Leaders* (New York: Harper & Row, 1985), pp. 92–93.

5. D. Kipnis, *The Powerholders* (Chicago: University of Chicago Press, 1976.)

6. For a synopsis of Xerox's efforts and successes in competitive bench-

marking see Gary Jacobson and John Hillkirk, *Xerox: American Samurai* (New York: Collier Books, 1986), pp. 229–38.

7. Ron Zemke with Dick Schaaf, *The Service Edge: 101 Companies that Profit from Customer Care* (New York: Penguin, 1990), pp. 88–89.

8. Ibid. pp. 477–85.

9. Ibid. pp. 352–55. William Davidow and Bro Uttal's *Total Customer Service* (New York: Harper, 1990), pp. 85–94 adds to the songs sung in praise of Nordstrom over the past two decades. Interestingly, Davidow and Uttal attribute Nordstrom's employees' reputation for initiative to its leadership.

10. Thomas Peters, "Secrets to Growth: What Makes 'Best Run' Firms Run?," in Y. K. Shetty and Vernon Buehler, eds., *Productivity and Quality Through People* (Westport, CT: Quorum, 1985), p. 27.

11. See, for example, Oliver Williamson, *Markets and Hierarchies: Analysis and Antitrust Implications* (New York: Free Press, 1975).

12. Warren Bennis and Burt Nanus, *Leaders* (New York: Harper & Row, 1985), p. 80.

13. *Business Week*, December 23, 1991, p. 69.

14. John Savage, "Nucor's Keys to Quality Approaches," in Y. K. Shetty and Vernon Buehler, eds., *Productivity and Quality Through People* (Westport, CT: Quorum, 1985), pp. 237–52.

15. Carl Rogers, "Active Listening," in Philip DuBose (ed.), *Readings in Management* (Englewood Cliffs, NJ: Prentice-Hall, 1988), pp. 194–96.

16. Powell Woods, "The Teening of America: Communicating with a Turned-On, Tuned-In Workforce," in Lee Thayer, ed., *Organization Communication: Emerging Perspectives* (Norwood, NJ: Ablex, 1986), pp. 18–33. The author argues that supervisors have to be prepared, even trained, to give greater credence to their employees' ideas. Employees, on the other hand, may have to be "weaned" (our term) from excessive dependence on hierarchic inputs.

17. Robert Waterman, *The Renewal Factor* (Toronto: Bantam, 1988), pp. 98–103.

18. Judith Vogt and Kenneth Murrell, *Empowerment in Organizations* (San Diego, CA: University Associates, 1990), pp. 48–50.

19. For a detailed review of these (and other related techniques) and their interconnected usage, see Richard Schonberger's *Building a Chain of Customers* (New York: The Free Press, 1990), pp. 96–115.

20. For a brief outline of the original list and the New Seven, see Masaaki Imai's *Kaizen* (New York: McGraw-Hill, 1986), pp. 239–42.

21. Eric Neilson, "Empowerment Strategies," in Suresh Srivastva and Associates, eds., *Executive Power* (San Francisco: Jossey-Bass, 1986).

22. Dennis Organ, *Organizational Citizenship Behavior: The Good Soldier Syndrome* (Lexington, MA: Lexington Books, 1988.)

7

INGRAINING: *PRACTICAL IDEALS*

CONSCIOUSNESS AND CULTURE

Two of the more influential scientific thinkers of this century were Einstein and Heisenberg. Einstein's life and achievements have received fairly wide public notice. His theories of relativity have undoubtedly opened our eyes to the world around us. The concept of the space-time continuum (with time as a fourth dimension), the "warping" or curvature of space-time, and the constant relative speed of light regardless of the observer's speed are just a few of his stunning theories, most of which have since been supported. Far less famous, though no less crucial to the development of modern science, was Werner Heisenberg, who, unlike Einstein, elected to stay in Germany when the Nazis assumed the reins of government. Building on Max Planck's postulate that energy is transferred in discrete packets called quanta, Heisenberg threw a huge monkey wrench into the smooth, satisfying progress of physics. He asserted the impossibility of determining both the velocity and location of a particle at any point in time. In dealing with small-scale phenomena (atomic and subatomic particles), predictions would have to be hedged in terms of probabilities and not framed in absolute terms. Quantum physics and the Uncertainty Principle made the observer an important part of a system under observation. There were immediate objections to this "iffy" state of affairs. Einstein reportedly protested that "God does not play dice."[1] These objections have continued to this day. Conversely, there have also been extensions of the notion of uncertainty even to the extent of suggesting that in a probability framework, a particle could be in two or more places at the same time. Some have gone further and theorized that this argues for the interconnectedness of *everything* with everything else. The quantum-extension is in essence that of a super-consciousness pervading the universe.[2]

The idea of a consciousness linking objects, particularly living things, together is not as ridiculous as it may at first appear to be. The sense of bereavement and horror that grips a city, nation, and even the world when an idealistic, youthful leader is struck down, the anger and frenzy that grips crowds in city streets or causes hysteria on a vast scale (as in Nazi Germany or in Maoist China) and the ability of many species of animals to sense the imminence of an earthquake well before the earth's crust actually starts shifting are all instances that bespeak the existence of a linkage among living things (and perhaps inanimate ones as well) that supersedes the tangible or *explicate* reality—the reality that we can sense as opposed to the underlying one.[3]

In organizations, as in nations and species, a consciousness going beyond what is seen, spoken, and done exists. A common understanding may exist among all employees. The understanding may be nothing more than their discontentment and disgust with the way they are being treated. On the other hand, the consciousness may be of a broad approval of the firm's treatment of employees, or even that there are different viewpoints among the workers regarding the equity and fairness displayed by top management. To take another issue, a widely accepted understanding may exist that ethical behavior with one's customer is essential. Or the organizational consciousness might clearly encourage an "anything goes" stance. The concept of an all-pervasive consciousness in organizations might appear to be cumbersome and farfetched. Yet, if it was feasible, what better way to ensure an unremitting search and a thirst for customer value than by creating a powerful consciousness of the need for value?

Fortunately, organizational consciousness belongs to the realm of neither physics nor philosophy but is firmly rooted in the reality of culture. Culture is one of those words that is often used and misunderstood. In the national sense it merely describes the attitudes, customs, and assumptions of a people though it is sometimes used, erroneously, in our view, in the sense of cultured or sophisticated. In the corporate context, on the other hand, it is not uncommon to find the word culture applied to a wide range of organizational situations, including the type of incentives offered, the nature of control exercised, the level of job satisfaction, and, in fact, almost anything that describes the inner workings of the firm. Our view of the consciousness we call culture is rather limited and focused. Culture is the foundation for any organization's mission of value. True, Interdependence, Integration, and Involvement are at the very heart of value. But how can they be made a permanent feature? How can we build the self-propelled, value-seeking organization? By creating a culture of value, an unquestioning assumption that product and customer value are paramount, not only because they are good for the firm and its employees, but because they are the firm's very reason for being. Except just what is a *culture* of value? And how does one go about creating such a culture or helping it along?

CULTURE AS A SYSTEM OF VALUES AND BELIEFS

To get things rolling, we offer the reader our view of the meaning of culture. Very simply, we see culture as a consistent set of Values and beliefs which are widely shared in spite of being implicit, are reflected in actions, behaviors, and decisions, and are easily transmitted to new members.[4]

Values—that word again! Except that in the capitalized form we distinguish Values from customer/product *value* and use the word in a quite different sense. The Values that define a culture are the composite of ideals that the organization considers worthy of striving toward. Values are what the organization desires, collectively, to become and to be known for.[5] The desire to maximize product and customer value by making the interfaces between the customer, product, and organization a continuously improving one is a Value we commend to the high-value organization. A Value of value—a continuous striving toward meeting the needs of customers, a striving which is a pervasive, ever-present consciousness of the centrality of value to a firm's mission. In addition to *customer value*, *cooperation* is another Value we enshrine in our Hall of Values. It is an ideal to strive for in the relationship among employees, customers, suppliers and other stakeholders. Rather than adopt an attitude of confrontation or alternate between cooperation and confrontation, depending upon the circumstances, we argue that the high-value firm is best served by setting its sights on cooperative, harmonious relationships. Essentially this emphasizes the high priority that *must* be attached to cohesiveness and unity in the high-value organization, not just as a means to an end but *intrinsically* and for its own sake. The strengthening of linkages within and among the Cs of value creation *demands* a cooperative endeavor as does the need to bridge hierarchic gaps. A third Value that seems critical to the value-seeking firm is a mutuality of respect, by which we mean taking the Golden Rule to heart. The relevance and importance of others to the aims and purposes of the firm have to be acknowledged. Mutual respect strikes to the very heart of the issue of the dignity of the individual and the absolute conviction that the success of the enterprise depends upon each one's contribution. This applies not only to employees but to every other stakeholder, particularly customers and suppliers. Lincoln Electric, a firm we have alluded to earlier for its obsession with customer value, epitomizes the Values we have commended. Not only does Lincoln's philosophy explicitly place customers on a pedestal, it clearly spells out its uncompromising stand on the dignity and respect attached to its employees and customers.[6] Even in firms such as IBM, which encourages competition among salespersons in achieving targets,[7] or Xerox,[8] in which teams are encouraged to emulate other and more successful new product teams, the fabric of cooperation is mostly retained. It is only the texture that is allowed to vary.

Along with Values that serve as beacons, drawing us (and our value-seeking firms) ever forward, are the beliefs that guide us in our unceasing quest. What types of beliefs? Primarily those that derive both strength and sustenance from the "lead" INs, Interdependence, Integration and Involvement. To illustrate, some of the beliefs worth considering for a high value firm are:

- progressively tighter dependencies between individuals and groups help unify the organization
- the best way to build value into a product is by making mutual adjustments, not by resorting to rules and procedures
- as people learn more about performing the other value activities in the firm, they will become more capable at doing their own jobs
- if supervisors communicate openly and often with their subordinates, greater levels of trust are likely
- when decision making devolves increasingly upon lower-level employees, value creation becomes an almost routine activity, and not something that needs special attention
- it is far better to admit deficiencies and correct them than to sweep them under the rug, and thus postpone corrective action
- honesty is indeed the best policy in dealings with employees, customers, suppliers, and all other stakeholders
- when things go wrong, it is more useful and practical to cooperate in setting them right than in pointing the finger at likely culprits

Values and beliefs are, of course, inextricably woven together and cannot easily be observed in isolation. For our purpose (that is, to show their relationship to each other and their part in forming culture), however, we shall treat them as being distinct from each other as shown in Figure 7.1. The juxtaposition of values and beliefs is designed to illustrate the linkage between the two and does not imply that these are the only beliefs serving the values shown or indeed that the values depicted are the only ones worth espousing. For example, "Resource conservation" (or elimination of waste) may be one of a firm's cardinal values or even be incorporated as a belief which appears to be the case in successful large

Figure 7.1
Keeping Values and Beliefs in Step with Each Other

Values: The ideals worth striving toward	Beliefs: The energy to get there
■ Highest possible product and customer value	■ More—and closer—dependencies help unify the organization ■ Mutual adjustments and flexibility make for a better product and higher value
■ Cooperative relationships among employees, and with suppliers, customers	■ Employees who learn different tasks are better able to deal with multiple perspectives on customer value ■ Downward communication engenders greater trust, a sense of belonging and a feel for the "big picture"
■ Mutual respect and realization of the importance of others to the enterprise	■ Continuous improvement is possible only when deficiencies are acknowledged and addressed ■ Honesty in dealings with employees, customers, and suppliers also creates trust and teamwork ■ Concentrating on seeking out roots of problems (not on affixing blame) helps make improvements permanent ■ A sense of ownership can only arise when people take the responsibility for their actions, and do so routinely

Japanese firms such as Toyota, Honda, and Matsushita.[9] Not only can the list of Values and beliefs be expanded while staying within the panorama of a value-enhancing firm, some may even be articulated that *contradict* the ones we have culled with great care. Mary Kay Cosmetics, as do many firms dependent on personal or direct selling, actively encourages competition *among* its salespersons ("beauty consultants" as they are termed by Mary Kay) in order to widen their access to and improve service received by customers. While the pursuit of customer value appears to be a strong concern at Mary Kay, this value resides in elevating women's self-image, particularly through the medium of beauty. Beauty consultants are encouraged to see themselves as entrepreneurs in competition with other entrepreneurs. They are not only rewarded based on sales achieved but also for recruiting new beauty consultants. All new consultants must make a minimum financial investment as any entrepreneur would, to cover the cost of their initial supplies. Even when beauty consultants move from one part of the country to another, they are free to commence operations in their new territory and, if possible, retain their old customers.[10] In such instances of pooled interdependence where the firm is a sum of parts which deliver value independently to customers, cooperation ceases to be the virtue it otherwise is in the high-value firm. Davis Cup tennis or Ryder Cup golf tournaments are rough analogies here. The results of the match-up between two countries is merely the sum of the individual results. And when, as in the case of Mary Kay, the value chain itself is a relatively brief one, with Value communication comprising the most prominent dimension (the roles played by C1 and C2 are routine and fairly unchanging over time) a belief in the efficacy of rivalry may be rather easy to buy into. Another illustration of divergence from our Value/belief package is provided by 3M.[11] The firm, which is well known for its ability to induce innovations from the general run of its employees, obviously regards creativity as a dominant Value buttressed by the beliefs that innovativeness is not the property of a privileged few, that curiosity, search and experimentation are the keys to new ideas, and that mistakes can and often will be made by those looking to improve the status quo. Each firm, therefore, needs to carefully analyze the Value-belief combination that best matches its value enhancement scenario.

Based on the cluster of Values deemed best for the firm and the corresponding constellation of beliefs, the entire package of Values and beliefs should be representative of the firm's value philosophy. Equally importantly, the Values and beliefs given expression to have to be *consistent within* themselves. Values that are contradictory of each other or beliefs that are at odds among themselves can only succeed in sending mixed signals and making the achievement of a value-creating organization even more difficult. For instance, attempting to combine Values such as creativity and innovation, on the one hand, with frugality and cost-efficiency, on the other, would be an exercise in sheer futility. A similar conclusion would be drawn if, say, wealth creation (shareholder value maximization) and customer value enhancement were sought to be maximized, both in the short run. Maximizing customer value would, as we concluded in chapter 3, lead to optimum shareholder returns *in the long term*. A belief in confronting deficiencies and eliminating them does not jell with the rather more common belief that larger margins for error make errors acceptable and thus disappear. Firms like Toyota have made a virtue out of the former credo. Inventory as a margin for error is a case in point. Similarly, espousing mutual adjustment and flexibility but being unwilling to see the need for employees who view their activities, as well as customer value, from diverse vantage points would be a perfect illustration of blowing hot and cold at the same time. Cultural inconsistency results from encouraging the adoption of Values and beliefs that contradict each other, due to incompatible Values/beliefs being held by different groups in the firm,[12] and from preaching one message ("see the big picture") and practicing another ("minimize interdepartmental links").

Organizations with consistent Values and beliefs acquire personalities, so to speak, best described by their distinguishing Values and beliefs. "Creative," "team-based," "stickler for service," "quality-obsessed" and so on are labels that are often applied to companies (they might fit 3M, Xerox, IBM, and Toyota respectively) whose dominant traits are thus singled out for attention. How do such personality tags attach to firms by a motley group of customers, employees, government agencies, and members of the public? The title of this chapter should give the reader a clue to the answer we offer—Ingraining.

THE ESSENCE OF CULTURE: SHARE

If a clear conceptual profile of the culture (in terms of Values and beliefs) has been drawn up, or at least visualized, the question still remains of how the culture can be made a reality. Just as value creation is a process, Value acceptance is also a process. It isn't by accident that large numbers of employees, in some cases come to *share* similar attitudes, ideals and assumptions. While the accidental evolution of culture is a possibility, the firm's strategy is undoubtedly a powerful influence in the molding of culture. 3M's strategy of value maximization through creativity and learning, IBM's strategy of value through service, and Mary Kay Cosmetics' successful fostering of entrepreneurship and commitment highlight long-term strategies which cannot but impact on the culture and vice-versa. Strong mutual reinforcement between strategy and culture goes a long way to creating a wide awareness of the core Values and beliefs espoused.[13] As mentioned earlier in our skeletal definition, unless the Values and beliefs are widely *shared*, one cannot claim that a culture exists, much less anticipate that it will be a linchpin in achieving the mission of value. It was, for instance, only when the notion of the supremacy of a free market and individual decision making became widely *shared* that much of the growth and economic prosperity we have seen in Western Europe, the U.S., and Japan became possible. On the corporate level, it is the *sharing* of certain dominant Values and beliefs (say, Dana Corporation's egalitarianism and Apple's early energetic entrepreneurship) that leads one to characterize culture in the terms used. SHARE indeed summarizes the essence of culture.

Symbols are an important part of experiencing and participating in a culture

Hero(in)es, notably past leaders, contribute to the traditions cherished by organizations

Actions of present-day managers and other employees serve as cues to be followed and add to the firm's lore

Reinforcement of behavior with a view to encouraging certain types of actions and discouraging others

Enabling employees to undertake actions and let them buy into Values and beliefs that *are* the culture

SYMBOLS

Unlike many important aspects and details of organizational life (quantity of output, absenteeism, timely service, avenues for feedback, and so on) culture is an abstraction, an intangible yet extremely powerful factor. Few question its existence but most have trouble relating to it. One way of coming to grips with the phenomenon of culture is by investigating the symbolism intrinsic to it. When a CEO takes the time, as did John Hanley of Monsanto Chemicals, to learn the names of his managers' and of numerous lower-level employees' spouses, even if only on a special occasion, there is no need to come out and declare his or her interest in them as persons.[14] When a CEO, on finding out that an employee or someone dear to him or her is ill, sends them a get-well card, as Reginald Jones of General Electric used to, it serves as one indication of his or her concern for the employees' well-being. Jones was also known to reply to some letters received from the shop floor personally (the rest were read and signed by him) and to call employees to congratulate them on a major achievement.[15] Companies in which the customer is never put on "hold" (unless there is *absolutely* no-one to take the call) and where the CEO takes a personal interest in customers' needs and concerns have indeed taken a big step toward spreading the message of customer value. Connolly of Crown Cork and Seal, who was responsible for turning the company around financially and, not by coincidence, culturally as well, often used to fly out to customers' offices to inquire into problems they had run into with Crown Cork's deliveries.[16] The size of the customer or the relative volume of their purchases from Crown Cork did not seem to concern him as much as the fact that they had expressed dissatisfaction with the product and/or the service accompanying it. Other instances of the use of symbolism include a top executive's publicly complimenting groups or departments for running the cleanest, safest, or otherwise most admirable operation in the company; everyone, whether CEO or janitor, sharing the same dining and wash areas, as well having to sign in in the morning; and praising workers for achievements going beyond the call of duty. Voluntary givebacks by workers as exemplified by Delta's employees[17] or by leading basketball players to bring their team under the National Basketball Association's salary cap also symbolize dedication to the organization.

While symbols may not *directly* have any effect whatsoever on the 3Cs of value or contribute to fulfilling any of the multiple customer needs identified, they shine a bright light on what the organization deems important. Once the sensory stimulus—of concern for employees, customers, the environment—has been activated, it is difficult to erase. The *impression* it leaves, particularly on the minds of employees, is what a symbol is all about. Care must obviously be exercised to ensure that the impression matches the reality. One of us once worked for a Chief Executive who was gung ho about employee participation. Every Friday afternoon a group of lower-level executives would be assembled to make suggestions and generally exchange notes and trade experiences with the CEO—symbolically, an excellent idea. In reality, it soon bombed when everyone realized that what they said was rarely treated with respect and that the meetings were an attempt to communicate the official line, albeit in small groups. Symbols are *not* an approach to performing impression management, perfecting the 30-second sound byte, or conducting a clinic of the spin doctor's profession. If symbols and reality do not match, all credibility will be lost and chaos will likely rule the cultural realm. In symbols, as with all messages, preach only what you can practice.

HERO(IN)ES

Heroes and heroines provide inspiration and are the stuff of which hopes and dreams are made in most societies. Some are *warriors* from days gone by: Richard the Lionheart, who was one of the prominent figures in the Crusades, is still commemorated for his bravery and sense of sacrifice; Arthur and the Knights of the Round Table who set a tone of chivalry and, as is true of Sir Galahad particularly, have been associated with the quest for the Holy Grail; Joan of Arc, who, in fighting injustice and inequity, gave her life for her cause; and more recently, General McArthur, whose unrelenting determination to liberate a major portion of the Far East made him a legend in his own lifetime. Heroes and heroines are not necessarily forged in the heat of battle alone. They can be a part of our *everyday* lives. Mahatma Gandhi and Martin Luther King, Jr., led compelling, irresistible, and nonviolent movements in their respective countries; Mother Theresa's life has been one of utmost dedication to the destitute and hopeless; Helen Keller devoted most of her life to bettering the lives of the visually impaired; and Edison utilized his natural talents to the fullest in inventing appliances, devices and equipment, many of which have radically altered the nature and pace of life in the modern world. Among the numerous heroes and heroines who fall into a third category are Robin Hood, with his partiality for the poor, William Tell, who took unerring aim at the apple on his son's head as well as at the injustice it represented, Florence Nightingale and her hard work, care, and compassion in the Crimea, and the little Dutch boy, who is credited with saving his country from a watery end by plugging a hole in the dyke with his fist. They are *ordinary* people who have risen to extraordinary heights of achievements. All three types of hero(in)es—those known for their bravery and love for action, others achieving prominence through dedicated service and thirdly, ordinary people for whom going the extra mile is the norm—play an important part both in a country's as well as a company's culture, inspiring and stimulating thought and action in their own unique ways. In national cultures, ingraining is, on the whole, not done consciously. Stories of hero(in)es, both mythical and historical, are repeated by parents to their children, teachers to their students, and by authors to their readers with a view to passing on, and being one with, a common heritage and tradition, and not because they are consciously trying to build a stronger nation. An exception might be the indoctrination that used to be practiced in some totalitarian states—we now know how successful *that* was!

Heroes and heroines play an equally significant and lasting role in an organization's culture, particularly when it comes to ingraining or getting people to buy into certain Values and beliefs. However, in the corporate context, the culture has to be communicated and strengthened. Depending on time and employing a trial and error approach to help arrive at a suitable culture is a luxury most corporations cannot afford. Unlike countries, most firms need to be constantly conscious of customer needs. They are locked in a struggle with competitors who stand ready to capitalize on mistakes. They need to instill in employees the ability to take responsibility for their actions. The process of ingraining can be accelerated through the medium of heroes and heroines. Of course, the firm with a "ready-made" model to present to its employees as an ideal to be emulated has an advantage in this respect. A brief, though certainly less than comprehensive listing would include

- Walt Disney's legendary creativity in animation, and ambitious vision as expressed in the EPCOT Center, continue to serve the corporation by encouraging innovation among present-day employees, even if on a smaller scale.
- Mary Kay Ash, the founder of Mary Kay Cosmetics, who sought to persuade women that they could make it in a business world dominated by men, by being entrepreneurial and believing in themselves.
- Tom Watson of IBM—one of the perhaps apocryphal stories has him insisting on photo IDs for all personnel to enter IBM plants. When he forgot his own ID

card he was reported to have been denied entry and was quite pleased at this evidence of an impartial application of the rules.

• James Lincoln of Lincoln Electric, who built an organization based on customer value and employee involvement nearly seventy years ago. His decision to form a joint plant committee to deliberate on issues of importance in plant operations and give workers benefits unheard of at the time have made James Lincoln almost as real a presence in the firm today as he was during his lifetime.

Not every firm, unfortunately, has its Watson, Lincoln, Mary Kay Ash or Disney to hold up as a paragon of the Values it wishes to see become the common currency of the firm. But the lack of a figure who has been widely quoted and written about, perhaps even become a household word, should not dismay the firm thus deprived. The absence of a heroic figure means only one thing—one has to be created. If one looks back through the history of any firm that has been in continuous existence for a generation or more, tales of corporate derring-do should not be difficult to unearth. These include stories of top executives who went to extraordinary lengths to find out what customers want and to deliver it to them—for example, the CEO or President who personally visited a dissatisfied customer, supervised repairs of urgently needed equipment, or drove overnight to investigate a complaint about poor packaging reported by a supermarket. Executives who simply refused to give up on a product which seemed to be going nowhere, stood their ground and took suitable retaliatory action in the face of dire competitive threats, faced down a powerful government agency in order to avert a diminution of customer value, and so on, can be added to the list.

While the first category of heroism, equivalent to the fearsome warriors of national legends, is important to the effort needed in ingraining bedrock Values and beliefs, the second type of heroic figure is as critical to ingraining, and probably less difficult to discover and describe. Unlike the flashy, aggressive corporate hero or heroine, the second group attains its aura not through confrontation but by building bridges and diplomacy, in relationships within the organization rather than outside it. Prime illustrations would be Chief Executives or owners who, in spite of their standing in the firm and in the industry were not above backing off from issues on which they had taken a firm stand. Walt Wriston of Citicorp was as decisive a CEO as any but when confronted by persuasive evidence or criteria which did not support his case, such as his objections to Citicorp manufacturing its own credit card reading terminals, he deferred to the consensus of the group entrusted with making the decision.[18] Top executives who continue to call on customers (as did Buck Rogers when he was one of IBM's top vice presidents) or continue to potter around the shop floor or design offices (as did Steinmetz at General Electric long after his early research days were over) are examples of the quietly inspiring role model. Another such exemplar is the Chief Executive who tries every option possible to avoid laying off anyone and, if it becomes inevitable, tries to help the individuals so affected in any way possible, through job retraining or alternative employment. Executives who roll up their sleeves to help the rank and file in an emergency (a machine breakdown on the shop floor, a computer failure at an airline's check-in counter or even a sudden surge of customers at the branch of the retail store the CEO happens to be visiting) may not provide glamorous examples, but they certainly help guide and point employees in the right direction. In the value-seeking firm, executives who devote time and energy to smoothing out interfaces among activities (say between Development and Engineering or between suppliers and manufacturing) or within activity groups (between two successive manufacturing operations or between room service, checkout, and billing in a hotel) occupy a special niche for low-key heroism.

The third category of hero(in)e, the workaday person, also has its parallel in organizations. These are people who go the extra mile in doing their jobs, who go out of their way to make sure the job, product, or service is done just right, who do not mind risking the wrath of their peers by returning a job not done well enough (even going to the extent of shutting down the flow of products or customers), and whose attitudes and actions are living testimony to the unity and cohesion a high-value firm so acutely needs. The display of extraordinary effort may be on an individual basis or in a group context. Instances of such achievement include taking the initiative (with internal customers) in making process improvements such as self-inspection and self-maintenance, in dealings with external customers by providing additional services, greater product flexibility, and so on. The unremitting efforts of Delta Airlines' operational staff, Federal Express' delivery people, of Lincoln Electric's production personnel, and of Wal-Mart's associates, to name but a few of the standout firms, in no way suffer by comparison with the better known heroic figures alluded to earlier. Value groups whose efforts have led to greater value delivered and customer-supplier teams that have established a symbiotic relationship to better serve the ultimate customer are powerful models as well. Specific problems addressed and solved by value teams and their impact on the firm's value journey are especially noteworthy. Teams that contribute to reductions in setup time, increased product variety, or improved design and punctuality are no less role models. Heroes and heroines, in fact, come in many shapes and forms. Well known or unknown, male or female, aggressive or passive, individual or team—it makes no difference, so long as the firm realizes the full potential afforded by its heroic figures. Unsung hero(in)es are difficult to emulate.

ACTIONS

The key to both Symbols and Hero(in)es is that people within (and, where necessary, outside) the firm must get to know about them. Symbolic actions such as the Chief Executive walking around the plant quietly picking up pieces of dirt and wiping extra grease off machinery have a greater impact if more people than those directly involved are made aware of it. Top executives may fly off in different directions to maintain close contact with the firm's customers and personally intervene to sort out interactivity linkages (say between Development and Engineering in order to speed up time to market) but if only the *immediate* actors know about the symbolic doings, it's going to take a long time for the information to percolate throughout the firm for it to have the desired effect (fostering the underlying Values and beliefs). As with symbols, so with hero(in)es. Keeping them under wraps is, in a sense, like stashing your cash under the mattress. Not only are they being wasted by being unused, stories (like cash) can be "lost" with the passage of time. Regardless of the species of hero(ine)—whether of the flamboyant, risk-taking type, the consolidating, transformational variety, or the "common" person capable of extraordinary effort—unless their exploits and/or achievements are widely known, their inspirational impact will remain localized at best and unknown at worst. Action as a stage of the Ingraining process is fortuitously placed since it trains the spotlight on playing the symbolism and heroism cards right.

The first card that almost suggests itself is that of Publicity. Pass the word along. Talk about the CEO's most recent visit to a customer's facility. Casually mention the value team's breakthrough in bringing the firm's advertising in tune with its manufacturing abilities or the willingness of empowered employees to take the initiative, such as shop floor workers calling customers to monitor product performance or helping suppliers meet tough product specifications. The "info-sharing" get togethers between the manager and his or her subordinates is a good avenue for publicizing the second and third types of hero(ine). The symbolism inherent in, say, instituting an "open-door" policy, a departmental manager acquiescing in a value team recommendation that runs counter to the department's interests, the VP (manufacturing) personally thanking and presenting an award to an operator credited with locating and rectifying a chronic machine problem—all these need to be brought to the attention of, and planted in, the collective consciousness. Low-key transmission of symbols and hero(ine) images (through the periodic meetings as suggested) is not merely an effective means of ingraining, it is also indispensable to it. Where Values are to be absorbed, a hammer won't get the job done! Gentle persuasion and tangential references are called for instead. Apart from the forum (managers' frequent meetings), the company newsletter, bulletin board, or just plain word of mouth will do the trick. Written communication could prove effective particularly when the channels of communication have not yet been fully unclogged due, say, to the lingering after effects of power addiction.

Word of mouth is *always* an effective medium for establishing symbols and hero(in)es in the corporate citizen's mind since person-to-person communication is, by its very nature, an interactive process that creates a sense of intimacy with the person, thing, or action being discussed. Interpersonal communication, particularly where it concerns today's hero(in)es and symbols, is a powerful agent for cementing Values and beliefs. Put differently, the grapevine is hijacked in the cause of Ingraining. Instead of carrying rumors and forebodings, the grapevine becomes a vehicle for culture building.

Actions, as denoted in this section, refer to any behavior that helps in the Ingraining process. In addition to bringing symbols and hero(in)es to life, actions have other purposes as well. For instance, executives should be in a position to tell their subordinates to do as they do (not just as they say). Management by Example (MBE) applies to every action that can strengthen the roots of culture. If Interdependence, Integration, and Involvement form the basic tenets of the doctrine of value, these three lead-INs have to be conspicuously practiced by top executives. The primacy accorded to customers in the value doctrine has to be practiced by its high priests. Calling on, conferences with, and feedback from customers have to become an important function of upper-level managers. Since the latter are in an excellent position to do so, they should also work hard to sort out interdepartmental issues, either through compromise or by referring them to adjudication by Value-teams. Beseeching the rank and file to become good team players isn't going to hold any water with them if the ranks of management are torn by dissension or dominated by an associate's shadow. The sense of disorientation, even turmoil, that accompanies a policy such as job rotation becomes a little less disturbing if people know that their superiors have also gone through the same experience or, if they haven't, that they will be subject to the same policy. Again, in attempting to stimulate greater involvement on the part of lower-level employees—an involvement that specifically seeks to draw employees into exercising levels of responsibility that reach into the traditional domains of their supervisors—managers must show a willingness to reach out to, assist, and encourage their subordinates. Isolation and aloofness are the natural enemies of any species. The empowering, involving manager is a rare and perhaps endangered one.

During recruitment and selection, a holistic approach to Action calls for recruiting individuals whose attributes are likely to make for a perfect fit with the culture. Interviewing and selecting the "whole" person means looking not just for task-related abilities ("Is he a capable fitter?" or "Is she a competent accountant?") but also for a meshing of Values and beliefs. The types of questions uppermost in the minds of holistic recruiters would be "Do they share our dominant Values, like linkage to customers, both internal and external, cooperative rather than confrontational interactions?" Assigning new personnel to work with "mentors" (the salesperson with the best customer record, the department's representative on an important team, the development engineer who best understands the translation of design into production) while a powerful signal and symbol, also acts directly upon the "disciple" who goes through and is hopefully better acculturated by this phase of Ingraining. Apart from recruitment and mentoring, actions speak volumes where the three lead-INs are concerned. Changing the arrangement or even location of offices, reducing the need for material handling and storage, bringing customers and suppliers into closer contact with the organization, instituting a fair and well-designed job rotation policy, flattening the organization, and making clear the firm's vision of its role in the industry, and in society, are some of the actions we have commended and continue to commend to the high-value firm. The medium (action) is, as is often true, the message (Values and beliefs).

REINFORCEMENT

The flow of the process of Ingraining, having led us from the relatively abstract concepts of symbolism and heroism to the more tangible area of action, now directs us toward an even more concrete stage, the methods of conveying approval of others' actions, or reinforcement. Incidentally, Reinforcement does not necessarily mean the conditioned responses made famous (and infamous) by Pavlov's salivating dogs or Skinner's decision-making rats scurrying around in their mazes. Bright lights, electric shocks and clanging bells (or their equivalents) do not figure in our visualization of Ingraining through reinforcement. Quite the contrary holds true in our view. Organizations too often devalue the resources (human, material, informational) they possess by designing tasks, specifying procedures, and creating barriers in order to reduce interdependencies and to enable supervisors to more closely monitor and tightly control the separate activities. Reinforcement in the traditional organization is geared to maximizing efficiency in insulated segments. Individuals and groups are urged to achieve goals (which they may not have had a hand in setting) whose importance to the rest of the organization, as well as to the well-being of the organization as a whole, is at best unclear.[19] Under such conditions, when behavior or actions are reinforced not only are the wrong signals probably being sent to employees ("Maximize your output and performance; don't bother with others' problems or with likely repercussions of present actions") but, even worse, they tend to reinforce negative self images prevalent among all grades of employees. In effect, the organization is telling its people, "We'll decide what you need to know. Just do what's assigned to you and leave the thinking to us." Once workers are ingrained into this sort of a disciplinarian, paternal culture, work itself can become demeaning and distasteful. In effect, organizations that provide reinforcement for pieces of work done ("piecework") without in any way attempting to draw them into the larger mission (the product-customer-organization nexus[20]) or to enlighten them about the Values and beliefs anchoring its philosophy, are, in a sense, treating their employees like the experimental subjects we mentioned earlier. Worse still, in many organizations this sort of reinforcement becomes taken for granted. People come to expect it and often do not come to grips with the negative effects of piecemeal reinforcement. In business firms, such an "islands of reinforcement" approach (whereby each activity or department signals its encouragement to employees to disregard the interdependence inherent among their activities) can, and often does, lead to an obvious lack of synchronism among groups. Conflicts among individuals and groups and the development of separate, conflicting subcultures are some of the potentially damaging side effects. Salespersons who are rewarded based on their achievement of sales quotas, production workers whose targets are in terms of unit/departmental production, and development engineers whose rewards are determined by the number of viable new products handed over to Engineering, are all instances of groups (one from each of the 3Cs) who will each march to the beat of a different drummer. Unless an attempt is made to *grow* a unifying view and culture in them (based on common interests and overarching ideals), they are unlikely ever to fall into step with each other.

A rather extreme but no less relevant illustration of reinforcing disunity and ingraining conflict comes from the sports arena—professional team sports to be specific. It has become an annual rite especially in basketball and football for players to be drafted out of college (either after graduation or as "hardship" cases). Once the draft is over, a waiting game is played by the teams (whether of the National Basketball Association or the National Football League) and by the players, represented by their agents, to secure the best possible contractual terms, from their respective, distinct viewpoints. It is not unusual for top draft picks to be rewarded with multimillion-dollar contracts and for them to miss preseason play (with detrimental effects on their performance during the first season and possibly subsequent ones) and even a part of the regular season, if the needs of negotiation so dictate. Continued reinforcement of the "hold-out" phenomenon perpetuates it and, given the transition that must be made from college to professional ranks, lowers individual and team performance. While veteran professional ball players, as a rule, are well paid with generous benefits, most of them (including last year's selection) probably earn less than this year's top draft choices. Most of us ordinary mortals might tend to dismiss any feeling of envy or deprivation experienced by the lower-income earners as the petty concerns of a spoilt athletic elite. However, the signal of reinforcement without performance that such negotiations send to the rest of the team could be potentially damaging to the morale, culture, and performance of the team. If last year's pick doesn't pan out, more cracks are likely to appear in the result-based, team-driven culture the coach may want to build. Of course, if last year's pick *has* been a success, he is likely to want to renegotiate his contract, probably driving up this year's going rate and the General Manager's blood pressure.

The Ingraining process, whether in business or sports or nonprofit organizations, has to emphasize the Values and beliefs of the entire organization. Moreover, acculturation (acceptance and voluntary pursuit of the Values and beliefs) is achieved by a reinforcement of employee actions that show dedication to these Values and beliefs. We propose a methodology of reinforcement that utilizes the 3Rs of reinforcement—repetition, recognition, and rewards.

REPETITION

Repetition should not be equated with nagging. In fact repetition often does not even have to be spoken. In a manufacturing organization intolerant of less than the best quality, repeatedly stopping the entire line when any one of the processes appears to be drifting out of control sends a message that no orator could possibly convey. Cypress Semiconductor, in a few short years, has become a global competitor achieving estimated sales in 1991 of $285 million with earnings of $38 million.[21] The firm's earnings increased at a rate of 16 percent a year when the industry's was growing at a rate of a mere 5 percent. Its CEO, T. J. Rodgers, is a firm believer in a flexible manufacturing process combining quick changeovers, "line stops" and small batch sizes. The "line stop" concept has been extended to activities other than manufacturing. For instance, if deadlines for deliveries are not met by suppliers, inventories held in excess of a specified number of days, or credit files not updated when needed, access to the relevant computer information is often denied to the user. This draws attention, compellingly, to the system deficiency, and demands that the necessary action be taken. The executive who constantly solicits opinions and suggestions from customers, or pays close attention not only to productivity and quality but also to working conditions, safety, and cleanliness doesn't have to preach these values. The argument has already been made and probably won. Reinforcement of key Values and beliefs, however, is accomplished not only through a repetition of actions by exemplars or role models. A few of the types of direct reinforcement action that suggest themselves are: a repetition of activities like training programs to widen job skills and/or an employee's value-perception; following through on empowerment initiatives and promises by expanding the range of decisions left to the discretion of individuals or teams; and making it easier for employees to meet regularly with a view to discussing and sorting out the problems of increased interdependence in work flow, problems that are bound to crop up when linkages are constantly being tightened to enhance customer value. Anything that serves to back up a statement or promise made about the path to be followed toward customer value or an action that builds on an earlier action serves as repetition. Just as effective, though rarely so when used alone, are oral appeals and exhortation. Their persuasive power slips considerably if not accompanied by action. Wallace, when he took over as Chief Operating Officer at National Westminster Bank, was shocked to find that customer contact was a lost art in the firm.[22] Rather than advise his subordinates to start calling on customers, he and Chief Executive Knowles personally reinstituted the practice. As they continued on their spree of customer calling, Wallace recalls that the lesson was quickly learned in the rest of the firm and resulted in a tremendous flow of information on customer needs and reasons for their dissatisfaction with the firm. At MCI, top officers are assigned specific accounts to be managed by them.[23] Not only does this set an example of greater customer contact, it also facilitates the learning of customer evaluation behavior. If the costs incurred in servicing certain customers are excessive, the need to lower the cost or service level is another lesson to be absorbed as well. Explanations of Values and practices are helpful, communication of strategies and problems are stimulating, and speeches on cooperation and unity may inspire, but without action to bolster the spoken word, ideas and ideals will, in all likelihood, meet their end prematurely, which is why we opened this section with a disclaimer on verbal reinforcement. It could serve as a beginning though it certainly cannot deliver the goods on its own.

RECOGNITION

Repeated behaviors (exemplary as well as direct action) and, where possible, verbally stressing the behavior which the organization wants to encourage are but the first phase of a program of reinforcement. The other Rs, that is, recognition and rewards, complete a trio of methods that really are inseparable from each other. While repetition comprises approaches to transmitting the desired message(s) most effectively, recognition en-

Figure 7.2
A Typology of Recognition

	Periodic	**Episodic**
Public	[1] Core	[2] Peak
Private	[3] Routine	[4] Niche

compasses methods of acknowledging, particularly to one's peers, the contributions made by individuals and groups. Essentially, recognition makes everyone more aware of *what* (e.g., customer value) really matters to the firm and *how* (e.g., the low-voltage organization) to achieve it. Recognition often occurs in a public forum, in the presence of one's peers to clearly emphasize the ideals and actions most desired. On the other hand, where the criteria are clear and well understood, and informal channels of publicity are almost certain to kick in, private recognition may be equally effective. Another way of looking at recognition is in terms of whether it is done periodically (say, every year for corporate-wide, standout actions) or whether it is episodic, such as on the achievement of a major breakthrough. Based on this classification of recognition systems we offer the typology above (Figure 7.2). Cell [1] is home to a highly effective culture-building method of recognition. Achievements and/or actions are recognized at regularly organized, public occasions. These may be held monthly, quarterly or annually and the participants range from the departmental or divisional to organization-wide. Obviously, at the less frequent, wider participation functions, such as Mary Kay Cosmetics' Award Night, elaborately planned and carried on live national closed-circuit TV,[24] the actions or achievements recognized typically would be those that have had a highly beneficial effect on the firm and/or demonstrate a dedication to the cultural traits that are sought to be ingrained. Delta Airline, for instance, instituted a "Feather-in-Your-Cap" award for recognizing extraordinary service. The firm confers further recognition by featuring outstanding performers in its commercials.[25] Extraordinary efforts to deliver customer value, a high level of cooperative endeavor, a supplier interaction team that has achieved dramatic turnaround in incoming quality, cost and delivery may merit recognition on an annual, highly-public basis. Relatively more frequent, limited publicity (monthly, departmental) occasions may be just the right level of recognition for less dramatic improvements such as devising a procedure for making sure that all the necessary tools are available before starting the changeover to another model or refining the information system used to help R & D engineers keep track of feedback received from customers through the Sales department. Whatever the nature of the function at which such public and periodic recognition is given, whether at a packed stadium rented for the purpose, broadcast on closed-circuit TV nationwide, or organized as a luncheon occasion in the cafeteria, the key is to acknowledge a person's or group's contribution in the presence of their peers. In doing so, the core Values and beliefs of the organization are reemphasized and a commitment to them stimulated.

The types of behaviors that characterize cell [2] are so rare, even unique, that they merit arranging a special function just to draw attention to them. The group that helped the firm develop a whole new generation of computers, the salesperson whose untiring efforts brought in the major order that saved the company, and the designer(s) who changed the entire philosophy of value conceptualization and succeeded in offering a greater variety of products at the same price and quality, are cases in point. The reason for recognition to be episodic (event-driven) is that it draws attention by making an *exception*. Periodic public recognition (the "core" category) seeks to make cherished Values and beliefs as pervasive as possible through reinforcement in the presence of one's peers. "Peak" recognition, however, verges more toward creating a heroic figure to emulate, as well as serving to disseminate corporate good news. The very fact that the firm or division deems the achievement worthy of a function all its own serves to sharpen the employees' awareness not just of the achievement itself but of the premises that guided the awardees' actions. A message that talks up emulation would certainly not be out of place on such occasions either.

The cell [3] awards are presented at regular intervals, without any accompanying publicity, either to individuals or to groups. Certificates for setting an attendance record, exceptional housekeeping and a meticulous observance of safety procedures would typically merit this recognition. Citicorp's Service awards,[26] based on quarterly performance evaluations are of the "routine" variety, as are Ryder's publicity in its newsletter of exemplary work.[27] The behaviors that occasion recognition are the type generally acknowledged as essential though not extraordinary. By labeling this cell Routine, we do not mean to imply that this is normal, everyday behavior and can be taken for granted. On the contrary, these seemingly minor actions are the building blocks of a culture (much in the same way that four, apparently insignificant proteins are the building blocks of DNA, our genetic core) and are indispensable to the process of acculturation. We use the word Routine more to emphasize how the behavior recognition should be viewed, as routine and expected. In that sense, this mode of recognition provides a contrast to the Core and Peak types. By eschewing the fanfare associated with the Core and Peak awards, the routine method serves to reinforce the commonplace and unremarkable attitudes and actions that provide the glue needed in the Ingraining process.[28] In a sense, since many will receive testimonials or token awards, it also serves as a reminder that those not receiving them have yet to learn and/or demonstrate the desired traits. Just as in the case of cells [1] and [2], the Routine cell also acts as an incentive for behavior change.

The recognition provided to individuals or groups in cell [4] is tagged "Niche" since it describes specialized achievements that are generally not honored at specified intervals but need to be acknowledged as they occur. As Harrington points out, the manager who provides this sort of recognition "makes a good job great and a great job fantastic." (p. 203.) A suggestion for improving the efficiency of the production process ought to be immediately recognized, in private if the scope of the contribution does not warrant convening a special function for it. American Airlines' AAchievers Points, awarded to an employee doing an excellent job in serving a customer under difficult circumstances or to an entire group, flight crew, gate agents, baggage handlers, for making up for lost time on a delayed flight,[29] are an instance of a relatively routine recognition mode. Niche recognition is especially appropriate when the action is of a highly specialized nature (say, when a chemical engineer finds a better way to treat pulp to increase a brand of paper's brightness and opacity) and may not mean much to employees outside the target individual's circle. Of course, a combination of recognition modes is possible in this instance— public (periodic or episodic) recognition within the department, and episodic private recognition by the division or company. Private episodic recognition, whether a pat on the back, a testimonial, a plaque or a cash award, can also be given to groups which, for instance, have helped develop or optimize flows of information and design of information systems, training and selection practices, and in any way strengthen the support systems or infrastructure of the 3Cs comprising the value chain. Of course, very little *can* be kept private in most organizations. When privately recognized work comes to light this is well and good! If and when the news of private recognition gets out, it should buttress the existing norms and expectations, provided these have been made sufficiently clear through the effective use of symbols, hero(in)es, actions and other approaches to reinforcement.

REWARDS: INTERNALIZING NORMS

Rewards are an indispensable third segment of the Reinforcement "trilogy." All three of them are an integral part of the Ingraining process. However, while Repetition and Recognition occur off and on, perhaps even frequently (as they should), rewards serve as a *constant* reminder of the organization's priorities. If, for instance, incentives are offered to shop floor personnel based on production output *quantities* alone, one can repeat till one is blue in the face that quick response to customer needs is imperative and even institute functions to award certificates and plaques for quality. Neither Repetition nor Recognition, however, is likely to have much, if any effect, in the face of a conflicting reward system.

Chester Barnard, one of the hands-on gurus of management from over half a century ago, described organizations as "cooperative systems"[30] (with which we concur completely) governed by an Inducement Contribution (IC) relationship between the company and its employees, with which we agree a little less than wholeheartedly. Though the IC model is generally true and probably the most commonly used model in practice, we hope to be able to transcend the IC approach in the value-driven organization. Inducements are unquestionably critical to encouraging employees to exert greater efforts to increase output, improve quality, be more courteous, and so forth. In fact, our first two Rs are designed to (at least in part) provide inducements to culture-supportive actions. Rewards, too, are meant to reinforce and strengthen the desired Values and beliefs. Why, then, do we disagree with the IC view of organizational life, when, in fact, the 3Rs seem to provide the inducement that Barnard himself envisioned?

Our qualified endorsement of the IC model does not stem from the *need* for inducements but from the *period* the inducements must be kept in place. In other words, we are strongly opposed to the notion of a *permanent* IC arrangement. Inducements should serve as a jump-start mechanism, not as the sole source of energy in the long term. The purpose underlying the 3Rs is, therefore, not to establish a permanent network of reinforcements, but to Ingrain a way of thinking and behaving that will persist indefinitely. The purpose is to help employees *internalize* the norms and practices that have been so carefully nurtured. In effect, people will not so much be responding to external stimuli as to internal ones. Ideally, things will be done not because they are repetitively suggested and enacted nor because they are recognized or rewarded, but because they seem intrinsically the right things to do. For instance, service to customers, cooperation with people in other departments, and improved relations with suppliers, through reinforcement, need to become a matter of habit, not a response that has to be evaluated every time the occasion arises.

Does this sound Utopian and fanciful? Probably just as Utopian and fanciful as telling a peasant in medieval Europe that individuals have rights that include freedom of expression and the private ownership of property. Reforms in society over a period of a few hundred years and the evolution of written and unwritten Constitutions have led to rights and choice being taken for granted in modern societies. The preservation of these rights requires that any government be one "of laws rather than one of men," and it is in the observance of laws that societies can avert the chaos of conflicting rights. In the long run, as people abide by the laws (and are not punished, maybe even experience reinforcement for it) or, contrarily, break the law (and are punished for it), a culture of lawful behavior gains ground and is shared by the bulk of the population. Few people will physically assault another for dressing informally when formal attire is indicated, publicly cast aspersions on someone's character without any basis for doing so, or try to force someone to change their opinion about a particular political candidate or issue. In most such and similar cases we behave in a particular way or we refrain from certain types of behavior not just because there are laws to guide us but because we have become *used* to doing so. Getting used to doing things in a particular way flows from a complex amalgam of laws, reinforcements, peer pressure, and parental (authority-based) admonitions. The governing purpose behind our Ingraining effort is to get people used to the high-value organization and its culture. Individuals must think and act the way they do, not just because they are rewarded or recognized for their thoughts and actions but because they *feel* it's the right, perhaps even the *only* way. Consider an illustration. A secretary in the H. B. Fuller Company, in the absence of her boss, received an urgent request for a certain type of glue from a customer who was running out of it. Going through a complicated process of determining the customer's precise needs, locating the glue, picking up 500 pounds of it, driving it to the airport, and paying for the freight out of her own funds were all in a day's work. The option of not responding immediately to the customer's request was not even considered an option.[31]

REWARDS LINKED TO VALUES AND BELIEFS

But we digress. Before internalization of norms can be achieved, much needs to be done. Establishing a viable reward system is particularly critical. Many options are available to accomplish ingraining through the deployment of rewards. Straight salary, commissions, profit sharing, stock options, merit raises, and promotions, are a sampling of the types of rewards from which to select the package desired. Two minimum criteria must be used in screening the method(s) chosen to reward people. First, the method(s) of choice should be in step with the Values and beliefs (articulated or not) of the firm. For instance, to take a rather extreme, though not improbable, example, rewarding a quarterback on a football team on the basis of straight salary plus the number of passes completed is likely to skew the team's offense toward a passing game, and perhaps alienate the offensive linemen and running backs. Or, to take an example from the business world, rewarding employees predominately on the basis of year-end profits could result, unwittingly, in reinforcing cost-cutting behavior at the expense of quality or timely delivery, which may not have been the original intention. Secondly, if more than one reward type is used in a firm, they should not send conflicting signals. An instance of this would be combining a piecework (payment per unit produced) or commission (payment per unit sold) method with a group incentive which is based on output achieved in cooperation with employees who, at the same time, are competing for the same piecework or commission payment. Rewarding basketball players based on total points scored as well as on team achievements (e.g., won-lost record) could lead to the same ambiguity of signals.

REWARDING PROCESS AND RESULTS

Rewards should also not be based solely on results or performance. Often results achieved are not necessarily due only to the efforts of the individual or group being evaluated. Salespeople who increase sales in excess of the targeted levels may be the beneficiaries of fortuitous circumstances, a sudden spurt in customer demand, a competitor going through a period of labor unrest, or a happy coincidence of being in the right place just when a customer's projected need was to be estimated. On the production side, orders during the most recent evaluation period may have been received for unusually large quantities, thus requiring fewer changeovers and little flexibility, incoming material deliveries may have been of a quality and timeliness far superior to that normally experienced, and so on. On the other hand, we also do not want to deny rewards to, or perhaps punish, those whose performance lags expectations due to no fault of their own, having been caused by recessionary conditions, price gouging competitors, or suppliers' unreliability.

In addition to not rewarding or withholding rewards from employees for results that are largely outside their control, we must also ensure we do not encourage the 'take the money and run' attitude. The following is a brief story about the manager who typifies such a philosophy. The firm in question sought to maximize profitability. Divisional managers were naturally charged with the same objective. The hero (though "villain" would do just as well) of our tale was a divisional manager who took his duties seriously. Since divisional managers', and, to a lesser extent, other divisional employees', bonuses depended on divisional profit, this man-

ager knew exactly what he had to do. First, he should not propose any
new investments since that would tend to deflate the figure for Return on
Investment in the short term. Second, he needed to look around for ways
in which costs could be cut. Anything that would not have a negative
effect in the short run (say, a couple of years) was viewed as axe-worthy,
including expenditures on preventive maintenance, development of better
products, efforts to improve manufactured quality, and so on. Cost reductions have an obvious and immediate impact on the bottom line. Not
increasing investment in fixed assets further improves profitability. Based
on his performance over a two-year period, the manager was promoted
and transferred. Then the roof fell in. Warranty claims and post-warranty
complaints came pouring in, long-ignored quality checks led to higher
reject rates within the factory itself, and the machinery, suffering from
continuous neglect, broke down repeatedly. His successor had to resort
to large-scale "crisis management" ("fire fighting" is a better description)
and had to deal with adverse management reviews ("It must be the new
guy's fault; things were okay till he took over!") and labor dissatisfaction
at bonuses missed. Inability to turn the division's performance around in
two years (during which it stayed in the red) resulted in the manager losing
his job and the firm never recovering its erstwhile position in the market.
Much later this firm substituted its performance measure with a combination of evaluation standards in order to discourage the myopic behavior
that characterized, but was by no means confined to, the divisional manager described.[32]

There are other problems that surface when results are used as the only
yardsticks of performance and rewards. We take up a fuller analysis in
the next two chapters. For now, suffice it to say that not only must *what*
is achieved be rewarded, *how* it is achieved is equally important. The *how*
is often called the process of performance. Its importance stems from the
need to avoid the pathologies associated with a pure output mentality.
But isn't a process approach pretty much like a professor telling a student
"Don't worry about how you do on the examination—as long as you work
hard you'll get a good grade" or a manager telling his or her subordinates
"Put in your best effort and you'll be rewarded. Even if we don't produce
or sell anything, it makes no difference." You can imagine the level of
trust, discipline, dedication to product, customer and organization, called
for in such a firm. We do not think it would be realistic to expect a process
assessment alone to do the trick. A combination of result and process
has to be designed for the reward system to be truly effective.

But what exactly are process-based rewards? Our answer has to be a
rather *inexact* one since the specific method of rewarding employees has
to be tailored to the needs of the organization. This isn't a cop-out. We
merely mean that the needs of sports organizations will differ from those
of fast food chains which in turn will be different from the requirements

of a manufacturing firm. Apart from the obvious differences in product, the nature of the activities that comprise product value created and customer value delivered can differ substantially. The reviewing of videos of opponents' games and, in general preparing separately for each opponent distinguishes, to take a sliver of their activities, professional football teams from manufacturing firms whose research activities include product design changes and customer value studies, and whose production concerns range from quality to quantity and from inventory to inspection. In spite of the obvious variations among organizations, we shall make some general observations in adopting policies for rewarding employees based on results as well as process.

REWARDING THE INs

The point we have been making is that organizations *must* constantly move in the direction of upwardly mobile customer value generated by the 3Cs of value creation. Maximizing value delivered through the 3Cs requires dealing with and heightening *interdependencies* between proximate value activities, establishing and managing *integration* among groups of activities with no direct links, evaluating the levels of commitment, empowerment and *involvement* so that they spread throughout the firm. Making these 3INs a matter of habit so they get built into the norms and assumptions of the organization, become part of the overall consciousness, so to speak, of the organization, is the very essence of *ingraining*. In order to actively cultivate the Values and beliefs that represent the 3INs, the reward systems adopted must reflect a focus on them.

Specifically, actions that could be considered in rewarding movement toward and the progressive attainment of the 3INs include improved performance in terms of less in-process inventories, quicker response to the next process or customer, and a greater willingness to help each other out, particularly on the part of self-contained *work groups*. Such groups include those that have complete responsibility for making an entire product or for carrying out a distinct part of the process for a product or service (e.g., the staff responsible for passenger services at a particular airport). If the performance of the group in question can be separately measured, the reward should be proportionate to the improvement detected. Of course, one should be careful that the future is not sacrificed for the present (like the myopic manager) or that other groups' work is not jeopardized. Apart from rewarding results, wherever they are measurable, the process of achieving interdependence must also be rewarded. For instance, the frequency with which workers (machine operators, stewards, cooks, etc.) help each other in the interest of the whole group and the level of satisfaction expressed by the next process with the immediate preceding one are examples of means or process that merit specific rewards. Rewards are apropos in the case of *teams* constituted for the purpose, or individuals, who are successful in developing methods to achieve lower set up times, hitting upon techniques for quality improvements, designing more effective self-maintenance and self-inspection procedures, and identifying/solving problems that invariably arise when interconnected activities have a minimum of rules to guide their coordination. The reward mechanism should not become an income augmenter so much as a communication of priorities. Management has, however, to be seen to be putting its money where its mouth is. Even where profits have not risen nor costs decreased and telephones have not yet started ringing off the hook with calls from overjoyed customers, rewards are distributed to employees for building an unshakable basis for self-generated value. Individuals or groups who suggest improvement in the existing system of interdependencies so that the *entire* system can reach a higher level of interconnection are also architects of stronger linkages and deserving of rewards as well. Typically, people who make such suggestions (e.g., changing the layout of the office, machinery, or customer service facilities) are not authorized to actually carry them out. Rewarding the suggestion therefore clearly transmits a signal that the firm indeed values higher interdependence and is serious about attempts to attain it. The reinforcement is aimed, in this instance, at rewarding an attitude, the attitude of dissatisfaction with things as they are. The ideas for improvement need not come under or even be related to the individual's job responsibilities. The types of ideas that would merit prime consideration are, for example, a suggestion that production workers and/or supervisors periodically track the level of satisfaction of a specific buyer or set of buyers or a proposal by an employee to reduce material handling time (or customer handling time in a service facility) in order to further tighten linkages among sequential tasks and make the system more alert and alive.

Rewards are different from *awards* in that the former serve not only to reinforce actions, attitudes and philosophies, they also call for an expenditure of resources by the firm to show it is serious about its mission of value creation. Expenditure, in fact, is not as apt a term as investment. In fact, rewards that emphasize the firm's investment in its employees are to be actively nurtured. Promoting from within (a longstanding tradition at firms such as Lincoln Electric and Procter and Gamble[33]) and converting bonuses into stock as Pepsico[34] does, or holding the monies in a separate fund to be paid on retirement (Wal-Mart) are instances of rewards that do additional duty as investment for the firm as well as its employees. The resources—time, energy, knowledge and cash—deployed to make the point that value and Values are of paramount importance will pay the organization many times its original investment. At the inception of a program for value renewal accompanied by rewards, executives have to be willing to spend time getting value-building efforts off the ground (teambased activities dealing with the problems arising from minimizing inventories of semiconductors or turnaround time of aircraft). The willingness and commitment to help implement value improvement efforts, particularly at the initial stages, also places heavy demands on the energies and patience of executives who are championing the cause of customer value. Designing reward systems calls for a further investment of time and energy to make sure that the right activities are being rewarded and to keep track of how well they are working. The expertise that committed executives bring to designing the reward system will obviously be critical to making sure that it stays fine-tuned with the passage of time, and as reactions to the value package are felt and expressed.

In addition to the personal commitment and zeal needed on the part of the point men/women for the 3C/5IN strategy to be implemented successfully, the material and financial resources of the firm must also be seen to be marshalled on behalf of the strategy. Equipment already available with the firm, items like video equipment, improved tool kits, or better procedures for maintenance and repair, should be shared with divisions that need it for value enhancement. Where necessary, new equipment may have to be purchased or made in-house. In either case, budgetary allocations to allow for investments to help the firm move ahead on the value track must be made. It is only when resources are seen to be set aside for the purposes spoken of that words become deeds and are taken seriously. To be taken even more seriously, additional resources have to be earmarked for rewarding the *process* by which actions were undertaken as well as the *results* of the actions. The amount allocated should not be so large as to make a dent in the firm's profit position but large enough to denote a commitment. A budget of 0.25 percent to 0.5 percent of sales revenue would be generous, without depleting the firm's coffers. Nucor, a ministeel firm which has prospered during the 1980s (sales of $1.27 billion, net income of $57 million, in 1989) has a primarily group-based incentive system that reportedly resulted in its employees earning about $5,000 per year each above the industry average. Assuming that most of the difference in salary can be attributed to incentive payments, Nucor's incentive payments to its 5400 employees would be in excess of 2 percent of sales.[35] For a firm attempting to reward within group and intergroup cohesion, seed money of under half percent to grow a culture of collaboration does not seem excessive. In a firm whose sales total $100 million, an investment of $250,000 to $500,000 for rewarding and building a value focus is not too steep a price to pay, especially in light of the impact it is likely to have in terms of managerial credibility. The amount budgeted should be demarcated into the three categories sketched out earlier: enhanced value within existing *work groups*, enhanced value within the framework *of teams*, suggestions for value improvement *anywhere*. As in the case of recognition systems, rewards should be directed to reinforcing group as well as individual ideas and actions. The individual rewards ideally would reward those whose suggestions and actions have led to improved group working, quicker information or material flow, or ideas for improved design for manufacturability, and so on. The total negation of individual effort is likely to lower interest and motivation levels and, paradoxically, vitiate group activity as well.

The actions that are deemed worthy of reward have to be recorded and subsequently monitored for main and side effects. A team or council consisting of top executives should initially be on the council. They need not, when an exemplary action is first reported, take any immediate action. Periodically, say every six months, the list of achievements should be updated and the value improvements claimed studied further. Once every year, and at least six months after a "claim" has been registered (this allows for a minimum gestation period for longer-term effects of the modification to show themselves), the various enhancements reported must be evaluated for their impact on value and for their importance relative to each other. Decisions on allocating the reward money are made at this stage. In order to avoid the damage often caused by bitter losers, debriefing would be useful in the case of those groups or individuals that "entered" but did not get any reward or received a smaller reward than expected. A re-emphasis of the criteria employed and an explanation of expected improvements that did not materialize would help in debriefing. Three points are worth noting in this connection. One, there should be no publicity attached to the initial recording of a value-enhancing action by a work group, team or individual. This prevents expectations being raised and the stoking of competitive fires. Two, the criteria employed should be made clear in advance so that no feelings of rancor and recriminations among groups sour the post-reward atmosphere. Three, as employee involvement in the value-creation process increases, the reward decision should become predominately an employee-run affair. That is, as individuals, teams, and work groups start exercising greater discretion and assuming more responsibility for their actions, they should logically be given a greater say in deciding what, how, when, and whom to reward.

REWARDING INTEGRATION

Unquestionably, in our view the nurturing of interdependence is a prime initial target for rewards since it clearly illustrates the organization's ability and willingness to invest in building a *value-tropic* (that is, constantly moving in the direction of customer needs) organization.[36] Value-tropism, much like tropism in plants, would be triggered by a stimulus, in this case unfulfilled or emergent needs in customers. It is a bit easier, obviously, to establish norms for and reward achievement of immediate dependencies than the more distant and less obvious ones. For instance, if a work group, in its day-to-day operations includes a set of machines, workers, and supervisors engaged in making a particular component, it does not need much reflection to identify the mutual dependencies *within* the group, and indeed *on* groups that immediately precede and follow it in the flow of work. Difficulties arise when activities are to be integrated that are neither *obviously* linked to each other nor require a constant linkage with each other for the performance of daytoday work. Instances of such "cross-functional" or remote linkages were cited in chapter 5 and include connections to be forged and tended between the shop floor and the process research people, between sales and production scheduling, between suppliers and user groups, and so forth. Encouraging cooperation and inducing coordination among less obviously connected activities calls for more persuasive abilities than in the case of directly linked groups. Rewards alone cannot get the job done: the adoption of job rotation, structure-busting teams (SBTs), and supplier/customer axes have to be suggested and urged during the face-to-face get togethers, the CEO/employee sessions, and through the use of visual display materials emphasizing the essential unity of the organization across its many activities. Of course, rewards can help (but only after the groundwork for their introduction has been laid) both by presenting the case for their introduction using some of the methods just described as well as through the gradual tightening of interdependencies among directly linked activities. Among the approaches to rewarding a holographic perception among employees are

- Higher wages for workers who volunteer for job rotation and pass the required skills tests. Embassy Suites hotels[37] and Lechmere, Inc.[38] operate a program of this type to encourage employees to acquire multiple job skills. In combination with effective communication of the firm's vision of value, a judiciously rewarded job rotation scheme not only gives the firm added flexibility in the event of unexpected worker absences or turnover, it can also instill an increasing sense of empathy, which is the essence of integration.

- For employees whose skills cannot be easily tested (salespersons, market, product and process researchers, and managerial personnel, in general) rewards based on an evaluation of job knowledge can be replaced by an assessment of the ability to identify and solve cross-functional problems. This sort of evaluation is necessarily less precise than a content-based test since recording, reporting, interpreting and conceptualizing customer needs are more abstract than day-to-day routine operations. Raises and promotions, particularly in a management job, could be tied to the extent of job rotation, and hence expansion of vision, the individual has experienced.[39] Ideally, job rotation at a frequency of about once every three years on the average could be made mandatory for all who seek promotion to the managerial ranks. Once career development and advancement in the firm are tied to broadening one's horizons, the tendency to dismiss it as another of management's passing fancies will disappear.

• The provision and distribution of reward monies should be delegated to the members of SBTs who have done a sterling job in opening the collective eyes of the firm to the roots of problems and opportunities in the value process. How to bring advertising in line with the product's environmental neutrality, improve the time to market of urgently needed products, make our suppliers not just *value-tropic* but also *consumer-tropic*, and find new ways of comparing our value performance to those of our competitors—these are a few of the issues that SBTs of all types can tackle and be rewarded for doing successfully. The rewards, of course, may take the form of a bonus (a one-time payment to all the team members). Other forms of reward possible are paid vacations, team meetings being held at "retreats," or congratulatory parties, depending on the nature of achievement and the magnitude of the reward.

In spite of the best of intentions and efforts, the rewards for Integration, being less immediate and tangible, will take longer to influence actions than will those for Interdependence. Be forewarned that a preoccupation with linkages within the immediate work group could even result in emphasizing its predominance rather than that of the organization as a whole. This could erode the value crusade considerably. To avoid such a derailment of mission, an organization-wide reward would have to be kept in place until the desire for Integration takes deep hold and need not be further evangelized. Overall firm performance as measured by profitability would be worth considering. For example, Return on Assets (ROA) calculated as net profits relative to total assets may be used as a performance standard. If a firm's goal for ROA, say, for the coming year is 15 percent, it may agree to share 20 percent of all profits above 15 percent with its employees. To assure that "myopic managers" do not embark on disastrous cost cutting and/or call a halt to all plans for new investment or preventive maintenance, some precautionary steps may have to be taken. The ROA could be measured on a scale of up to five years. That is, the bonus would be figured on an average calculated over five years to avoid "short-terming" the firm to death. Any actions undertaken in year one will affect the second or third year's bonus. Also, investment levels in the divisions and departments would be agreed upon in advance and no variation allowed from them. Preventive maintenance expenditures and all actions needed for the upkeep of productive assets would have to be shown to be at safe levels. A farsighted approach to profit sharing is Wal-Mart's plan, in which employees are eligible to participate after a full year of service during which they have worked 1000 hours or more. The employee's share of the profits is invested (e.g., in Wal-Mart stock) and can be withdrawn upon retirement. In the event of the employee resigning, the amount reverts to the common pool.[40]

Reward systems for achieving greater Interdependence and Integration, are indeed complex and call for a great deal of care in designing, in proposing to all levels of employees, in implementing, and in tracking their functioning or malfunctioning for the purpose of fine tuning. No such complexity prevails in rewarding Involvement. In fact, one would not be completely facetious in saying, "If you reward involvement, it isn't involvement anymore!" Since Involvement is supposed to spring from an amalgam of willingness, empowerment, responsibility, ability, and self-motivation, an external incentive could be said to defeat the very purpose of seeking Involvement as one of the keys to self-generative value. Obviously, it would be ludicrous to exhort subordinates in a newly "flat" organization to exercise greater decision-making discretion and pay them for doing so. It would be equally absurd to encourage employees to talk more freely to supervisors, and vice versa, regarding the firm's customers, competitors, suppliers, and, in general, its value strategy, by telling them they would be paid for these conversations. Involvement is, and must be seen to be, its *own* reward.

Involvement through stock ownership appears to flout the intrinsic reward theory of involvement. But in reality it does not. Through a scheme such as the Employee Stock Ownership Plan (ESOP), employees, in effect, become part owners of the firm and, as owners, are driven to do what they can to make the firm succeed. A willingness to adapt to others' needs in the best interests of the firm characterizes the actions of employees, and involvement follows hard on the heels of this flexible, giving attitude. Moreover, the empowerment of employees is partly due to ownership, not purely one of knowledge, capability, and supervisory acceptance. While ESOPs and similar plans do indeed possess the potential to foster high levels of zeal and commitment, they are also subject to certain limitations. Where much of the stock is closely held, getting outside capital may be difficult, thus constraining the firm's expansion. Majority ownership by the employees can, in addition, result in an inordinate interference by them in the running of the company. This may sound like heresy coming from us, considering we have been preaching the gospel of shifting decisions and control downward in organizations. However, we have been making the point that a well-articulated plan for delivering customer value based firmly on tight Interdependencies, binding Integration, and evolving Involvement has to be carefully executed, thus creating common ground and a pervasive consciousness of the Values and value that must endure. Without such a consciousness, attempts to create involvement through stock ownership are likely to result in interventions based on power (of the workforce this time), not knowledge, and will only meet with short-lived, if any, success.

ENABLING

Enabling, the final pillar supporting the firm's SHARE of ingraining, is both a catalytic and residual factor. It is catalytic in the sense that it can get things started but should not become a permanent feature of the process. It is residual because enabling may be called for when things appear to be stuck or going nowhere, and a gentle shove would help. Suggesting how changeovers may be speeded up (whether on shop floors, in hotels or in airlines) does not imply that management is seeking to strip employees of the authority delegated. The sharing of prior experiences helps provide the occasional jump-starting that all groups need. Modifications in facility or office layouts and the installation of visual tracking methods (charts to show performance improvements in the various groups or that remind employees of their pre-eminent concerns—"Quality comes First!" or "On Time every time") are some illustrations of Enabling behavior. Training in job performance and problem-solving skills is an area where Ingraining occurs through Enabling. More knowledge regarding machine operation, material properties, statistical process and quality control, Pareto analysis, and so forth, imparts abilities on which the individual and group can further build and grow. An unmistakable message is, in the process, transmitted: "Learning is highly valued here. If you want to learn, we can help."

THE JOURNEY ENDS . . . AND BEGINS

From the preceding exploration of culture and of the Ingraining process summarized in Figure 7.3 it is clear that Ingraining calls for a gradually increasing emphasis on the desirable dominant Values and beliefs which flow from the firm's strategic thrust. For our model value-seeking firm, the Values and beliefs are of a customer-tropic nature, laying particular stress on Interdependence, Integration and Involvement. True, the evolution of a culture of value is driven by implementing the 3INs and the process of SHAREing—unless there is already an organizational culture in existence which is different from or hostile to the evolution of a high value system. Change is called for and Enabling actions like explaining the need to be continuously more responsive to customers (internal and external), identifying, and pointing out the evils of waste and insulation, and initiating changes in layout and work procedures, and so forth, can get the ball rolling. But, in most ongoing firms, systematic action to *override* well-established beliefs and conventions must also be undertaken if the "new" value-driven ideology is to have a chance of taking root. To start with, a culture audit must be performed.[41] The dominant Values and beliefs presently held (or implied) need to be listed and the points of conflict with the desired Values and beliefs delineated. For instance, if, in an organization, individual work carried out in isolation is a deep-seated Value, an obvious conflict arises with the cooperation-based high-value firm. Similarly, belief in authoritarian control, obviously, runs counter to the belief that employee involvement leads to commitment and dedication.

Figure 7.3
Ingraining—A Look Back

The Concept of Universal Consciousness

Organizational Consciousness — Culture

Culture as a System of Values and Beliefs

Symbols   —   Actions and Words with great leverage

Hero(in)es   —   Three Types of Individuals/Models to emulate and
                                    inspire

Actions   —   Publicity, MBE, Recruitment, and Monitoring

Reinforcement   —   Avoiding "Islands of Reinforcement"
                           —   the 3Rs: Repetition, Recognition and Rewards

        Repetition   —
        Recognition   —   public vs private; periodic vs episodic

        Rewards   —   the IC view
                           —   salaries, commissions
                           —   profit sharing, stock options, etc.
                           —   short term vs long term
                           —   process vs result rewards
                           —   investment, not expenditure, on rewards
                           —   rewards for the 3INs

Enabling   —   catalytic and residual
                           —   facilitates value achievement

Knowing the specific Values and/or beliefs that are totally contradictory
to the ones sought by the value-seeking firm helps focus the change efforts.
Using a guide such as Figure 7.1, the dominant cultural traits that need
changing can be targeted, and extra time and energy invested in the problem areas. For instance, if the current value system has emphasized cooperation among equals but strong hierarchic separation, more attention
would be directed to the latter belief than to the former. Ingraining, in
the case of a currently operating firm or division, therefore, isn't just a

matter of "getting there from here." It requires a judicial evaluation of what "here" is, anticipating the problems likely to arise in changing the aspects of "here" that need changing, and constantly trying to communicate and reinforce the culture we visualize for the firm, the one over "there."

Ingraining is a slow, evolutionary process and one cannot expect quick results. A preoccupation with customer needs is not likely to appear overnight in a firm which hitherto had been most concerned about production convenience and efficiency. The various aspects of SHARE, moreover, are slow-acting remedies whose results will take time to make themselves apparent. Meanwhile, the organization has to exist and, hopefully, continue to improve its performance. Firms that are embarked on the INroad to value, however, must find out what, if any, progress they have made and where they presently are. In the next chapter we lay out a variety of milestones to serve this purpose.

NOTES

1. For a fascinating account of the quantum quandary see Michio Kaku and Jennifer Trainer, *Beyond Einstein: The Cosmic Quest for the Theory of the Universe* (Toronto: Bantam, 1987), pp. 40–60.

2. Michael Talbot's *Beyond the Quantum* (Toronto: Bantam, 1988) argues that the universe itself is a "super hologram" and develops hypotheses of interconnectedness among living and inanimate things, past, present, future.

3. This distinction is emphasized by David Bohm, *Wholeness and the Implicate Order* (London: Routledge and Kegan Paul, 1981).

4. Our definition of culture is based upon Edgar Schein's (*Organizational Culture and Leadership*, San Francisco: Jossey-Bass, 1985, pp. 5–21) perspective. We have focused our attention on what Schein refers to as the Level 2 of culture (values) since we feel Level 1 (artifacts) is too mundane in nature and Level 3 (assumptions) too abstract. See also Bernard Arogyaswamy and Charles Byles "Organizational Culture: Internal and External Fits," *Journal of Management*, 1987, Vol. 13, No. 4, pp. 647–59.

5. Bernard Arogyaswamy and Charles Byles, "Organizational Culture: Internal and External Fits," *Journal of Management*, 1987, Vol. 13, No. 4, pp. 647–59.

6. Arthur Sharplin, "The Lincoln Electric Company," in John Montanari, Cyril Morgan and Jeffrey Bracker *Strategic Management* (Chicago: Dryden, 1990), pp. 807–20, and *Quality*, August 1983, pp. 14–15. While both cited pieces, as do most material on Lincoln Electric, emphasize the incentive system, the parallel evolution of mutual respect and recognition among hierarchic levels stands out as an equally plausible explanatory factor for Lincoln's success.

7. Buck Rogers. *The IBM Way* (New York: Harper & Row, 1987).

8. Gary Jacobson and John Hillkirk. *Xerox: American Samurai* (New York: Collier, 1986, pp. 247–48).

9. Taiichi Ohno, Toyota's manufacturing chief for many years, said his ob-

jective was to eliminate all waste and that by far the biggest of all wastes is overproduction. See Masaaki Imai, *Kaizen* (New York: McGraw-Hill, 1986), pp. 88–93.

10. Robin Romblad and Arthur Thompson, Jr., "Mary Kay Cosmetics, Inc.," in Arthur Thompson, Jr., and A. J. Strickland III, eds., *Strategic Management* (Homewood, IL: Irwin, 1992), pp. 917–54.

11. Gifford Pinchot III, *Intrapreneuring* (New York: Harper & Row, 1985), pp. 200–20.

12. Bernard Arogyaswamy and Charles Byles, "Organizational Culture: Internal and External Fits," *Journal of Management*, 1987, Vol. 13, No. 4, 647–59.

13. Ibid.

14. Harry Levinson and Stuart Rosenthal, *CEO: Corporate Leadership in Action* (New York: Basic Books, 1984), p. 145.

15. Ibid., pp. 34–36.

16. As reported in *Fortune*, October, 1962, p. 164.

17. Fred Rollins, "Delta's Teamwork Approach to Labor/Management Relations," in Y. K. Shetty and Vernon Buehler, eds., *Productivity and Quality Through People* (Westport, CT: Quorum, 1985).

18. Harry Levinson and Stuart Rosenthal, *CEO: Corporate Leadership in Action* (New York: Basic Books, 1984) pp. 75–76.

19. This situation is almost diametrically the opposite of Management by Objectives (MBO) where objective and standards clarity between employee and supervisor is emphasized. See, for instance, Alan Filey, Robert House and Steven Kerr, *Managerial Process and Organizational Behavior* (Glenview, IL: Scott, Foresman, 1976), p. 319.

20. This refers to the Product-Organization-Customer nexus discussed in chapter 6.

21. *Business Week*, December 9, 1991, p. 64.

22. Charles Smith, "National Westminster Bank, U.S.A," in Neil Snyder, Alan Rowe, Richard Mason, and Karl Dickel, eds., *Strategic Management Cases* (Reading, MA: Addison-Wesley, 1991), pp. 475–76.

23. Lynn Daniel, "Overcome the Barriers to Superior Customer Service," *Journal of Business Strategy*, January/February 1992, pp. 18–24.

24. Robin Romblad and Arthur Thompson, Jr., "Mary Kay Cosmetics, Inc.," in Thompson and Strickland, eds., *Strategic Management*, pp. 918–27.

25. Ron Zemke with Dick Schaaf, *The Service Edge* (New York: Plume, 1989), pp. 86–89.

26. Ibid. p. 193.

27. Ibid. p. 264. Recognition in the newsletter is termed "private" since it does not take place in the presence of others. In that sense it is similar to individual recognition which subsequently gets around by word of mouth.

28. H. J. Harrington, *The Improvement Process* (New York: McGraw-Hill, 1987), p. 203.

29. Ron Zemke with Dick Schaaf, *The Service Edge* (New York: Plume, 1989), p. 92.

30. Chester Barnard, *The Function of the Executive* (Cambridge, MA: Harvard University Press, 1938).

31. Ron Zemke with Dick Schaaf, *The Service Edge* (New York: Plume, 1989), pp. 458–59.

32. This situation reportedly occurred in General Electric during the period GE was increasing its profit center emphasis. Melvin Salveson, "The Management of Strategy," in Neil Snyder, Alan Rowe, Richard Mason, and Karl Dickel, eds., *Strategic Management and Business Policy* (Reading, MA: Addison-Wesley, 1986), pp. 88–89.

33. Ron Zemke with Dick Schaaf, *The Service Edge* (New York: Plume, 1989), p. 336.

34. *Wall Street Journal*, June 28, 1989.

35. See Charles Stubbart, Dean Schroeder, and Arthur Thompson, Jr., "Nucor Corporation," in Arthur Thompson, Jr., and A. J. Strickland III, eds., *Strategic Management* (Homewood, IL: Irwin, 1992), pp. 489–552.

36. For a discussion of the phenomenon of tropism (related to light, gravity, electricity, water, etc.) see an introductory text in botany, e.g., Carl Wilson and Walter Loomis, *Botany* (New York: Holt, Rinehart, and Winston, 3rd ed., 1962), pp. 205–08.

37. William Davidow and Bro Uttal, *Total Customer Service* (New York: Harper Perennial, 1990), pp. 115–16.

38. Richard Schonberger, *Building a Chain of Customers* (New York: Free Press, 1990), p. 127.

39. This could be ensured by making rotation a prerequisite for promotion into managerial ranks as Wal-Mart does, or by rewarding managerial employees for knowledge acquired as Richard Schonberger, *Building a Chain of Customers* (p. 130) recommends.

40. See Arthur Thompson, Jr., Ken Pinegar and Tracy Kramer, "Wal-Mart Stores, Inc.," in Arthur Thompson, Jr. and A. J. Strickland III (eds) *Strategic Management* (Homewood, IL: Irwin, 1992) p. 980.

41. Insights on deciphering culture are provided by Vijay Sathe, *Culture and Related Corporate Realities* (Homewood, IL: Irwin, 1985), pp. 16–24. The specifics of a culture audit are addressed by Robert Allen, "Four Phases for Bringing About Cultural Change," in Ralph Kilmann, Mary Saxton, and Ray Serpa, eds., *Gaining Control of the Corporate Culture* (San Francisco: Jossey-Bass, 1985).

8

INDICATORS: THE MEASURES OF VALUE

THE BOTTOM LINE

A British member of Parliament, when confronted with seemingly irrefutable numbers, is reported to have exclaimed, "There are three kinds of lies—lies, damn lies, and statistics!"[1] While not all statistics are necessarily misrepresentations or even misleading, the point is well taken. Consider the television manufacturer whose overall defect rate on outgoing sets dropped from 5 percent to 1 percent. The "superior" quality achieved was celebrated and publicized, and the firm basked in a self-congratulatory glow. It didn't last long. What no one had observed was that batch-to-batch deviations were unreasonably large. Sometimes, there would be one defective in a batch of 1,000; other batches of the same size would have ten times as many defectives. Compounding the inconsistency in process was the statistical reality that an "acceptable" defect level of 1 percent when applied to a sample does not guarantee that the population will conform to the same standard. That is, samples with 1 percent defective may, in fact, be drawn from populations which have, let us say, a 2 percent defect rate, unless sample sizes are large, which could prove expensive. To top it all, as everyone knows, while it's better to have one rather than five dissatisfied customers out of a hundred, it still means that for every 10,000 sets that were sold, 100 were potential sources of bad publicity, wasted time, and costly rework. The manufacturer soon realized that shooting for a single target, though glamorous and dramatic if achieved, tends to ignore other and possibly equally important measures that need to be tracked.

Most of us have at one point or the other, as did our prematurely pleased company, talked about bottom lines and goal achievement. Managers may empathize with their subordinates' hard work but will typically chide them for not keeping customers satisfied, allowing machinery to break down frequently, failing to anticipate competitors' actions, and so on. Irrespective of how industrious or intelligent the employee, in most firms and in the eyes of many managers success or failure depends on one's bottom-line performance. Evaluation primarily on the basis of an implicit or explicit bottom line, or of a single measure, pervades our everyday lives. Teachers regularly grade students on the basis of performance in exams and often tend to ignore other factors such as time and effort expended, interest shown, feel for the subject, and (critical to some students) examination-related anxiety. If my broker advised me to sell a particular stock, which then happened to spiral dizzily upward, I'd probably be very upset with him or her and would have little patience with explanations of how the decision to sell was reached. The broker's courtesy, promptness and efficiency in previous dealings might even count for little unless this was just one glitch punctuating a row of successes, a circumstance which only serves to further stress the importance of the bottom line. If a car you've just had repaired needs to go back to the repair shop, you are unlikely to be impressed by the mechanic's claims, however valid, that the present problem is unrelated to the previous one and was not discernible from the various diagnostic tests performed. You are likely to attribute the present failure to inefficient procedures employed earlier, and the systematic nature of the shop's search-and-repair routine will probably be lost on you. In our various roles as supervisors, subordinates, teachers, students, investors, customers or vendors we often judge others, and accept their judgment of us, based on the end results achieved.

Examples of our interest in the bottom line abound in sports as well. Fans are likely to notice that an NFL quarterback's rating this year was 68.4 and conclude that he is at best a mediocre passer or, if he were normally a star performer, that he has had a bad year. Few apart from the truly committed are likely to inquire how many passes were dropped, the degree of pass protection he received, and the effectiveness of the running game. Again, if a regular season batting champion managed to hit only .100 in the World Series, faring no better with runners in scoring position, few would hesitate to use the word choke freely in connection with his name. Only the die-hard fan might be moved to point out the unfortunate hitter had been robbed of a couple of home runs and a few base hits by near-miraculous fielding. A few inches the other way could have made the difference between goat and hero. Conversely, of course, few will notice, and quite rightly so, how much the top-rated passer or World Series MVP benefitted from lucky breaks and happenstance.

We are *not* arguing against the use of bottom-line measures in evaluating individuals or groups in business, sports, education, and so on—quite the opposite. Without the use of such yardsticks, people might not be motivated to put forth any effort at all. Imagine a situation where your boss says any level of performance you achieve is acceptable or a course in which you automatically receive a passing grade just by registering. The less conscientious among us might be tempted to construe this as an invitation to slacken off. At any rate, unclear or unstated expectations are the equivalent of no expectations at all. And if you expect nothing, you will not be disappointed. We are not against the use of measures of performance. What we do oppose is reliance on a single bottom-line measure to judge individuals, departments, organizations, or even countries. (In addition to economic yardsticks such as the GNP growth rate, one can evaluate a country's political system and its stability, its culture and expectations, and the importance of religion and spirituality, in order to better estimate its past performance and its potential.)

MANY MEASURES FOR VALUE DESIRED

Evaluation of the value-driven company ought to be similarly based on a diversity of measures or *Indicators*. Keeping in mind the need for multiple, overlapping methods of assessment, we shall in this chapter propose ways in which a firm's ability to deliver value can be measured, predicted, tracked, and, where necessary, improved. We will not confine ourselves to developing indicators of output achievement (that is, measures of final value created) but will also explore a variety of indicators of successfully cultivated interdependence, exceptional integration, and stimulating involvement.

In the absence of a symbiotic relationship between the firm and its customers, through the medium of value, a firm's good performance in any other area (shareholder returns, employee satisfaction, supplier cooperation) will remain at best a nine days' wonder. Measures of customer value are therefore crucial to the firm's continued success. The other constituents' requirements must also, no doubt, be fulfilled to ensure that service to customers is not interrupted, for example, through the loss of shareholder confidence, employee discontentment, and governmental regulatory action.

Ascertaining the firm's value-performance means measuring the firm's ability to deliver the *components* of value that are deemed important by customers (using a device such as Figure 2.3). Not only must the relative weights of the components be drawn from expressed customer needs, the firm's delivery capability must also be evaluated by customers. In the case of products that are targeted at a wide range of customers, the analysis and fulfillment of customer needs could become a complex, lengthy process. For example, airline travel, microcomputers, hotel accommodation, automobiles, and lawnmowers are some of the numerous products which have to satisfy a wide range of customer needs. Expectations are not likely to be in agreement from one customer to another. Some may accord prime importance to price and routing and others to courtesy and convenience (in the case of airlines); to styling and comfort versus fuel efficiency and warranties (for automobiles); and software versatility and machine size as against promptness of service and easy availability (microcomputers). Questionnaire surveys sent to recent purchasers of the product, with incentives provided to participants such as discounts on the next purchase, are useful in helping determine the critical components of value. Personal interviews and focus groups could then be made use of to collapse the various value components into a few meaningful ones.[2] Statistical techniques come in handy during this stage of the value process, when the criteria for measurement are being specified, and some of them are sketched out below.[3]

- **Cluster** analysis could be employed to consolidate two or more components of value into a single factor. In the case of vacuum cleaners, for instance, cluster analysis might help decide whether "Lightness," "Quick turning" and "Convenience in handling" may be combined into a single factor, "Easy maneuverability." When the number of attributes that customers expect from a product becomes unmanageably large, composites of attributes bring a degree of focus to the task of specifying and evaluating value delivery.

- **Conjoint analysis** enables the value researcher to arrive at an assessment of the relative importance of the diverse components of value. The techniques of monotone regression (based on customers rating the various *combinations* of attributes against each other) or trade-off analysis (whereby the attributes are rated against each other, pair by pair) are generally used to determine the ideal profile of benefits the customer expects from the product.

- **Multidimensional scaling** (MDS) is a technique that can help with value-based benchmarking relative to leading competitors. A convenient aspect of MDS is that, based on a pair-by-pair comparison, by customers, of the product's overall value, it is possible to display pictorially the differences among competing products in terms of the components of value. That is, MDS takes a one-dimensional benchmarking and breaks it down into a multidimensional one, each of the latter dimensions corresponding to a value component (response time, warranties, etc.).

Techniques such as the above which help combine components of value under a few labels or descriptions when there are too many components (cluster analysis), figure out the optimum combination of the components of value (conjoint analysis), and compare competing products on some of their value dimensions given only an overall comparison (MDS), are but a few of the statistical analyses that could prove invaluable in probing the nature of value and the organization's ability to conceptualize, con-

struct, and communicate it. It might appear that these are rather complicated approaches to diagnosing value—and they are. But measuring
value (as perceived by customers) is not a straightforward matter. Things
get complicated, particularly when the product has many components of
value (i.e., benefits expected by customers), which are dynamic (changing
over time and due to perceptions of competitors' value), thus making the
need for a relatively precise estimation of value delivered all the more
indispensable.

MEASURING VALUE DELIVERED

It is all too easy, if one isn't careful, to succumb to the trap of pre-
sumption or fall into the pit of despair while gauging the firm's ability to
meet the exacting needs of the marketplace. The trap lies in assuming
that a careful cataloging of needs is, however complex, the entire story.
Finding out what customers need is one thing. Providing for these needs
and evaluating how satisfied customers are is another and at least equally
important part of the firm's journey of value. While providing for the
value needs of customers has been documented throughout this book,
determining customers' reactions to the company's offerings can be ignored or taken lightly only with serious and perhaps terminal repercussions. Characteristic of the despair syndrome, on the other hand, is a
genuine attempt to come to grips with what customers feel about the
product and the value they receive from it. However, as they realize the
difficulties inherent in arriving at a specific and general sense of customer
needs and reactions to the product, these firms take the easier way out.
They decide to content themselves with gross and surrogate measures of
customer need fulfillment. Sales and market share, for instance, become
the yardsticks by which customer value is measured. We have nothing
against the validity of either of these and similar measures and will, in
fact, champion their use shortly. Using them as complete substitutes for
customer perceptions of value delivered, however, would be a mistake.
Imagine you want to find the height of a tower by measuring the length
of its shadow. Knowing the sun's elevation, the height of the tower can
be fairly accurately estimated. If, based on this, we were to assume that
there was a fixed relationship between the length of shadow and height
of tower, we would be right—but only at a specified time and on a specified
day. Using the ratio at other locations would be even more erroneous
since factors such as the slope of the land, and its height above sea level
must be considered in addition to the sun's elevation. Using sales to
measure customer need fulfillment likewise has many drawbacks. Other
factors like competitors' actions, seasonal variations, and the supply of
substitutes or complementary products can inflate or depress sales levels
independent of value delivered to customers. Assuming that the shadow

of sales represents and completely defines the tower of customer value may be valid, but perhaps no oftener than in the real-world physical analogy.

Let us return briefly to the case of the presumptuous firm. Its critical failing lies not in ignoring customers' needs but in the rather complacent assumption that it knows, or at least has a sense of, what customers' reactions are. This incomplete application of the marketing concept[4] is downright dangerous since it tends to both isolate the firm from external stimuli as well as subtly reinforce the basis of value without an external reference. For example, Polaroid's instant movie camera, following hard on the heels of its tremendously successful instant camera and film, was a big flop. It was a forerunner of the video camera and may, in fact, have never achieved much success in any case, since it was on a different branch of evolutionary progress, so to speak, from the mainstream audio/ video industry. However, the fact that the picture was very grainy and that viewers, particularly children, found the persistent noise irritating doomed it to extinction.[5] Briggs and Stratton, a legend in the lawn mower (and outdoor engine) business, faced difficult times in the late 1970s and early 1980s due in part to the entry of Honda.[6] Honda's experience with small engines, particularly motorcycles, and its ability to make a lawn mower with an integrated, made-by-one-firm look gave it an instant edge over Briggs and Stratton, whose engines were fitted onto other firms' lawn mowers. Irrespective of how long the product has been around (Polaroid's problems surfaced at the introduction stage while Briggs and Stratton's arose during the maturity stage of the life cycle) tracking the extent to which customers' needs are being satisfied or denied never ceases to be critical to the firm's continued health. In Polaroid's case, the value deficiency was intrinsic to the product and essentially related to conceptualization (design improvements) and communication (deciding what improvements were needed to satisfy customers) while in Briggs and Stratton's encounter with the Japanese multinational the value deficiency was based in the first two Cs. The development of integrated mowers needed design and manufacturing modifications if it was to erode Honda's edge. Customer needs must be identified if they are to be satisfied. Bridging the two (identification and satisfaction) is the firm's value capability.

TRACKING VALUE ALONG THE CHAIN: QFD

Clearly, therefore, however trivial and trite it might appear to be, not only must important customer needs be determined, measuring how well these needs are being provided for is also critical. The two aspects are indeed the two faces of the coin of customer value. And, in measuring success at meeting customer requirements, one has to go back to the court of customer opinion again. In chapter 2, we outlined a technique called

Quality Function Deployment (QFD) aimed at ensuring that the needs of the customer are not translated wrongly (by, say marketing research, development, or engineering people). As Ishikawa and Lu point out clearly and powerfully, quality as designed may differ from quality as produced, which in turn may not match quality demanded by customers.[7] Such quality gaps can make the pursuit of value a frustrating experience, since the attainment of internal quality targets does not ensure satisfaction of customers' quality needs. Distortion in communication is not the exclusive preserve of hierarchies. Wherever information crosses boundaries (whether between value activities or hierarchic levels) distortion and even loss or suppression of information can occur. We often hear what we want to hear. Sometimes we only convey what presents us in a favorable light or makes life a little easier. Omissions, embellishments and changes are either rationalized away or not considered serious. In light of the tendency of communication to go astray, QFD performs a unique and vital role in the value process. It tries to bind the parties concerned to specifics. The needs of customers are stated in the terms acceptable to and used by customers themselves. ("Easily moved around" and "Quiet" are two requirements of a mower or vacuum cleaner.) An internal translation is needed to make the requirements workable from a design/operations standpoint. ("Light," "Centering of weight," "Handle access," "Low vibration," "Noise insulation," "Beater speed" are some of the possible internal criteria directly corresponding to market needs.) Generally, more than one level of translation is needed to make the consumer's down-to-earth needs intelligible to the scientist or engineer since the latter has to convert everyday ideas into specifications. The situation is analogous to two people, one of whom knows only English and the other only Chinese trying to strike up a conversation. If they can locate English/Chinese interpreters a reasonably faithful translation can be expected in both directions. But if the only interpreters available are English/German, German/Arabic, and Arabic/Chinese, strict rules for translation must be specified if original meanings and intent are to survive. QFD attempts to create the rules for translating needs into specifications even if multiple levels of translation are needed. The techniques, incidentally, can be applied with equal validity to services as to products.

QFD should not be viewed as a panacea for spanning the customer-company chasm since it has its limitations and pathologies. One such limitation is obvious even from the rather elementary mower or vacuum cleaner illustration earlier. Lightness and less vibration, for instance, could prove contradictory since lowering the level of vibration might require a heavier machine body. In reaching a compromise between the two criteria, one has to remember that the conflict arises not from design or marketing decisions but from a tension between customer needs. A priority or weighted list of customer needs can be consulted to make a determination of the benefits that could be de-emphasized at the expense of the most important ones. Not only must choices be made between conflicting criteria, resulting inevitably in a less-than-optimal decision, customer needs are rarely static. Dynamic needs cloud the picture even more and may arise from:

- Intrinsic changes in customers' preferences, as when widespread perceptions of environmental degradation lead customers to increasingly prefer products made from recyclable materials;
- Improvements in competitors' offerings which cause shifts in customer needs. Examples: Honda's introduction of an integrated mower triggered a demand for this type of machine,[8] Miller's light beer[9] ignited a need for an "athlete's brew," and Adidas' and Nike's concept of a sneaker for all occasions changed the meaning of casual footwear. The relative calm pervading an industry can be rudely shattered by such changes in the value game;
- Interactive, gradual changes that result from satisfying existing needs. As industries mature and/or products deliver increasing value, customers become more sophisticated. That is, as initial and more basic needs are fulfilled, other, more advanced needs take their place in a variation of Maslow's needs hierarchy, according to which as individuals progressively satisfy their needs, other types of needs arise. The sequence Maslow proposed was physiological, safety, social, and actualization.[10] This phenomenon is easily observable in a broad context. Winter heating and pneumatic tires are no longer luxuries in a car, and multi-function, handheld calculators are no longer novel in terms of value delivered. Antilock braking and programmability respectively are likely to be the current important needs where these products are concerned. Just as an escalating customer awareness leads to the progressive ascent of customer needs, satisfaction of customers' needs by individual firms also can lead to emergence of hitherto submerged needs. Polaroid's development of an instant movie camera, described earlier, brought dormant requirements such as "quiet running" and "high resolution picture" into the foreground of benefits desired. In the food retailing business, as Kroger and Safeway diversified their product range, customer satisfaction grew and, almost simultaneously, expectations rose too: specialty departments (baked goods, video rentals) and personalized service were the prominent requirements that arose to magnify the demand for one-stop shopping. Success in satisfying customer needs generates higher expectations and often creates other needs such as lower-priced products as well. The growth of superstores, on the one hand, and of wholesale clubs, on the other, exemplifies the insatiable nature of customers' expectations.[11]

The shifting sands of customer needs do not invalidate a technique like QFD; rather they make it all the more useful, provided the need for change and flexibility is understood and built into its implementation. Not only does QFD play an invaluable role in the definition and translation of customer value, it can also help in adjusting to shifting value perceptions. For example, if buyers of a make of small cars, satisfied with the product's fuel efficiency, shift their focus to easy serviceability, QFD, if geared to be flexible, would facilitate making the necessary internal changes for adaptation.

A danger that lurks within QFD's role as "value messenger" is that the medium could become the message. The technique becomes more important than the objective of customer satisfaction. Problems arising from a too narrow focus and inflexibility can be rather easily overcome by using external reference points. In judging whether QFD or, for that matter, any customer-to-firm communications are functioning effectively, ask the customer. Don't ask the intermediate people how the product measures up to their criteria ("Are the mean and variances in amplitude of vibration acceptable?"). Rather ask the user how well it meets their needs ("Is it quiet?"). In the earlier instance of speakers of different languages, if the Chinese person who asked a question ("What's the weather like in England during the summer?") received a plausible reply ("It rains a lot"), she would conclude that the sequence of translations worked quite well. If, on the other hand, the reply she got was absurd ("Dubrovnik had an old world charm"), she would conclude the mechanism was a failure. The results of QFD have to be judged at the court of customer opinion. Internal mechanisms are only as good as the external results. In a sense, evaluating these methods of functioning serves a purpose that is analogous to that of the Turing test. Turing proposed that a machine such as a computer could be called intelligent only if an observer in a separate room could not tell the difference six times out of ten between the machine and a human when communication has been established with both.[12] As in machine "intelligence," so in value: external perception is at least as important as internal capability. The validity of any approach to building better value rests upon assessment by the recipients of value and not on second-hand criteria. QFD, quality and process control, the 3Cs, the 5INs, and all the other guides to action outlined must pass this test of value received if they are to be deemed effective. The customer keeps us honest, alert, and humble.

VALUE AND SALES/PROFIT: MATCH OR MISMATCH?

Customers, as we have seen, have divergent, changing, and conflicting needs. Feedback can help reduce performance gaps through redesign, improved response time, user information, and so forth. However, it is unlikely that any firm will achieve perfection in the eyes of its customers. Either it suffers by comparison to its competitors or to its own past prowess or its achievements engender a rising tide of expectations. Either way, the firm is constantly "pulled" by or drawn in the direction of specific customer need satisfaction, which is the origin of all efforts at continuous improvement. Firms that have recently improved value delivered consid-

Figure 8.1
Value (Process) and Sales/Profitability (Results)

	Sales Growth		Profitability	
	Rapid	**Anemic**	**Excellent**	**Poor**
Superior	**1** Matching Value and Results (Ideal)	**2** Well Kept Secret — Small is Beautiful	**1 1** Best of Both Worlds	**2 2** (a) Things will pick up (b) Easy popularity?
Customer Value (received)	**3** Enjoy it (While it Lasts)	**4** Matching Value and Results — Snap out of it!	**3 3** Are we gouging?	**4 4** Matching Value and Results — Snap out of it!
Inferior				

erably (video parlors with longer rental periods for the same price, airlines with sharply lower fares or more direct flights, automakers providing you-name-it options delivered in three days) will, of course, experience a surge in customer approval. However, as competitors adopt matching strategies, customers are, justifiably, quick to ask, "What have you done for me lately?" Moreover, some strategies, like price cutting, may not be sustainable in the long run. Falling profits could force a firm to reevaluate its choice of a way to its customers' collective hearts.

To business organizations, results provide not only a barometer of performance but also serve as a stimulus to further effort. Sales, market share, and profitability are useful indexes of corporate achievement when used in conjunction with customer value. High sales growth (say, at twice the rate of the other firms in the industry) in a firm whose customers rate the firm a value leader is mutually reinforcing evidence. Sales growth without matching customer value perception, on the other hand, indicates that the market success might be short-lived and could be due to aberrations in the industry such as competitors' mistakes or seasonal peaks. The opposite situation (low growth in sales and superior value received) may indicate an inability or lack of effort to communicate the product's inherent value capabilities. If the component-capability chart of Figure 2.4 showed a distinct deficiency in C3, it would be additional evidence of such a failing.

The left half of Figure 8.1 illustrates four combinations of Customer Value and Sales growth with cells 1 and 4 indicating a perfect fit between process and results. Cell 1 is the ideal situation, typified for the most part by firms such as Wal-Mart[13] and Lincoln Electric[14] that are customer favorites, have the sales volume to show for it, and want to achieve even more. Not only do they excel in value delivery, the firms also draw upon the energies and talents of their employee base in doing so. Sears, which for most of its long and colorful history, had been second to none in delivering customer value has of late foundered both in value and in sales. It is trying to snap out of its sojourn in the cellar (cell 4) through a variety of methods. One such initiative is "Kid Vantage," a program based on parent focus group feedback offering free replacement of children's clothing items if the child's size is still the same. Another is the use of frequent-shoppers cards, which allows customers to earn discounts and monitor spending levels.[15] National Westminster Bank's President Knowles, entrusted with turning the bank around, commissioned a comprehensive investigation of customer need fulfillment which pointed up numerous failings in value delivery—failings which seemed correlated to the poor financial performance.[16] Firms in cell 2, as mentioned earlier, get rave reviews from their limited customer base but have not successfully communicated their value capabilities to the bulk of potential customers or have chosen not to do so. Adopting a strategy of focus with low sales levels is a perfectly viable strategy adopted by most small businesses and by bigger ones as well. Luxury carmakers, upscale jewelry stores, and exclusive colleges often decide not to expand for fear of compromising quality, while commuter airlines and local breweries have little room for expansion given the nature of competition they face.[17] For businesses with ambitions of growth, however, being positioned in cell 2 is, to say the least, damaging, if not disastrous, and is clear evidence that their message of value has found few listeners. Disastrous is hardly the label one would apply to occupants of cell 3; they are riding high but may be due for a crash. This cell is transitional in that firms headed from cell 1 to cell 4 spend time in cell 3 (as did Sears during the early 1980s). The bubble must burst, as it did for Detroit's automakers starting in the mid 1970s, since the tension between the process (customer satisfaction or the lack thereof) and the result (growth in sales) is inevitably resolved in the customer's favor. Cell 3 firms drift into cell 4 and if the latter want to escape, they often must spend time in the limbo of cell 2. Lee Iacocca has, for the past few years, been trying to get Chrysler out of cell 4 into cell 1. Considering that its quality, warranty terms, and price have undoubtedly improved, why is Chrysler still battling the ghost of failures past? For one, the Japanese haven't exactly been rooted to the same spot; their performance parameters have improved too. Another and perhaps equally valid explanation is that the perception of *present* value takes a back seat to *past* value. Customers have to first be informed that today's value is far superior to that of yesterday. Then, they must believe it. Even more important, they have to be convinced that, if the product is once again elevated to cell 1 status, it will not become presumptuous enough to sneak back into the exploitative mode of cell 3. Communication has to first focus on reassuring customers that they will not be taken lightly again.

The right-hand half of Figure 8.1 employs the Profitability-Value match (or mismatch) as an indicator of the company's health. Profitability refers to dollar profits measured in relation to sales generated, assets invested, equity held, or some combination thereof. Profitability ratios such as return on sales (ROS), return on assets (ROA) and return on equity (ROE) are preferred over absolute dollar profits since they keep profits in perspective relative to resource usage or market performance and make improvements over time easier to track. Just as before, the northwestern and southeastern cells (11 and 44, respectively) represent firms that are getting exactly what they deserve, favorable or unfavorable. Cells 22 and 33 again serve as indicators of something being not quite right. A firm in cell 22 has to investigate whether the dissonance between profit and value arises from charging below par prices, which elevates value perceived while depressing profits. If prices *are* unusually low (and the firm's costs are not) other methods of achieving popularity may have to be explored. On the other hand, profitability in terms of ROA often will be low soon after a major investment has been made, since such investments (airplanes in an airline, high plant and equipment costs in a manufacturing firm, new construction in a hotel firm) frequently have an extended "gestation" period with marginal profits. Depending on the firm's diagnosis of why it finds itself in cell 22, the choice between urgent action and waiting patiently must be made. Organizations in cell 33 (as in 3) may experience no such urgent call to action and may choose to wait it out. But, just as in cell 3, success may be fleeting unless value enhancement is carried out. High-priced products that sell well due to the exit of major competitors or due to the fact that the product has been introduced recently and has not reached its "natural" level of competition are not exactly firm foundations for long-term success. Products in the growth stage of the life cycle often go through such a value-profit imbalance until industry demand increases to draw other firms in and stabilize the competitive picture. Unless the firm's customers get the value presently being denied to them, the countdown to occupying cell 44 will be brief.

Value delivered to customers is a top priority for any firm. Indeed, as we have asserted at every opportunity afforded us, it is *the* top priority. While, in the long run, the value-maximizing firm will emerge as the most successful whether evaluated by market, financial, technological, human or other yardsticks, firms cannot and do not live on visions and long-range views alone. Employees have to be paid, shareholders expect dividends or stock appreciation, government regulations are to be complied with, and local communities have claims on the corporation's resources that may not brook denial or even delay. Though no firm should lose sight of its value mission, the humdrum necessities of everyday existence call for a judicious mixture of the long and short terms, of detail and outline, of microscope and telescope, so to speak. Figure 8.1 demonstrates one way of bringing value into practical focus by keeping tabs on it along with sales and profitability. Other factors that could be considered as co-indicators of performance, besides sales and profitability, include market share, degree of compliance with regulations, rate of product innovation and extent of community involvement.

One of the tenets of Roman law was that justice must not only be rendered but also be *seen* to be rendered. We suggest a similar principle for customer value. Not only must value be delivered, it should be achieved in the right way. Value enhanced through inappropriate or questionable means could be counterproductive, short-lived and encourage value-destructive behaviors. In other words, the *process* which an organization employs is at least as important as the *results* achieved. The short-term view exemplified by the myopic manager often leads to excellent results which may peter out and quickly lead to decline and decay further down the road.

We do not advocate total absorption in the means as opposed to the ends. Our interest in "how" is aimed at neutralizing the homage most organizations pay to the bottom line. We argue that process and results, as Indicators of value must be given equal importance. The reader who has stayed the course with us thus far must have realized that we are not mystics or philosophers. We do not go around preaching, "It's not whether you lose or win that matters—what's important is how you play the game." As long as one plays fair, winning is good, for the sports team, for the military commander, and for the business firm alike, because it almost always means that the organization has to be competitively *dynamic*. It cannot hope to succeed unless it is constantly moving, alert, and concerned. Even St. Paul, who was satisfied that he had "run the good race" and "fought the good fight," was no slouch when it came to results. His zeal, energy, and inspiring oratory helped build an edifice that has survived and grown through the centuries. In scientific inquiry, too, it is equally important to realize that the ends are important while adhering to the prescribed methods. If Darwin, after his extensive travels had penned a fascinating account of the various animals and plants he had seen, documenting and classifying them in the accepted fashion, he would certainly have been lauded for his accomplishment. However, the process of science culminating in his theory of natural selection assured Darwin enduring, perhaps unmatched, respect among the scientific community and the public at large. Process and results were equally important and superlative.

As can be seen from the chapter summary (Figure 8.2), in the long haul, customer value is the prime Indicator of corporate performance; in a more

Figure 8.2
Indicators—A Look Back

Pervasive Nature of Bottom Line Measures

Need for Multiple Indicators

Value — an important indicator

— customer feedback and statistical methods

— measuring ability to provide for needs

QFD — its role in ensuring fidelity of communication

— its ability to deal with shifting expectations

Process and Results

— Value and Sales

— Value and Profit

— the implications of consonance and dissonance within these pairs immediate sense, value is a *process* which has to be reconciled with important performance indicators or results. In addition to an overall output assessment of customer value, the input process of value creation must also be tracked and corrections made as needed. In the odyssey of value, minor navigational errors could later cause major discrepancies and require the type of radical traumatic change that a program of continuously improving value seeks to avoid. A convenient framework of indicators for the process of value is provided by the other INs themselves. The levels of Interdependence, Integration, Involvement, and Ingraining achieved by the firm are fairly reliable indexes of how effectively the firm is pursuing its stated ultimate end. To this, we now turn our attention.

NOTES

1. Attributed to Benjamin Disraeli. Lawrence Peter, *Peter's Quotations* (Toronto: Bantam, 1987), p. 477.

2. Thomas Kinnear and James Taylor, *Marketing Research: An Applied Approach* (New York: McGraw-Hill, 1979). The book provides an overview of (pp. 44–45) as well as the methodology and rationale underlying focus groups (pp. 425–30).

3. Joseph Hair, Jr., et al., *Multivariate Data Analysis* (New York: Macmillan, 1984).

4. Frederick Webster, *Marketing for Managers*, (New York: Harper & Row, 1974), pp. 10–11.

5. *Fortune*, April 7, 1980, pp. 66–70.

6. Richard Hoffman, "Competition in Outdoor Power Equipment: Briggs & Stratton Versus Honda," in Arthur Thompson, Jr. and A. J. Strickland III, *Strategic Management* (Homewood, IL: Irwin, 1992), pp. 489–552.

7. Kaoru Ishikawa and David Lu in *Total Quality Control* (Englewood Cliffs, NJ: Prentice-Hall, 1985).

8. See Richard Hoffman, "Competition in Outdoor Power Equipment: Briggs & Stratton Versus Honda."

9. Douglas Workman, "Anheuser-Busch Companies, Inc.," in Neil Snyder et. al., *Strategic Management Cases* (Reading, MA: Addison-Wesley, 1991), p. 132.

10. Abraham Maslow, "A Theory of Human Motivation," *Psychological Review* 80, 1943, pp. 370–96.

11. *Standard and Poor's Industry Surveys* (New York: Standard and Poor's, 1992), pp. R86–89.

12. For an absorbing exploration of machine/human interaction see O. B. Hardison, Jr., *Disappearing Through the Skylight* (New York: Viking, 1989), pp. 317–32.

13. The largest retailer in the world does not rest on its laurels. Sales through customer service is the message employees hear all the time. See *Fortune*, September 23, 1991, pp. 47–59.

14. In spite of its uninterrupted stream of profits over the years, Lincoln Electric

has started revamping some of its policies (e.g., promotion from within) and encourages workers to constantly think quality. Complacency is being eschewed. See *Industry Work*, March 5, 1989, 15–18.

15. *Business Week*, Nov. 11, 1991, p. 140.

16. Charles Smith, "National Westminster Bank, U.S.A.," in Neil Snyder, et al., *Strategic Management Cases* (Reading, MA: Addison-Wesley, 1991), pp. 496–500.

17. Richard Levin and Brent Callinicas, "The Golden Gate Brewing Company," in Neil Snyder, et al., *Strategic Management Cases* (Reading: MA: Addison-Wesley, 1991), p. 230–31.

9

INDICATORS: EVALUATING THE INs

MEASURING THE PROCESS OF VALUE

Mystery novels and mystery movies have a wide following all over the world, and some of their charm surely lies in the revelation of the identity of the criminal. For some mystery buffs, the more startling and unexpected the ending the more satisfied they are. However, even the most rabid whodunit fan will readily admit that the plot and its development, the richness of characterization, the careful planting of clues, and the personality of the detective also contribute greatly to the success of the overall package. The meticulous search for clues and the deductive abilities of Sherlock Holmes and his exchanges with Dr. Watson are as celebrated as Miss Jane Marple and her simple, yet sinister English villagers or Phillip Marlowe's ability to get himself into all sorts of trouble and joke about it. Even in the "Columbo" series, where the viewer, unlike the detective, knows the identity of the perpetrator, our attention tends to be held by the twists and turns of the action, as well as by the idiosyncrasies and feigned ignorance of the detective.

Detective fiction offers a simple analogy to the value-maximizing organization. The ending (result) is important but so too are the plots, characters and action (process). The vehicles of value, so to speak, are as important to measure as the attainment of value. Interdependence, integration and involvement are our three central vehicles to deliver value, with ingraining serving to build them into the fiber of the organization. In a general sense, interdependence comprises the degree of linkage, the immediacy of impact, and the absence of slack resources or insulation between any two successive operations. Carried to its logical conclusion, interdependence may be extended to and measured across the entire value chain stretching from supplier to customers. One indicator of tight linkage between successive activities lies in their being part of a closely-knit group. This is particularly true when there are numerous activities to be performed and a large number of work centers as in the case of large manufacturing facilities. If the flow of product(s) is not confined to a prespecified routing, but is based on operator preference, machine availability, etc., responsibility for the output and a sense of identity with other operations are likely to be eroded. Linkage between successive operations can be tightened by establishing a self-contained production or service cell. The cellular group's distinctiveness from other such groups is clearly demonstrated by its exclusive machine layout and its autonomy in controlling its pace, methods, and atmosphere. One indicator of interdependence is, therefore, the extent to which self-contained work groups (SCWG) are deployed in an organization. This may be expressed as

$$\text{Human resource linkage (HRL)} = \frac{\text{Total number of employees in SCWG}}{\text{Total number of employees}}$$

and

$$\text{Equipment linkage (EL)} = \frac{\text{Total equipment investment level (\$) in SCWG}}{\text{Total equipment investment level (\$)}}$$

These indicators measure the prevalence of human resource and equipment interdependencies in any organization. When used in combination, HRL and EL provide a first-cut appraisal of the resource linkages present in the department or firm. The maximum attainable is a level of one, which indicates a completely autonomous grouping of the firm's resources, an unlikely eventuality since some resources such as computers, buildings, and supervision are generally shared among work groups even if the latter are otherwise autonomous. The linkage indicator is best applied department by department and need not be confined to manufacturing groups. For example, interdependence within the sales department can be assessed using the same measures. Of course, the interdependence may not be serial in nature as it often is in a manufacturing context. Sales linkages are more likely to be reciprocal or multiple, especially where the salespersons are responsible for similar or identical products and for customers who have at least a few value characteristics in common (e.g., a widely shared need for quick manufacturer response, product flexibility, and information). In both the manufacturing and sales contexts, providing reinforcement to the members of the SCWGs based on an evaluation of the group's achievements is likely to further cement group linkages. Layout changes aimed at bringing geographically dispersed sales groups and individuals together periodically could help foster interdependence to an even greater extent within SCWGs. Geographical concentration of SCWGs could help in increasing interdependence at other points of the value chain as well. For instance, R & D groups organized and spatially configured on a SCWG basis would bring a greater sense of direction to the value conceptualization effort. Even without organizing New Product Teams (see chapter 2), which are specifically focused SCWGs, the stimulus of interaction within clearly distinct (as opposed to larger and undefined) groups tend to generate a sense of identity, belonging, and responsibility for actions.[1] Triggering and maintaining more numerous and stronger dependencies in organizations will promote equally cohesive SCWGs. Airlines, hotels, department or discount stores, and food retailers are among the types of businesses that could benefit from the within-groups unifying effect of tighter interconnections. The HRL and EL indicators suggested earlier would work equally well, even if it be only to provide an overall sense of how well the stage has been set.

TIME: THE DOMINANT DIMENSION

Self-contained work groups and their measurement are, in a sense, the warm-up act. Who or what is the main performer? In one word, Time. Time has been the subject of intense research effort, especially in physics,[2] and some of the findings have been quite fascinating, if not startling— time as an extension of space, the slowing down of time at high speeds, gravity's effect on time, and so on. The managerial view of time is nowhere near as exotic. And yet, for the value-conscious organization, time and its measurement are vital to success. Stanley Davis[3] urges organizations to analyze the "time value of information" and to contract activity-times where they will have maximum impact along the value chain. Time as value can be progressively enhanced until, at the extreme, "ideas are acts."

Time as a component of value has been mentioned and discussed by us earlier (chapter 2, Figure 2.1 particularly) in terms of responsiveness to customer needs. One indicator of the ability to respond quickly is, in manufacturing firms, referred to as the cycle efficiency.[4] We refer to it here as operational cycle efficiency (OCE) and apply it to both manufacturing and service firms. Essentially, it measures the proportion of time spent on value-creating activities.

$$\text{Operational cycle efficiency (OCE)} = \frac{\text{Value creation time}}{\text{Total time}}$$

Value creation time refers to time actually consumed in processing the product or service, while the total time includes waiting, storage, rework,

material handling, and other "waste" activities to use the Japanese terminology. An OCE of one is ideal though a level as low as ten percent
is not uncommon.[5] Adopting the conventional approach to analyzing this
conventional monitor may not help very much. Typically, for instance,
foremen strive to "keep the machines running." While this certainly increases value creation time, it may also increase total time expended if
the items produced in a frenzy of capacity utilization lie unused (since
the next machine is down), are found to fall short of quality criteria, or
are not yet needed by customers. As Suzaki[6] observes, what matters is
whether a piece of equipment is available when needed ("on-demand
utilization factor") and not what proportion of the time it is in production.
In reality, then, the OCE could go down even when machines are being
run instead of being allowed to remain idle, clearly belying the maxim
that "A busy plant is a productive plant." A sign worth hanging over any
Operations Manager's desk is one that says, "Judging plant performance
solely or mainly by machine utilization rates could be injurious to your
health and your job!"

On second thought, all managers might benefit from taking this motto
seriously. Sales and Engineering managers who worry about how busy
their individual employees are (or are not) could profit by paying more
attention to linkages between the resources at their command and by
making sure that a balance exists among them. Facilitating interactions
and reciprocal linkages among people as well as ensuring a balanced flow
of information and tasks so that no bottlenecks result are beyond doubt
both critical managerial responsibilities.[7] Time is both an irreplaceable
resource and a prominent dimension of value. It also plays an indispensable role in unifying an organization by vesting customers' needs with
a sense of urgency. Organizations facing a crisis, for instance, typically
feel a sense of urgency which in some cases serves to bring the organization together. Johnson and Johnson, in the wake of the Tylenol tragedy,
closed ranks in the face of a near disaster. The sense of urgency precip-
itated by the crisis served to bind the firm more closely together than it
ever had been before.[8] Obviously, we are not advocating that crises be
engineered in the interest of cohesion. However, efforts to reduce the
time taken in responding to customers' needs has the effect of exposing
bottlenecks in capabilities and resources. Dealing with "mini-crises"
(caused by a lack of inventory, shutdown of machines, straying from
quality conformity, an increased need for rapid changeovers, customer
expectations of frequent product change, etc.) can increase organizational
agility, consciousness, and cohesion, and can help avert the occurrence
of major crises (such as customers being turned off by the firm's inflexibility and poor quality). Heeding internal prodomes or warning signals
could help thwart crises,[9] but first these warning signals have to be allowed
to surface.

TIME: MARKET, RESPONSE, AND SETUP

George Stalk, Jr., and Thomas Hart[10] have devoted an entire book to exploring time as a competitive weapon. "Time compression" is viewed as central to productivity, quality, and innovation enhancements, which are the harbingers to superior value and profitability. We propose *time-to-market*, *response time*, and *setup time*, as three indicators that clearly illustrate the pervasive need for a time-based linkage and balance. Time-to-market denotes the time elapsed between customers' felt need and the arrival of the ready-to-sell product in the showroom, on the shelves, or wherever customers can buy it. Time-to-market[11] includes elements like

1) Expression of need for a particular product
2) The organization's awareness of customer need
3) Acceptance of the economic viability of the product
4) Conceptualization
5) Establishing the form of the product, its design, and the benefits it will provide
6) Specifications for materials, people and other input resources
7) The process of manufacturing or service operation
8) Pilot testing and trial runs
9) Test marketing
10) Troubleshooting

Encouraging tighter and multiple linkages will have a favorable effect on time-to-market. To illustrate, as the time that elapses between 1) and 2) is progressively reduced (that is, the customer to market research/sales connection is made stronger), the firm will find itself responding more quickly to customer needs and gaining a head start over its rivals. Again, as linkages between 5) and 6), and between 6) and 7) are tightened (that is, the time delays between them decrease), the transition of a product from design to manufacturing becomes streamlined. One way of improving linkages is by performing two or more activities simultaneously. Consultation with manufacturing personnel/process or service engineers at the design stage can drastically reduce time taken up later developing a suitable sequence of operations. Similarly, conceptualizing the nature and functions of the proposed product could be linked to the current product specifications, materials used and personnel capabilities. Designing for operations[12] is one way of achieving this sort of incremental innovation. There is a caveat. Close coordination between, or even the collapsing of, two or more activities, however, discourages radical changes being made in the product. Though substantial value enhancements may follow the use of time-to-market as an indicator of interdependence and customer value, it is *not* meant to stimulate radical innovations. The latter, whether effected through sharp price reductions (BIC's nineteen-cent ball point pen when first introduced), dramatically enhanced functions and capability (Apple's first microcomputer), or clearly superior quality (the Japanese cars that stood in stark contrast to their American counterparts), depend more on being able to satisfy customer needs in uniquely different ways from those currently available, and time-to-market may be less important than economic viability, technical competence of the design and of the manufacturing process, and all the other steps essential to ensure the success of a completely new product.

While tightly linking two or more activities together (by ensuring interaction between them or even assigning them to the same individual or group) helps reduce the time consumed in the separate activities and enhances customer time value, this sort of splicing and joining should be done judiciously. For instance 2) and 3) above (that is, awareness of customer needs and establishing a product's viability), if assigned to the same individual or group, could result in progressing naturally from need awareness to assuming the product fits the needs. In other words, conflicts of interest are likely. Moreover, the time-to-market chain has to be recognized as a highly interrelated set of activities, not as a relay race in which one's responsibility ceases once the baton is passed. Market researchers need to update customers' needs and keep in touch with designers, technologists and engineers to share the information. If troubleshooting runs into delays, R & D, sales, and anyone else, even if not directly required to, have to consider it part of *their* problem. Holding periodic review meetings after product introduction to discuss product performance and identify areas for further support is useful in building the value consciousness needed in the campaign to shorten the time-to-market. Improvements achieved by reducing time delays in bringing customers the products or services they value can be evaluated in different ways:

- Simply measuring the improvement over time in each time indicator
- Comparing total time-to-market to the prior figure, to competitors, to the length of the product life cycle (a time-to-market that is of the same order as the length of the cycle is too long, even if it shows improvement over past years)
- Benchmarking specific components of time-to-market (e.g., design, pilot process development, test marketing, etc.) against leading competitors separately.
- Identifying activities (through Pareto analysis) that take up a disproportionate share of the time consumed. This could be followed up by assigning more resources (say, more people) to these activities[13] and doing some of the work at an earlier stage (e.g., keeping the manufacturing or service process in mind while designing the product or service).

Though time-to-market might appear to be one facet of our next important Indicator, response time, there is a distinction between them as employed here. We use response time to denote time taken to respond to customers' needs where they concern the existing product, whereas time-to-market applies to new or modified products. Response time is a "time umbrella." Simple indicators such as "How quickly do we provide information to customers?" and more complicated ones like "What are the critical components of our product's lead time?" rub shoulders with each other under the rubric of response time. Federal Express's guarantee of providing information about the location of any piece of mail at any time may appear trivial to some, but through its instant tracking capability, the firm allays the fears of its customers, including those who may never use this tracking service. Being able to offer information to customers on demand is an indicator of tight linkage along the value chain, particularly when the information needed spans many activities.[14] Toll-free numbers are an approach to collapsing different value-chain activities into one. Questions about conditions of sale, assembly, operation, malfunction, and maintenance are fielded from one location. Procter and Gamble, for instance, segments its telephone answering service by customer and puts its representatives through an orientation program to give them an overview of the firm's background and range of activities.[15]

Though information flow is a significant component of timely response, other types of activities could assume importance as well. Customers who, for example, would like material delivered in smaller lots every day rather than in large batches every week are not just asking for information about the firm's capability. They want a decision, a commitment, and demonstration of the ability to deal with the new set of circumstances. Of course, improvements in operating cycle efficiency (OCE) achieved by chipping away at the "waste" times like storage time, material handling time, waiting time, and time lost due to quality lapses can certainly help. But we have to remember that though improvements in OCE typically increase both the firm's emphasis on value creation activities as well as the output rate (more cars produced per day, more guests checked in per hour, and so on), OCE still remains an *efficiency* measure. In a standardized operation where efficiency (resource utilization) and hence costs are the predominant considerations, OCE and allied efficiency indicators might suffice as performance measures. On the other hand, for firms that wish to deliver continuously rising value through tight linkage to the customer, flexibility/responsiveness indicators must be tracked to supplement the efficiency meter.

In a manufacturing context, setup time strongly influences a firm's ability to respond quickly to changes in customer demand. If machine settings, material specifications and quantities, and human skills are dedicated to the needs of a particular product and its convenient production (the "Production View" of the firm) the ability to change, so to speak, gets shortchanged. We as customers put up with such a corporate philosophy of emphasizing manufacturing ease all the time, because we assume that standardized products mean lower prices and increased availability. Steel furniture, fast food, airline transportation and computer terminals are typically available only in models or packages their vendors deem efficient to offer. Bringing customer choice and product customizing into the picture, we have been conditioned to believe, will make the product more expensive, delay its availability, and perhaps render it in some way inferior to the standardized version. However, firms that work at flexibility can break with the traditional belief that customers really want standardized products made efficiently because, after all, it's to the customer's benefit. Once this important commandment of manufacturing ("You shall not produce in small quantities or customize, if you want to be price-competitive") is questioned, and subsequently broken,[16] the road and rationale to setup reduction become almost obvious and attainable. As is true of many organizational change situations, demand determines ability, and ability dictates practice. "Need not be done" often becomes "Can't be done" resulting in "Won't be done."

Firms like Toyota have, almost literally, made a living out of setup time reductions. Changeover times are reckoned in minutes—not in hours as they used to be a bare two decades ago. Designing equipment and training people to speed up the switch from one product to another, planning carefully so that the procedures for setup changes become a well-executed drill, and doing as much of the changeover activity while the process is up and running, are just a few of the technologies the Japanese have used in parting company with the large batch tradition in manufacturing.[17] The large batch syndrome is not confined to manufacturing alone. The tradition is alive and well in the service industry too. Some fast food chains impose a time penalty on customers for orders that deviate even slightly from the listed ingredients of any item. Hotels assign some employees to receive payments and others to check guests in even if the demand for one service is far more than another (usually at the designated checkout time), presumably because the records and procedures for the transactions differ markedly. Improving changeover practices would, in both cases, enable switching back and forth without missing a beat and in enhancing value delivered in terms of service-time by the customer.

Measuring setup times (time taken to fully switch from one type of product or service or transaction to another while maintaining the desired output criteria, such as quality, service/production rate, etc.) is relatively straightforward. Efforts to measure setup times must of necessity be relative to past setup times or to what competitors have achieved. Time benchmarking is an integral part of value maximizing.

Desirable as setup reductions are, they must be coordinated. In facilities where the product goes through a sequence of operations, reducing changeovers on machine A from two hours to one hour means and achieves little if machine B's setup time is still two hours. Bottleneck setups need to be targeted if any real gains in flexibility are to be realized.

Figure 9.1
A Confluence of Time

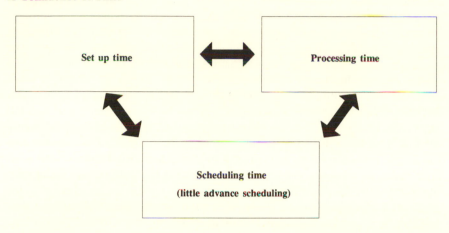

Remember, these are bottlenecks in setup, not bottlenecks in operations, so adding machines or people is not the answer. Product or service process time will go down with this augmenting of resources but setup bottlenecks will persist. To find out if setup bottlenecks exist, calculate the ratio of

$$\frac{\text{Maximum setup}}{\text{Minimum setup}}$$

(which we shall term the setup range) in a multioperation production or service process. Ideally, as setup times are reduced, the ratio should hover around one, indicating a well-coordinated attack on setup times and on inflexibility. Another indication of responsiveness through setup contraction is the average batch size (or the number of batches run per day, which is the obverse of the same coin). As smaller batches are run, setup times must necessarily go down. Of course, as batch sizes go down (due to which, incidentally, the firm can accept smaller orders for products or services with a diversity of products to be delivered at shorter notice) the responsiveness of internal operations to one another comes under fire as well. Even if the next operation's requirements are known in advance, they cannot be produced or delivered until the need has been signaled. Instant communication, computerized or visual, and the ability to respond to the signal ("Ten more of Style C with a five-inch diameter" or "Three hamburgers, two fries, and an apple pie") call for not only low setup times but synchronized processing times as well. Idle time may increase when a work center's output is strictly determined by the needs of subsequent operations. But the three-way interaction of times shown in Figure 9.1 goes beyond merely preferring flexibility, alertness and cohesion to internally convenient response times, inventories and continuous (often unwanted) production. Emerging from the confluence of these streams of responsiveness, so to speak, is a force whose impact is potentially greater than that of any or all of them—quality.

TIME FOR QUALITY

Manufacturing or service quality improvements are an almost natural outcome of attaining the time reductions and balance shown above. To be sure, quality is not simply or solely a matter of putting parts together right or serving customers with speed, accuracy, and courtesy. Product design, whether it be VCR, room service, a restaurant's atmosphere, an amusement park's rides, or a seamless aluminum can for soft drinks, is tremendously important in the quality actually built into the product. An amusement park which cannot boast the terrifying attractions offered by its nearby competitors, the VCR that requires complex procedures to be followed before a program can be taped, and an airline with old or obsolete aircraft, are all struggling against imposing odds. Their products as conceived may be so severely flawed that the best of efforts at constructing value (through quality consciousness, thorough testing, and instant service) may fall far short of customers' expectations. An assertion often made (and rarely contested since it is difficult to verify or refute) is that eighty to ninety percent of quality is determined at the design stage. We do not wish to dispute this belief which counts among its adherents some of the leading practitioners of quality in the United States and Japan. Taguchi[18] has taken this argument one step further in calling for the conduct of experiments to determine the combined effect of all the parts' design variations on the performance of the completed product. Robust quality, he asserts, helps minimize the quality loss (that is, cost of subsequently rectifying the product to suit customers' needs and other stakeholders' requirements). While the important transition from quality-as-designed to quality-as-delivered is beyond dispute, we are not so sure we support the implied conclusions that (a) if quality is to be improved, it is best to focus on the product's design and, as a corollary, (b) any enhancement achieved in quality during the operations phase (stage C2 of the value chain) is marginal and not deserving of all the attention showered on it by writers and managers alike. Our objections to this line of thinking must be obvious. Value delivered lies not only in what is done at each stage but equally in how the stages are connected to each other. Undoubtedly, early stages of the 3C chain limit the potential of later stages. A poorly-designed product severely constrains how much value can be built into it, just as there is only so much marketing one can do with a poorly-made product. However (and this is the core of our argument) a well-designed product does not necessarily result in a well-manufactured and made one. Even if ninety percent of a product's or service's quality sprang from its concept and design, the other ten percent could mean the difference between top-notch and second-rate final quality. Granted, quality as designed (stage C1) is an important determinant of final quality and it could be crucial to newly-introduced products since unexpected defects and malfunctions may have to be designed out. But as products mature, competitors come out with copycat offerings, and in general, design know-how gets diffused across the industry, value construction (C2) tends to emerge as the determinant both of quality delivered to customers and of quality differences among competitors. A poorly-designed product, therefore, will almost certainly be deficient in quality. A well-designed product, on the other hand, is no guarantee of superior quality.

Having stated our stand on the strategic importance of quality constructed into the product, we return to our assertion that the nexus of setup, processing, or scheduling times can have a strong impact on quality. There are many measures of quality applicable to both manufacturing and service businesses that are in popular use:

- Percent defective in a lot is compared to a yardstick acceptable level and the lot is either accepted or rejected, with rework following in the latter case. But what percent defects is acceptable to pass on to customers? With low acceptable defect rates, how do we deal with mounting rework costs?
- Customer complaints and returns and frequency of warranty and other repairs indicate the level of quality experienced by customers. While the frequency of repairs may indicate the level of output quality (or lack of it), customer complaints are a broader indicator of value in general, not of quality alone, and serve better as indicators of the broader concept.[19]
- Statistical process control procedures which monitor whether the specific process is within control or is tending to stray out of control. Rather than serving as an indicator of quality after the fact, as output quality measures do, process control tries to bar the stable door before the horse has bolted.[20]
- Small sample procedures like the so-called $N = 2$ regimen in which the first and last item in each batch are inspected, preferably jointly, by the worker and his or her supervisor. If the extremes are of the desired quality, the intervening items are assumed to be within the same acceptable limits, and the entire batch is passed.[21]
- Self and/or successive-inspection programs which first encourage, then insist that workers take responsibility for quality. They also ensure that incoming quality is being maintained as required by the process.[22]

Clearly, both output and process quality measures are essential to establishing a culture of quality and to focusing attention on value as a cardinal organizational Value. The purpose underlying all quality assurance efforts, as is true in a broader sense, of value enhancement efforts in general, is, at one level, to establish both methods and philosophies of working which lead to improved outputs (quality and value) as well as techniques for keeping track of progress toward these output goals. At another, more important and more permanent level, quality assurance must become internalized and not continue as an externally introduced remedy for a recurring illness. Employee responsibility for quality and the realization that lapses in quality, in effect, snap the ties that bind one activity to the other, are the ultimate objectives of a successful quality program. Good quality must become self-sustaining. And the three-way time confluence in Figure 9.1, by urging the firm to be more flexible, responsive and focused on specific, rather than standardized, customer requirements can help fuel the organization's progress toward internally generated quality assurance. As the time-linkage becomes stronger (through a reduction in response time, setup times, time-to-market) concerns over fulfilling customers' needs become internalized. Features of the product, particularly aspects of quality, almost immediately, tend to show the beneficial effects, of this time compression. In *Zen and the Art of Motorcycle Maintenance*, Pirsig[23] conducts an extensive inquiry into the meaning of Quality. While Quality, in his eyes, is a panoramic concept encompassing Beauty and Truth, there are important implications for our discussion of value as well. Just as Pirsig's Quality is difficult to define and explain, and even more difficult to measure, so too is value. Rigidity is equally an enemy of Quality and value attainment. And harmony among the constitutent parts is as much a determinant of Quality as it is of value (e.g., balance among the 3Cs as well as among the components of value). Though customer value is by no means a metaphysical notion, grounded as it is in specific needs, resources and actions, there is a sense of order underlying it and a sense of beauty in its achievement that transcends physical assessment. In suggesting that the limited concept of *quality* is partly determined by the combination of the three time indicators mentioned, we are, therefore, emphasizing the need for a time-harmony in order to better serve customers' quality needs. Time-to-market, setup time, and response time represent respectively the conceptualization, construction, and communication stages and product quality depends on their being in balance with one another as well.

INTEGRATION INDICATORS

Indicators of value range from the precise to the elusive. The more exact indicators include long-term profitability and the time-based indexes such as OCE, while at the other extreme are indicators one can do no more than get a general feel for. Most of the measures of value and interdependence explored earlier lie at or in the proximity of precise measurement, particularly if improvement is to be evaluated. We now embark on a review of indicators, most of which are far less precise. In fact, most indicators of integration and involvement can best be compared to relying on one's sense of touch to tell temperature instead of using a thermometer. Getting a general sense of the effectiveness of the coordination among activities as well as of the level of commitment, belonging, and initiative demonstrated by the workforce may seem a bit like reading tea leaves to tell the future. We have to tolerate fuzziness in our indicators, however, as we move from measuring results and activities to assessing cooperation and empowerment. This applies even to high-technology firms (which, essentially are firms with relatively high expectations and stakes in the C1 stage of value creation). As Naisbitt pointed out in *Megatrends*, high-tech undoubtedly carries with it the imperative for high touch.[24] Precise estimation and sensory judgment are coexistent indicators in the high value organization.

Measuring the effectiveness with which value is transferred across activity boundaries, as well as to and from external entities like suppliers, can take many forms. The irreducible core of integration is the emergence of a holistic view, the holographic organization. The different bases of value have to be understood, shared and cooperatively achieved by cross-functional groups or value teams which may diverge in goals, styles of work, skills, educational background, etc. The extent and success of job rotation programs provides one indicator of integration. The number of jobs employees can perform, on the average, provides a rough measure of the extent of job rotation, a level of 1 (one) being the minimum and anything of the order of two or higher indicating a versatile and probably empathic workforce. Similarly, calculating the number of successive years spent, on the average, within any activity area (or function, in the case of managerial employees) gives one a feel for how rigidly bound people are, to their jobs or departments, in a particular company. These evaluations could be carried out on an organizationwide basis or, if within-company comparisons are to be made, on a departmental basis as well. Firms that score high on the first indicator (average jobs per person) and low on the second (average successive years per job) rate high on a *job rotation index*, given by

$$\frac{\text{Jobs per person}}{\text{Successive years per job}}$$

with a higher index rating favorably as an indicator of job rotation. In addition to job rotation, membership on value teams helps get an additional read on how well the value creation process is supported by a networking of resources across multiple activities. A rough measure of the presence of value-teams is provided by calculating the

$$\text{Value team index} = \frac{\text{Membership in value teams}}{\text{Total number of employees}}$$

A ratio of around one suggests a fair cross-functional effort, though it does not mean that everyone is on a value team. Some may be on more than one while others may be on none. However, combining the job rotation and value-team indexes would paint a consolidated picture of the skill and perspective diversity that characterizes the organization. A third input measure of integration (input, because it gauges the effort and not necessarily the achievement) is the frequency of CEO/"vision executive" contact meetings held. These informational sessions are aimed at locking everyone onto a common value wavelength and supplement job rotation and value teams in the integration and value endeavor. Once every six months to a year is about par (depending on the size of the firm) if people are to be updated on the strategic and operational changes occurring in the firm and its external environment. More frequent get togethers are desirable but often not possible in large firms. Top executives capable of communicating the vision of value can fill in for the CEO so that the "Vision Session" index (the number of such sessions per year) is at least one.[25]

What with all this talk of indexes, it appears that an organization can evaluate its efforts at integration satisfactorily if not accurately. Realistically though, these numbers furnish rough, perhaps superficial, measures of integration. For instance, if the average number of jobs per person worked out to be three (excellent rotation), it still does not tell us how well individuals can do other tasks besides their present ones, whether workers really visualize customer value from multiple viewpoints, and so forth. In this, as in most business applications, the numbers must be in accordance with reality. If in a firm with a high job rotation index employees rarely fill in for each other and jealously guard their narrow interests, obviously something is not quite right with the index. However, if in a firm with a rising job rotation index, there seems to be an increasing willingness to step into others' shoes, the story of the numbers would appear to be borne out by the facts.

Evidence of integration achieved is difficult to evaluate and even the approximate indexes covering the *effort* at integration may appear precise by comparison. The frequency with which information is exchanged among diverse activities and the intensity of this interaction would be a valuable pointer to the extent of coordinated and unified endeavor in the firm. However, apart from counting the number and duration of such communications or obtaining self-reported assessments of them, both of which are likely to be as tedious to compile as they would be unreliable and inconclusive, there seems to be little to do but depend upon informally gauging whether any improvements in cross-functional information sharing, cooperation, and empathizing are indeed occurring. In a single-product firm or a small business, such improvements are noticeable since they are likely to result in more face-to-face meetings between the different functions (R & D and Marketing, and Marketing and Production, and so on) as well as in the reduction of disputes to be mediated. However, where the value exchange has to occur between different product groups or divisions ("value extensive" as opposed to "value intensive" transfers, to use the terminology of chapter 3) conversational or even hearsay reports may, in part, have to serve as indicators of integration. To be sure, the *basis* of value sharing can be spelled out and communicated. For instance, one division may gainfully learn from another's experience in reducing time-to-market, or in improving product quality, particularly when the divisions concerned have a similar or identical value focus. But how does one measure whether the divisions are indeed helping each other build on their common value foundation? "Objective" methods of assessment, where observers agree upon a method of measuring the transfer of resources, do not seem feasible. One again has to rely on a general feel for how frequently the concerned groups meet with each other, the nature and atmosphere of these interactions, and the outcome, or how well the transfer of resources seems to have been carried out. Do both divisions seem to be improving in the time-to-market measure? Is one group's setup time reduction matched by that of its collaborating group? A combination of the process (frequency and type of interactions) and result (matching value improvement) indicators provides a method of cross-checking the efficacy of value sharing. For diversified firms whose products share elements of commonality across the board (General Motors, IBM, Campbell Soup, Exxon) or diversified firms in which similar products are gathered together in SBUs or some such product cluster (General Electric, Procter and Gamble, American Express), monitoring value transfer by both methods, and periodically correcting imbalances, is essential to generate economies of scope (value sharing across products).

Similar yardsticks apply to the geographically dispersed firm as well. The economies of scope stem, in this instance, from the ability to reproduce the components and capabilities of value (arrayed in Figure 2.1) in different countries. The gaps that need bridging are those of space and distance, culture, ideology, government policies, infrastructural facilities and many more.) Transnational coordination, as articulated by Bartlett and Ghoshal,[26] is therefore no mean task regardless of whether the activity to be integrated is relatively "simple" or "complex." Simplicity refers to value arising from a narrow range of value attributes as in the case of a product with a unique design, while complexity would apply, for instance, to a manufacturing process in which the tight linkage between R & D and manufacturing has to be reproduced in each new location.

The process of global expansion somewhat superficially resembles reproduction by living creatures. In the case of organizations, however, international replication creates "children" that have to survive in entirely different environments than that of their "parents," and the latter often learn as much from the former as the other way round. In the world electronics industry, Matsushita has attained its position of dominance partly due to its ability to diffuse centrally innovated products. Phillips, on the other hand, has successfully diffused numerous innovations from its local operations to its headquarters in Holland.[27] Learning the value lesson (or lessons) is the key to the success of a global strategy of value for firms that seek to replicate the basis for value globally, as well as for those firms that try to adjust the value activity to be responsive to local needs, or as part of an international network of vertical integration.

The integration of global value, horizontal or vertical, poses obvious problems of measurement. How does one assess the extent of integration across activities, sources of value, countries and perhaps even product variations? First, the architects of global strategy must realize that they cannot themselves assume the entire burden of ensuring integration; carrying a worldwide strategy through successfully requires active involvement right down the line. The activities (C1, C2, C3) and the basis for value to be coordinated have to be specified and communicated to the activities concerned—say, Distribution Managers for a particular product in Brazil, Canada and Germany; or Development Engineers located in China, England, Poland, and South Korea. Each discrete group should be clearly informed and updated on the value sharing expected. Even where global sharing occurs through vertical integration, spelling out the specifics of the value exchange visualized keeps the protagonists informed and energized. In this, as in the multiproduct instance, the frequency and depth of interaction are indicative of how well the global strategy is working. This again calls for an informed "guesstimate" of the rate of resource transfer. Looking at Figure 9.2 we can see why "objective" indicators are hard to develop. A and B are final product or service facilities which exchange information on value (V_1) at a specific stage of the chain (C_1). E, on the other hand, functions purely as a material (M_2) supply center with the same value basis as A (V_1). D is again different. It supplies material, say M_3, to B, and exchanges final product information on Value (V_3) with B as well. The multiple locations, operational charters, bases of value, and exchange possibilities open up a wide range of options for action and for measuring their results. Transactions in the four location case are shown purely for illustration and can be far more complex. Firms with more than four locations are faced with greater complexity and can do little more than make a judgment call about the effort expended and the achievements in integration. Make no mistake about it though. The effectiveness with which the sharing of capabilities is conducted is critical

Figure 9.2
Global Integration

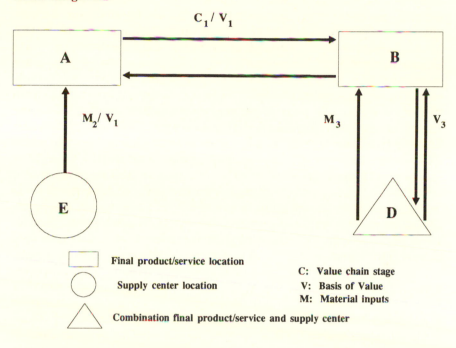

C_1 / V_1

A   B

M_2 / V_1 M_3 V_3

E   D

□ Final product/service location

○ Supply center location

△ Combination final product/service and supply center

C: Value chain stage
V: Basis of Value
M: Material inputs

to successfully transplanting the firm's success in other products and/or geographic locations. In fact, as Stalk, Evans, and Shulman[28] observe, competing on the basis of shared capabilities was central to the success of firms like Wal-Mart and Honda, and has emerged as a pivotal element of any successful corporate strategy.

As we saw in chapter 5, tight linkages are an essential part of the supplier relationship as well. For example, if response times and flexibility are to stand any chance of improvement, suppliers have to be enlisted and must avidly buy into the cause. Coopting suppliers onto coordination teams and increasing exchanges of visits with suppliers facilitates locking into the same customer needs. The proportion of suppliers who are on the firm's coordination teams measures how well suppliers are interlocked with the organization in the service of the customer. A rising incidence of contacts, meetings, and visits (even if they are for troubleshooting) are also an indication of supplier relations moving in the right direction. Supplier lead times should compare favorably with response times required by customers and as the latter time contracts so should the former. In general, links that stretch from supplier to customer, if encouraged, not only facilitate suppliers becoming time-responsive but taste-responsive and preference-responsive as well. For instance, Englehard, Inc., a supplier of additives like gypsum to paper firms (such as International Paper), by establishing direct links with printers and publishers, anticipates changing needs to benefit not only itself and the consumer but also to better understand the problems and opportunities likely to arise in its relationship with its direct customer. Owens-Illinois (beverage containers) and Briggs and Stratton (mowers and engines) are in a similar position vis-à-vis the buyers of their final and intermediate products. Tightening supplier linkages is relatively difficult with a large number of suppliers, since the effort it requires would be stupendous. Moreover, the effort might be wasted as well, particularly if the list of suppliers changes frequently. Strengthening bonds with one's suppliers and establishing a modicum of trust in the relationship demands that there be as few suppliers per item as is feasible. We realize that the one supplier norm applied in Japan is probably unrealistic in the United States given the vagaries of transportation, the possibility of labor unrest, and so on. However, as the *number of suppliers per item* is reduced and approaches two, the strategies for tightening interdependence with suppliers (and customers) become all the more viable.

INVOLVEMENT INDICATORS

Even less amenable to direct and objective measurement are the involvement processes in a firm. As we did not hesitate to assert, power can be a dangerous and distinctive force to unleash, but it remains a rather abstract entity. Power-addicted managers are often detrimental to a firm's health. They tend to conceive of the firm as a territory to be carved up and ruled rather than being fertile ground for empowered workers to cultivate and to nurture customer value. Trying to measure the power of managers and supervisors relative to workers will open up a Pandora's box of problems instead of the solution we seek. Asking managers how much power they have relative to their subordinates creates distortion and bias and could even sour the atmosphere in a firm. Those who have conducted studies dealing with the concept of power in firms report that the term means different things to different people and responses are therefore unreliable. We suggest, instead, that indirect indicators be used—for instance, the height of the hierarchy. An organization with fewer levels this year than it had last year is probably moving toward greater empowerment. Two organizations in the same industry and of comparable size can be assessed similarly. Coupled with becoming flatter, more decisions must also be made at lower levels. Trimming layers off must be accompanied by greater delegation. That is, the proportion of time managers spend on decision making relating to their subordinates' task areas should go down as hierarchic levels are reduced. If, a year after the elimination of hierarchic levels, managers are bogged down responding to crises in their subordinating domain, empowerment is probably little more than an illusion. Assuming that the conversion of a tall organization into a relatively flat one automatically transforms it from a high-voltage to a low-voltage status as well is little more than wishful thinking.

We have periodically, especially in this chapter, strongly opposed the tendency many of us have for using a single indicator for any result or goal. We also recommend that, in a scheme such as

$$\text{Action} \quad \rightarrow \quad \text{Result}$$

if the Result is achieved, we also need to investigate what other side-effects arise. For instance, promising a bonus proportionate to the profits achieved might very well result in higher profits. However, if the level of machine maintenance and product quality also go down, the apparently simple picture becomes considerably clouded. Even worse than the one-dimensional perspective is the *un*dimensional one—*assuming* that because a particular Action once led to the desired Results, it *must* have the same effect here. Assuming that having fewer levels in the firm necessarily means greater empowerment is an unjustifiable leap of logic, perhaps of faith. The complementary assessment of managerial decision-making time required is therefore essential to gauging changes in the extent of empowerment.

As decision-making authority appropriately devolves to lower levels, information flow downward needs to increase as well. In addition to holistic information conveyed by top executives, which we touched upon earlier, specific job-related information relevant to decision making has to be transferred to empowered groups and individuals. Reports on quality, costs relative to budget, company-wide summaries, and any other types of consolidated information could be usefully shared in order to provide a context for decisions. Without some background on other departments, both similar and diverse, in addition to a feel for one's own activity area, the setting for decision making would be incomplete. Whether computerized or manual, the flow of reports downward must increase if empowerment is to be more than an ideal. The traditional paradigm   of "Information upward, Instruction downward" has to give way to one where reports and information flow downward. The *number of reports* made available to lower-level employees should increase. Even better, the organization of reports at lower levels ought to be encouraged wherever data is collected at that level. Increases in both the downward flow of reports and in self-generated information are unmistakable indicators of rising involvement, when looked at in conjunction with hierarchy flattening and reduced day-to-day managerial decision making. In firms where employees have become conditioned to being told what to do, not only information but training on how to respond to various job eventualities must be provided. Machine operators who are expected, as a first resort, to cope with problems of production (quantity and quality) and maintenance themselves, must be trained to reach a higher plane of functioning. Exchange of knowledge goes hand in hand with delegation of responsibility. The knowledge transfer is not of job content alone, but job management as well—how it relates to other tasks, the costs that go with various options, whom to consult and how to respond under different situations. An entire gamut of issues arise when one goes from job *performance* to job *responsibility*, and training to deal with and anticipate them is a necessary part of the ability to make decisions. In a sports setting, a quarterback who is told that, from now on, he will be calling his own plays is likely to feel lost, even if he has many years' experience leading the team.

Training helps in the development of judgment and discretion, particularly when the employee has all the job skills needed. It is almost a truism with the Japanese that quality begins and ends with training.[29] Training in the form of classroom instruction, job simulation, seminars, or workshops could be designed to cover both individual and group milieus. Techniques like Pareto analysis, fishbone diagrams, the 5 Why methods, statistical process control and the like are excellent stepping stones to developing employees' analytical and decision capabilities. Since the ability and opportunity to make decisions could progressively evolve into an individual effort, the interdependence that is critical to any high-value firm also has to be carefully cultivated. Training in group processes and dynamics is invaluable in organizing work teams—product teams, setup teams, supplier teams, structure busting teams, and any other type necessary—charged with the responsibility of tightening linkages within and among activities. They also make it easier for managers to delegate authority. Groups typically consider a more diverse range of options than individuals do, and are less likely to make decisions hastily. Adopting a flat organizational configuration and increasingly empowering workers often strikes managers as a risky proposition even if information and training in job-specific and managerial skills are provided. Group-based or group-dependent working makes delegation a more palatable reality.

In sum, therefore, assessing the extent of involvement is a rather fuzzy business. And yet one needs at least a general sense of whether the organization is headed toward increasing involvement or toward heightened power differentials. Some of the indicators proposed are

- changes in organizational height,
- the rate of managerial decision activity,

- the flow of information and knowledge downward,
- the frequency with which training programs for job-related activities are conducted,
- and the extent to which groups are relied upon for enhancing interdependence and integration, as well as for decision making.

INGRAINING IS SELF-INDICATED

In trying to measure the extent of Ingraining that has taken place, we find that some measures of ingraining are impossible to design while the others are unnecessary. A review of the SHARE model of ingraining makes it obvious that the extent to which Symbols and Hero(in)es are being incorporated into the culture is, at best, a matter of judgment. Precise indicators of symbols would be a contradiction in terms while assessing whether heroic figures are being brought into the mainstream of corporate life is not something one can attach a number or estimate to. Actions, Reinforcement, and Enabling on the other hand, are more amenable to exactness of measurement but, since they are by themselves indicators of culture, measuring *them* would be redundant.

PRECISION IN COST MEASUREMENT

Profits are often called the lifeblood of capitalism because of the incentive they provide to entrepreneurs and investors alike. They represent the resource surplus that accrues as a result of the firm's ingenuity, efforts, and abilities. While we have in this book focused primarily on the delivery of continuously increasing value to customers, we have also made it clear that an organization must satisfactorily meet the needs of all its important constituents, the government, shareholders, local community, employees, and so on. Instead of separately pursuing these diverse goals, we have argued, firms can best attain them by working toward the objective of customer value. The latter is, therefore, both a destination and a way station on the road to success. It is, however, difficult to convince a shareholder to ignore recurring losses or marginal profits since customer value is at a peak level. Value is all very well, but reality provides the ultimate test, and profits are perhaps the most important reality for a business firm. Our discussion earlier in this and in the preceding chapter makes clear our balanced stand, one leg placed squarely in the ideal of value, the other firmly in the reality of profits.

Laudable as this approach may sound, problems can arise that make it difficult to implement. Not the least of these problems is how to measure value—and we have tried to address this and related issues through much of this chapter. Not quite so obvious is the problem associated with measuring profits.

Everyone knows that profits equal sales revenue minus costs. In the case of firms whose stock is publicly traded, the results of operation have to be filed with the Securities and Exchanges Commission. Most firms typically generate an Income Statement (or some variation of it). Nearly every business firm should, therefore, know at the end of the year, what its operating performance has been. So far so good. Things aren't quite so clear, however, where multiproduct forms are concerned, especially if value sharing is required. The cost of common or shared resources has to be allocated where value-extensive functioning is the norm. Even in the case of single product, value-intensive organizations, cost allocation has to be resorted to in order to monitor costs periodically (say, every month or quarter) or to compare costs among different departments.

Without going into excessive detail, we might explain that the typical *standard costing*[30] system estimates costs for a future period, such as a year. The direct costs, which are attributable to or vary with the volume of operations, are added to the indirect costs, whose magnitude is relatively independent of production or service levels. Period demand is forecasted so that the indirect costs can be spread out evenly over the operations performed throughout the year. One of the more popular ways of allocating these overheads has been on the basis of labor costs incurred for the product or service. The quotient

$$K = \frac{\text{Total indirect costs}}{\text{Estimated labor costs}}$$

is computed, and for each labor dollar incurred in a car repair garage, amusement park, VCR assembly line or power station construction site, K dollars of overhead costs are deemed to be incurred as well, and are included in the computation of product costs.

As Drucker argues, this basis for cost allocation is becoming increasingly unrealistic, unfair and frustrating.[31] In many firms, for instance, labor costs are shrinking as a proportion of total costs. In fact, they are often as low as ten percent of the total, meaning that overheads are allocated on a dwindling base and may be wildly inaccurate. Further, if sales do not reach the levels expected, overheads remain underabsorbed. That is, some costs would have been incurred but not allocated. Even worse, if due to improving productivity, labor costs per unit of product or service are trimmed, some overheads would again go unabsorbed. Mid-year hikes in the absorption rate (K) or (and this is even more bizarre) opposition to labor cost reductions, on the grounds that they make the costing system hard to apply, are among the pathologies of such a costing system. When the means (costing system) start dictating the ends (type of products/

services and operational methods), you know that something is not quite right. When Convenience calls the tune to which Ideals and Goals must dance, the firm cannot remain focused on customers' and other stakeholders' needs for very long. Not only does the absorption costing system slowly, deceptively, and imperceptibly turn its back on reality, it also sometimes appears to be inequitable in allocating costs among the products made or services rendered at a particular facility. Standard costing does not distinguish between two products on which the same labor or machine costs, whichever the basis for allocation, are incurred. One product may need an intense and sophisticated promotional effort, a second may require special testing, and a third may have to undergo a lengthy holding period (say, for curing and maturing), all of which contribute to the indirect costs of the various products and increase the overhead absorption rate of every product, including those that do not need any of these additional support services.[32] Standard costing, by spreading indirect costs around evenly, becomes a bit like socialism. It takes costs, so to speak, from the more costly operations and tags them onto the less costly ones. Not only is this unfair on cost-efficient products, it also obscures the true costs of operation. Cost reduction efforts could be misdirected and even meaningless when working costs are a distortion of the true costs.

Explaining and justifying cost structures become arduous tasks especially when lower- or intermediate-level employees want to know why product prices are inflated in spite of their bare-bones type of operation. In the superior value, total involvement organization we have been fashioning for the reader's consideration, clear and open communication downward has to be more than a formality. It must be seen for the cohesive force that it actually is. And cost information, credible, fair, and clear cost information, must be passed on, discussed and, where necessary, justified as well.

The needs of modern-day customers—diversity of products, low prices, quick response to service needs, adoption of product/service improvements—makes an across-the-board cost allocation system an anachronism. It would be ironic if, in a firm seeking high value through closer linkages, the costing system were to do exactly the opposite. A little reflection will make it obvious that when indirect costs are allocated, it is almost like an inventory of costs from which costs are doled out to various products. This inventory of costs succeeds in insulating operations from each other, which is just the result we are trying to avoid. Another strike against pure allocation to deal with indirect costs is that the pivotal importance of employees internalizing the cause of value and making it *their* crusade cries out for an easily understood and balanced approach to cost calculations. Just as the costing system should reflect the preoccupation with interdependence and integration which the value maximizing organization has to imbibe and demonstrate, the empowerment and commitment that are an inalienable part of value creation have to stand out in the approach to costing as well. Costs are an important value component. Any firm that wishes to deliver increasing value to its customers has to tap the creative and cooperative energies of its employees on all aspects of value, not the least of which are costs.

Activity costing tries to moderate the insulating and esoteric character of traditional costing by identifying so called *cost drivers*.[33] These cost drivers are, in effect, the causes that generate costs. For instance, if the Purchasing Department determines that order placement is a cost driver, the product concerned would be charged a predetermined amount for each order placed on suppliers (the cost, incidentally, would include, besides the actual communication of the order, costs of all the associated activities such as floating bids, negotiation, evaluations, monitoring, and so on). If the order pertains to a known volume of output, costs could be computed per item of product which is extremely helpful when one needs to keep a "running meter" on costs as and when they are incurred. The artificial distinctions among costs for different products can also be avoided if, in this case, the activities (such as order placement on suppliers) are demarcated clearly, by product. Even where supply orders are placed by combining two or more products, a proportional allocation of costs on a per product basis would be relatively realistic and fair compared to the standard method of allocating costs on the basis of an arbitrary multiplier. Whether the indirect cost incurred is in research and development, marketing, finance, or even in operational support activities (such as production planning), cost drivers can be clearly delineated and activity costing is a viable option. Possible cost drivers are the hours spent on design improvements or developing improvements in layout, or the number of visits paid to customers to promote and sell the product. A direct linkage between cost driver and cost makes it easier to focus on cost and treat it as a value driver. The alternative, figuring in an overhead absorption rate for R & D, Marketing, Purchasing and other support activities, does not establish a direct and obvious connection between costs and their sources. Overheads and their absorption rates not only effectively delink activities from each other, they also erect barriers between activities absorbing costs.

Activity costing, on the other hand, explicitly takes into account the sequence of cost generation[34] shown below:

Resources   →   Activities   →   Products

Human, material, informational and financial resources are consumed in performing activities like advertising a product, forecasting demand for services, placing orders, and expediting payments by customers. When the factor(s) influencing activity levels are identified, the resource usage corresponding to the activity can be determined as well. The cost for the activity in question follows from an estimate of the resource usage rate. *Product* improvement through developmental *activity*, for instance, consumes resources like human and equipment time, material, and information as well. If the rate of consumption of these resources is known, their cost as dictated by the cost driver (development) can be targeted to the concerned product. A similar procedure would be followed for all the other indirect costs associated with this product. The reverse flow, signified by the double arrows, represents the sharp control that one expects of all operations in tracking all the activities and resources that add to their costs. Cost monitoring is a right, not a privilege. Activity costing makes the right a reality, an important element of any organization's value-thrust.

The moral of this chapter is summarized in Figure 9.3: "Don't assume you're delivering value and don't take anyone's word for it—verify!" Verifying that customers are getting what they want may require the use of formal (say, statistical) and informal (conversational) methods, but it can and must be done. And if value is being delivered, can financial and market success be far behind? Yes, they can! We diagnosed possible reasons for these gaps earlier in the chapter. The process by which value is generated is as important as the end result of value. Indicators of interdependence, integration and involvement are extremely useful in tracking the process of value and keeping it on an even keel. Indicators based on spatial and temporal linkages, the job rotation index, global value-sharing assessments, and empowerment and communication measures have been suggested to get a sense of the extent and permanency of value creation embodied by the firm. We have not recommended specific magnitudes for the indicators since variations from firm to firm are more than likely based on the nature of the product (consumable or durable; growing or mature, etc.), type of competition (price-based, international), customer requirements (price, quality, responsiveness), and so on. In the spirit of continuous value improvement, which has been our preoccupation throughout, the indicators should, however, show a movement in the *appropriate* direction. That is, response time and time-to-market should show decreases, extent of value sharing (in a diversified or global firm) should increase, as should the flow downward of systematized information, while the proportion of managerial time devoted to decision making on behalf of subordinates should fall, and so forth.

Some of our readers probably object to the use of "touchy-feely" indicators like "getting a sense of the extent of interaction between two groups," in the case of value sharing across products or transnationally. Unfortunately, subjective assessments are unavoidable in most aspects

Figure 9.3
Indicators: Evaluating the INs—A Look Back

INDICATORS

Interdependence

- — Human resource linkage
- — Equipment linkage
- — Operational Cycle Efficiency
- — Time to market
- — Response and set up times

Three-way interaction of set up, processing, and scheduling times

Importance of interdependence to quality

- — Design vs manufacturing in the quality story

Integration
- — Relative fuzziness of indicators
- — Job rotation index
- — Value team index
- — Value exchanges and sharing
  - — diversified firms
  - — global firms

Involvement

- — Organizational levels
- — Managerial decision time
- — Information downward
- — Training - job related, group processes, techniques

Accounting systems — traditional vs activity costing

of management and are often useful complements to other indicators. By focusing on specific measures, however, we hope we have drawn attention to their importance and that this encourages additional effort at improvement, regardless of the imprecision involved. The use of multiple indicators builds in some redundancy and fail-safing. Finally, the measurement of measurement also often needs alteration. Accounting systems, which keep track of and record results are typically tied to modes of value creation that have been or need to be jettisoned. Just as the temperature indicated by a thermometer depends on how it is calibrated, the value indicated depends on the measuring system. In sum, a value sensitivity has to pervade individuals and groups in an organization and the activities they perform in concert with each other and with suppliers and customers. Value sensitivity is central to the indicators of value as well. As the firm evolves its unique value focus, the Indicators too will evolve with it. And changes in the measures of value must be achieved in the same way value maximization ideally should be, internally and voluntarily.

NOTES

1. This phenomenon is likely to become increasingly evident if the members of the group are personally compatible with one another and if, moreover, there are other similar groups as well. See John Adair, *Effective Technology* (New Delhi: Rupa, 1991), pp. 74–78.

2. Stephen Hawking, *A Brief History of Time* (Toronto: Bantam, 1988), pp. 15–34.

3. Stanley Davis, *Future Perfect* (Reading, MA: Addison-Wesley, 1987), pp. 19–21.

4. Mark Beischel, "Improving Production with Process Value Analysis," *Journal of Accountancy*, September, 1990, pp. 53–57.

5. Ibid.

6. Kiyoshi Suzaki, *The New Manufacturing Challenge* (New York: The Free Press, 1987), pp. 57–58. Suzaki also recommends the use of a feature called "autonomation" whereby machines are automatically shut down when they produce defective items—a further devaluation of capacity utilization (pp. 91–94).

7. In any "adhocracy" the distinction between staff and line function tends to disappear, which means the manager becomes a purveyor of information, attempts to foresee problems, and in general becomes the facilitator of value creation. See Henry Mintzberg, "The Innovation Context," in Henry Mintzberg and James Bryant Quinn, eds., *The Strategy Process* (Englewood Cliffs, NJ: Prentice-Hall, 1991), 2nd ed., pp. 732–39.

8. Steven Fink, *Crisis Management* (New York: Amacom, 1986), pp. 202–18.

9. Ibid., pp. 20–25.

10. George Stalk, Jr., and Thomas Hart, *Competing Against Time* (New York: The Free Press, 1990), pp. 1–36.

11. Ibid., pp. 123–28.

12. See Richard Schonberger, *Building A Chain of Customers* (New York: The Free Press, 1990), pp. 317–24.

13. See, for instance, Masaaki Imai, *Kaizen* (New York: McGraw-Hill, 1986), pp. 56–58.

14. For a discussion of the various information loops between customer and firm see Jay Forrester, "Modeling of Market and Company Interactions," in Philip Kotter and Keith Cox, eds., *Readings in Marketing Management* (Englewood Cliffs, NJ: Prentice-Hall, 1972).

15. Ron Zemke with Dick Schaaf, *The Service Edge* (New York: Plume, 1989), pp. 334–37.

16. See, for example, Bernard Arogyaswamy and Ronald Simmons, "Interdependence: The Key to JIT Implementation," *Production and Inventory Management*, 1991, Vol. 32, No. 3, 56–60.

17. Ibid.

18. Genichi Taguchi and Don Clausing, "Robust Quality," *Harvard Business Review*, January-February 1990, 65–75.

19. Value encompasses product and support quality in relation to the price charged. While some authors assign dollar amounts to value we stress its ability to satisfy customer needs economically. For a monetary perspective on value see, for instance, J. M. Greecock, *The Chain of Quality* (New York: John Wiley & Sons, 1986), pp. 41–45.

20. Shigeo Shingo, *Zero Quality Control: Source Inspection and the Poka-yoke System* (Cambridge, MA: Productivity Press, 1986), pp. 59–64. Shingo evaluates $\bar{X}.R$ versus P control charts and stresses the need for action based upon inspection.

21. Richard Schonberger, *Japanese Manufacturing Techniques* (New York: The Free Press, 1982), pp. 70–71.

22. Shigeo Shingo, *Zero Quality Control: Source Inspection and the Poka-yoke System*, pp. 67–82).

23. Robert Pirsig, *Zen and the Art of Motorcycle Maintenance* (New York: William Morrow, 1974).

24. John Naisbitt, *Megatrends* (New York: Warner, 1982), pp. 39–53.

25. Dana Corporation, Wal-Mart, and IBM are well known for bringing top, if not chief executives in direct contact with their rank and file, frequently more than once annually if possible. We have settled on a minimum frequency in arriving at this indicator.

26. Christopher Bartlett and Sumentra Ghoshal, *Managing Across Borders* (Boston, MA: Harvard Business School Press, 1989), pp. 66–71.

27. Ibid., pp. 121–28.

28. George Stalk, Philip Evans and Lawrence Shulman, "Competing on Capabilities: The New Rules of Corporate Strategy," *Harvard Business Review*, March-April 1992, pp. 57–69.

29. Masaaki Imai, *Kaizen* (New York: McGraw-Hill, 1986), pp. 58–59.

30. See, for instance, Arthur Francia, Mattie Porter, and Robert Strawser, *Managerial Accounting* (Houston, TX: Dame, 1982).

31. Peter Drucker, "The Emerging Theory of Manufacturing," *Harvard Business Review*, May-June 1990, 94–102.

32. For a succinct discussion of the need to make the transition from standard costing to activity-based costing (ABC) systems see Robert Kaplan, "The Four-

stage Model of Cost Systems Design,'' *Management Accounting*, February 1990, pp. 22–26.

33. Ibid.

34. The identification of resource usage for distinct activities not only helps in developing accurate costs for different products but for the same product marketed in different segments as well. For a value-chain based approach to "focused" accounting of this nature see Robert Howell and Stephen Sovey, "Customer Profitability: As Critical as Product Profitability," *Management Accounting*, October 1990, pp. 43–47.

10

CONCLUSION: VALUE FOR ALL SEASONS

RESOURCE LINKAGE: A GAIA ANALOGY

Everyone knows that the physical environment plays a big part in the quality of our lives. The indiscriminate discarding of plastic, glass and metal containers; the use of chlorofluorocarbons in refrigeration and in aerosol sprays; and the emission of carbon dioxide, methane, and other atmospheric pollutants are just a few of the many ways in which environmental changes (albeit engineered by humanity) affect and even limit our lives. Indeed, environmental shifts, such as the thinning out of the ozone layer and the greenhouse effect, have the potential for seriously altering not just the quality but also the course of life on the planet. Natural calamities such as volcanic eruptions, lightning induced fires, tidal waves, and floods in major river systems have over the centuries had a similar and lasting effect on living things both in a localized and planetary sense. Adaptation is probably the most popular and widely accepted model to describe the evolution of living things. As the environment changes, species and life forms that adapt most successfully are likely to flourish while those that fail to adapt would tend to be at a disadvantage in the survival sweepstakes. Plants, reptiles and mammals are all subject to the rule of survival through adaptation. The Gaia hypothesis, named after the Greek goddess personifying the earth, proposes a *joint* evolutionary process, one in which both the living (humans, animals, plants) and the nonliving (water, atmosphere, rocks) continuously act to change and adapt to each other. Just as living creatures adapt to their inanimate environments, the reverse is equally true. James Lovelock, who first proposed the theory, argues that ever since the process of photosynthesis in plants started about 3.5 billion years ago, the effect on the atmosphere and rocks has been dramatic. Subsequently, with the entry of oxygen into the atmosphere and the reduction in methane due to ultraviolet action, life proliferated causing, in turn, even more changes in inanimate nature. And so it has gone through the millennia, the unified evolution of Gaia, the living Earth.[1]

Since we are not experts in any of the sciences involved, we do not feel qualified to comment on the theory and processes underlying Gaia. We have introduced the notion of a living earth, however, because it offers an inspiring model of the value-seeking organization we have been trying to articulate in this book. The oneness, so to speak, and importance of all entities on the planet is paralleled in organizations by the critical nature of relationships between all resources, human and nonhuman. Whether the resources consist of machines, raw materials or information, they are only as good as the effectiveness with which they are deployed, conserved and shared. The Gaia view of organizations, on the other hand, recognizes that the remarkable thing about the high-value firm is that it is *alive*. Not just the people but the other and seemingly sterile entities as well. A machine that does not produce at the rate and quality expected, in some way, *diminishes* its operator; software designed to access data from files with diverse structures *enhances* the performance of analysts using it. And when the systems analyst helps the machine operator improve the performance of his or her machine, an indefinable synergy of animate and inanimate entities takes place that is, in a sense, similar to the Gaian mixture.

Interdependence is the key to both Gaia and the organizational Gaia model. Almost equally critical to both is the process of mutual adjustment, which makes interdependence workable and internally generated. Lovelock suggests that the adaptive mechanism follows an incremental route, changes being made in different processes over long periods of time. Value-enhancing firms too, as we have repeatedly emphasized, entrust the value creation and adaptive process to the *activity* level through a progressively increasing empowerment and involvement.

TAKING AIM AT VALUE

Authors of books in business and management strike a sympathetic chord with managers when they decry "paralysis by analysis"[2] and call for effective and immediate action. In fact, the more successful companies have often been described as possessing a "bias for action."[3] We don't dispute this since the absence of action could mean stagnation and possibly degeneration since competitors' moves and customers' needs are not likely to remain static. However, we do recommend carefully treading between the extremes of constant evaluation and planning, on the one hand, and continuous, unreflecting action, on the other. At the risk of appearing to oversimplify the issue, our perspective on continuously rising value leans heavily on a firm's ability to take AIM at value both in a literal and—as the reader probably has come to expect by now—in an acronymic sense. Literally, and obviously, value is an overarching goal to aim for. AIM also represents Actions, Ideas, and Message which, at one level, are substitutable terms for the 3Cs, Construction, Conceptualization, and Communication respectively. In this view, Ideas are the essence of value conceptualizing and precede the Action-intensive stage of value construction. Getting the Message out to customers falls within the domain of value communication activities. While separation among the value stages is helpful in getting a clearer picture of what they comprise and how best to manage them as well as their linkages, we are driving at more than a watertight division of responsibilities.

Firms whose AIM is value must also be alert to the fact that Actions, Ideas, and Messages do not merely correspond to the 3Cs, they need to be pervasive *within* each of them as well. Actions are not the sole responsibility of Operations people, they are integral to the success of R & D, which must learn to *act* based upon information received from Operations (for instance, by designing for quick setups) and from Marketing (say, by improving product characteristics to match changing customer needs). Specific ways of addressing different needs have to be worked out, perhaps by incorporating the time-to-market, response time and allied indicators covered in the preceding chapters. All too often, when faced with conflicting needs, the C1 stage of value can become a burial ground for ideas and suggestions emanating elsewhere. If decisions and actions (based on highest value delivered) are postponed or not made at all, the resultant drift could prove catching, even terminal. Similarly, C3 does not hold a monopoly on communication, even with the customer. Often, in the case of services, those responsible for actually performing the service (airline stewards/stewardesses and counter associates; retail sales persons; advertising copywriters) are best positioned to participate in two-way communication with the customer. In manufacturing organizations, the notion of direct production-to-customer linkages could also result in the direct delivery of value. A department normally insulated from customers thus experiences the stimulus of direct customer contact. The latter gains likewise by communicating with those responsible for physically building value into the product. Internal customers (e.g., other departments) should be treated no different than external customers. Delays, deviations and improvements ought to be promptly notified. The voice of the customer should not be devalued merely because it originates from within the firm.

Just as signalling value delivered is not purely a value communication activity, creativity and idea generation should not be considered the sole preserve of the R&D people. Process improvements, layout changes, and mutual adjustment procedures are matters from which Operations can be excluded only to the detriment of value creation. *Ideas* to improve particular activities, for instance, distribution, promotion and sales, must similarly originate in the activity of first resort, in this case the communication stage of the chain, after which *actions* flowing from these ideas are undertaken (daily deliveries, joint displays, more frequent personal visits) and their message communicated both inside and outside the firm. Action that is bereft both of ideas and of the message underlying the actions and ideas is a good way of getting nowhere fast. Taking AIM at value places action in an organized, two-tiered framework. It helps moderate the Jesse James (shoot first, ask questions later) and Don Quixote (tilting at windmills) syndromes that comprise the radical extremes of a passion for action on the one hand and the quicksands of eternal analysis on the other.

NO STRINGS ATTACHED

The vision of high value management we have offered in this book is not a conditional one. Irrespective of cultural setting, industry characteristics and economic conditions, the 3C/5IN approach will lead unerringly to customer value enhancement. Some of our readers might argue that ratcheting the level of interdependence ever upward will be accepted, and can succeed only in a culture and society that is itself based on interrelationships. The Japanese ethos, for instance, is built on an edifice of lasting relationships among individuals and groups that makes it easier to deal with the problems created by interdependence in the workplace.[4] Does that mean that cultivating interdependence is a concept that must remain confined to Japan and to the pages of this book? No. It does mean, however, that interdependence has to be approached warily. The use of small teams is probably the most pragmatic transition from islands of efficiency to completely interdependent activities. Such "closed loop" teams (with members drawn from adjacent, sequential activities) have been used by AT&T in new product development and design, and by John Deere to strengthen the linkages between development, engineering and production, compress the time-to-market, and facilitate implementation.[5] After Firestone was acquired by Bridgestone Tires (a Japanese-owned firm) the concept of "rootbinding" (emphasizing the overlapping, interconnected nature of manufacturing activities) was publicized and actively fostered.[6] Employees gained a sensitivity of the impact their tasks had on proximate tasks as well as on the organization as a whole. Hand in hand with the increased interdependence is the need for greater involvement attained by eliminating the power addictive tendencies typical of most organizations. A small teams transition helps move firms further on the road to increased involvement as well, since close supervision is inadvisable if teamwork is to be effective. Cray Research's tremendous success in supercomputers is built in no small part on the amazing creativity, flexibility and decision-making ability of the small teams the firm established.[7] The active tightening of linkages has not, however, been a part of the conventional wisdom of management, particularly in the United States (see chapter 4). But that does not mean it has to be confined to firms based in interdependence-receptive cultures. The experience of Toyota, Honda, Nissan, Matsushita, and other Japanese firms in their North American operations suggests otherwise, as does the success of Cray, AT&T, John Deere and the like in organizing small teams on the road to stronger interconnections.

It might appear that the high-value methodologies developed in this book would be of little if any use if the product were a commodity (coal, salt, steel), and that the recommended panoply of methods to enhance value would be far more useful for products that can be and are expected to be differentiated from competitors' offerings (e.g., electric appliances, automobiles or hotels). This, again, is the conventional "wisdom" and its plausibility stems from assuming that costs are the only ways in which commodity producers compete and prices are the only criteria employed by buyers in selecting a product. However, additional information on assembly, use, and maintenance, and updates on future availabilities, special services such as convenient transportation, reservation system, and engineering support, and features like the use of environmentally neutral materials or equipment, when thrown into the "commodity" package, make value delivery much more than a matter of price reduction. What appeared to be a product/service with a single value dimension could easily turn out to be a multidimensional and complex value opportunity.

Again, while custom-made products, tailored as they are to individual requirements, have to be treated differently from standardized ones, they too can successfully attain value through linkages. Doctors' clinics, for example, need to be conscious of the need to conceptualize value (range of services, waiting room decor, walk-in or appointments), construct it in terms of the expertise of the attending physicians and capability of the equipment and support staff, as well as communicate value to the patients through a caring manner, accurate billing and post-consultation follow-up. In small operations, hierarchic distinctions may not be a major obstacle to communication and certain other factors, like time-to-market may even be irrelevant, but an awareness of the centrality of value delivered, tightly linked and balanced, to business success is universally applicable.

An unceasing quest for value is not strongly economy-dependent either. Typically, during economic downturns, many firms have to hit the operational brake pedal because their customers have stopped placing orders or are placing fewer of them than before. Lower consumption leads to a decline in production (of both products and services), in investments in new plant and equipment, and in employment as well, all of which leads to a further downward movement in buying by consumers. Under such conditions, only firms charging low prices and/or providing superior product benefits can hope to succeed—which may not seem very different from customer behavior during "normal" times, except that consumers' selectivity becomes considerably sharper. They'll look longer and probably be more successful in finding the best product-organization combination around (that is, the highest product value and the strongest organizational support to suit their needs). The internal arrangements in a value-seeking firm are more favorable to ride out a recession. Lower wastage rates mean lower costs, greater involvement often produces a high degree of sensitivity to customers' needs, and mushrooming cooperation and self-generated coordination make tough decisions less difficult to work out. Cutting working hours across the board, postponing bonuses, and transferring employees are likely to meet with less opposition than in firms where the traditional barriers and boundaries are in place.

We started this book with the commonly heard refrain that the United States has emerged second best in the contest of industrial competitiveness with Japan and the other countries of the Pacific Rim. The countries of the European Community which are going through the rigors of unification are going to prove no less able and tough as competitors in the years to come. Down the road, honing their competitive skills, are China, India, and many other less-developed nations. Competition is going to get more intense in world markets and, as we pointed out earlier, negotiating, pleading, and hectoring can iron out unfairness but will do little to prepare us for the coming century (which has, prematurely, in our opinion, been dubbed the "Pacific century"[8]). Firms in the United States have to enhance their capabilities to compete against well-armed rivals who will become, if anything, more selective and well informed. We hope we have succeeded in drawing up a practical and conceptual plan of attack based in large part on ideas and precepts once native to the United States. We hope we have rallied our readers around the battle cry of "Value!"

NOTES

1. James Lovelock, *The Ages of Gaia* (New York: W. W. Norton & Company, 1988), pp. 15–41.

2. Igor Ansoff and Edward McDonald, *Implanting Strategic Management* (New York: Prentice-Hall, 1990), p. 163. The phrase denotes the stagnation that accompanied the separation of planning and execution, with the latter often unwilling and unable to buy into the former's ideas.

3. See, for example, Thomas Peters and Robert Waterman, Jr., *In Search of Excellence* (New York: Harper & Row, 1982), pp. 13–14.

4. Edwin Reischauer, *The Japanese Today* (Cambridge, MA: Harvard University Press, 1988), pp. 128–39.

5. George Stalk, Jr. and Thomas Hunt, *Competing Against Time* (New York: The Free Press, 1990), 183–89.

6. Mary Walton, *Deming Management at Work* (New York: G. P. Putnam & Sons, 1990), p. 194.

7. Donald Gifford, Jr., and Richard Cavanagh, *The Winning Performance* (Toronto: Bantam, 1985), pp. 178–84.

8. *The Economist*, 4 January 1975, p. 15. While the high growth rate experienced since 1975 by the countries of the Pacific Rim seems to support the implied prediction, the jury is still out on the sustainability of economic growth in the Rim and its relative influence on the rest of the world.

SELECTED BIBLIOGRAPHY

Abegglen, J. and George Stalk, Jr. *Kaisha*. New York: Basic, 1985.

Adair, John. *Effective Teambuilding*. London: Pan Books, 1987.

Adam, Everett and Ronald Ebert. *Production and Operations Management*. Englewood Cliffs, NJ: Prentice-Hall, 5th Ed., 1992.

Akao, Yoji. *Quality Function Deployment*. Boston: Productivity Press, 1990.

Allen, Robert. "Four Phases for Bringing About Cultural Change," in Ralph Kilmann, Mary Saxton, and Ray Serpa, eds. *Gaining Control of the Corporate Culture*. San Francisco: Jossey-Bass, 1985.

Andrews, Kenneth. *The Concept of Corporate Strategy*. Homewood, IL: Irwin, Third Ed., 1987.

Ansoff, Igor. *Corporate Strategy*. New York: McGraw-Hill, 1965.

Ansoff, Igor and Edward McDonald. *Implanting Strategic Management*. New York: Prentice-Hall, 1990.

Arogyaswamy, Bernard and Ronald Simmons. "Interdependence: The Key to JIT Implementation." *Production and Inventory Management*, 1991, Vol. 32, No. 3, 56–60.

Arogyaswamy, Bernard and Charles Byles. "Organizational Culture: Internal and External Fits." *Journal of Management*, 1987, Vol. 13, No. 4, 647–59.

Barnard, Chester. *The Function of the Executive*. Cambridge, MA: Harvard University Press, 1938.

Bartlett, Christopher and Sumantra Ghoshal. *Managing Across Borders*. Boston, MA: Harvard Business School Press, 1989.

Beischel, Mark. "Improving Production with Process Value Analysis." *Journal of Accountancy*, September 1990, 53–57.

Bennis, Warren and Burt Nanus. *Leaders*. New York: Harper & Row, 1985.

Bohm, David. *Wholeness and the Implicate Order*. London: Routledge and Kegan Paul, 1981.

Carlzon, Jan. *Moments of Truth*. New York: Ballinger, 1987.

Chandler, Alfred. *Strategy and Structure*. Cambridge, MA: MIT Press, 1962.

Cherunilam, Francis. *Business and Government*. Bombay: Himalaya Publishing House, 1990.

Clausewitz, Carl von. *On War*. Harmondsworth, UK: Penguin, 1985.

Coase, Ronald. "The Nature of the Firm." *Economica*, new series, 1938, 4: 386–405.

Copulsky, William. "Balancing the Needs of Customers and Shareholders." *Journal of Business Strategy*, November/December 1991, 44–47.

Corballis, Michael. *Human Laterality*. New York: Academic Press, 1983.

Cyert, Richard and Kenneth MacCrimmon. "Organizations," in Gardner Lindzey and Elliot Aronson, eds., *Handbook of Social Psychology*. Reading, MA: Addison-Wesley, 1967, 2nd ed., Vol. 1.

Daniel, Lynn. "Overcome the Barriers to Superior Customer Service." *Journal of Business Strategy*, January/February 1992, pp. 18–24.

Davidow, William and Bro Uttal. *Total Customer Service*. New York: Harper Perennial, 1990.

Davis, Stanley. *Future Perfect*. Reading, MA: Addison-Wesley, 1987.

Day, George S. "Strategic Perspective on Product Planning," in Philip Kotler and Keith Cox, eds., *Marketing Management and Strategy, a Reader*. Englewood Cliffs, NJ: Prentice-Hall, 1980.

Deming, W. Edward. *Quality, Productivity and Competitive Position*. Cambridge, MA: MIT Center for Advanced Engineering Study, 1982.

Drucker, Peter. *Innovation and Entrepreneurship*. New York: Harper & Row, 1986.

Drucker, Peter. "The Emerging Theory of Manufacturing." *Harvard Business Review*, May-June 1990, 94–102.

Drucker, Peter. *An Introductory View of Management*. New York: Harper's College Press, 1977.

Fallon, Carlos. *Value Analysis to Improve Productivity*. New York: Wiley-Interscience, 1971.

Filey, Alan, Robert House and Steven Kerr. *Managerial Process and Organizational Behavior*. Glenview, IL: Scott, Foresman, 1976.

Fink, Steven. *Crisis Management*. New York: Amacom, 1986.

Forrester, Jay. "Modeling of Market and Company Interactions," in Philip Kotter and Keith Cox, eds., *Readings in Marketing Management*. Englewood Cliffs, NJ: Prentice-Hall, 1972.

Francia, Arthur, Mattie Porter, and Robert Strawser. *Managerial Accounting*. Houston, TX: Dame, 1982.

Gifford, Donald, Jr., and Richard Cavanagh. *The Winning Performance*. Toronto: Bantam, 1985.

Gilbreth, Frank. *Motion Study*. New York: Van Nostrand, 1911.

Greecock, J. M. *The Chain of Quality*. New York: John Wiley & Sons, 1986.

Hackman, Richard and Greg Oldham. *Work Redesign*. Reading, MA: Addison-Wesley, 1980.

Hackman, Richard and Greg Oldham. "Development of the Job Diagnostic Survey." *Journal of Applied Psychology*, April 1975, 159–70.

Hair, Joseph, Jr., et al. *Multivariate Data Analysis*. New York: Macmillan, 1984.

Hamel, G. and C. K. Prahalad. "Strategic Intent." *The McKinsey Quarterly*, Spring 1990, 36–61.

Hardison, O. B., Jr. *Disappearing Through the Skylight*. New York: Viking, 1989.

Harrington, H. J. *The Improvement Process*. New York: McGraw-Hill, 1987.

Hawken, Paul. *Growing A Business*. New York: Simon & Schuster, 1987.

Hawking, Stephen. *A Brief History of Time*. Toronto: Bantam, 1988.

Hay, Edward. *The Just-in-Time Breakthrough*. New York: Wiley, 1988.

Hein, Tony. "Japanese Management in the United States," in Sang Lee and Gary Schwendiman, eds., *Management by Japanese Systems*. New York: Praeger, 1982.

Herrick, Neal. *Joint Management and Employee Participation*. San Francisco: Jossey-Bass, 1990.

Herzberg, Frederick. "One More Time: How Do You Motivate Employees?" *Harvard Business Review*, January-February, 1968.

Hill, Charles and Gareth Jones. *Strategic Management*. Boston: Houghton-Mifflin, 2nd Ed., 1992.

Howell, Robert and Stephen Sovey. "Customer Profitability: As Critical as Product Profitability." *Management Accounting*, October 1990, 43–47.

Hughes, Jonathan. *The Vital Few*. New York: Oxford University Press, 1986.

Huxley, Julian. *Evolution in Action*. New York: Harper, 1953.

Imai, Masaaki. *Kaizen*. New York: McGraw-Hill, 1986.

Ishikawa, Kaoru and David Lu. *Total Quality Control*. Englewood Cliffs, NJ: Prentice-Hall, 1985.

Jacobson, Gary and John Hillkirk. *Xerox: American Samurai*. New York: Collier, 1987.

Juran, J. M. *Quality Control Handbook*. New York: McGraw-Hill, 1979.

Kaku, Michio and Jennifer Trainer. *Beyond Einstein: The Cosmic Quest for the Theory of the Universe*. Toronto: Bantam, 1987.

Kaplan, Robert. "The Four-stage Model of Cost Systems Design." *Management Accounting*, February 1990, 22–26.

Kelly, John. *Scientific Management, Job Redesign and Work Performance*. London: Academic Press, 1982.

Kinnear, Thomas and James Taylor. *Marketing Research: An Applied Approach*. New York: McGraw-Hill, 1979.

Kipling, Rudyard. "The Ballad of East and West," in *Collected Verse of Rudyard Kipling*. New York: Doubleday, Page & Company, 1916.

Kipnis, D. *The Powerholders*. Chicago: University of Chicago Press, 1976.

Kotha, Suresh and Daniel Orne. "Generic Manufacturing Strategies: A Conceptual Synthesis." *Strategic Management Journal*, 10, 1989, 211–31.

Lawrence, Paul and Jay Lorsch. *Organization and Environment*. Cambridge, MA: Harvard University Press, 1967.

Lele, Milind. "How Service Needs Influence Product Strategy." *Sloan Management Review*, Fall 1986, 63–70.

Lele, Milind and Jagdish Sheth. *The Customer is Key*. New York: Wiley, 1987.

Levinson, Harry and Stuart Rosenthal. *CEO: Corporate Leadership in Action*. New York: Basic Books, 1984.

Levitt, Theodore. "The Globalization of Markets." *Harvard Business Review*, May-June 1983, 92–102.

Likert, Rensis. *New Patterns of Management*. New York: McGraw-Hill, 1961.

Lovelock, James. *The Ages of Gaia*. New York: W. W. Norton & Company, 1988.

McCraw, Thomas K. "From Partners to Competitors: An Overview of the Period Since World War II," in Thomas K. McCraw, ed., *America Versus Japan*. Boston: Harvard Business School Press, 1986.

McGregor, Douglas. *The Human Side of Enterprise*. New York: McGraw-Hill, 1960.

McKelvey, Bill and Howard Aldrich. "Populations, Natural Selection, and Applied Organizational Science." *Administrative Science Quarterly*, 28, 1983, 101–28.

Maslow, Abraham. "A Theory of Human Motivation." *Psychological Review*, 80, 1943, 370–96.

Melcher, Arlyn, Bernard Arogyaswamy and Ken Gartrell. "Leading Strategies: The Trade-offs of Financial, Production and Marketing Activities," in William Guth, ed., *Handbook of Business Strategy 1986/1987 Yearbook*. Boston: Warren, Gorham and Lamont, 1986.

Melcher, Arlyn, et al. "Standard-Maintaining and Continuous-Improvement Systems: Experiences and Comparisons." *Interfaces*, 20: 3 May-June 1990, 24–40.

Melcher, Arlyn and Bernard Arogyaswamy. "The Shifting Playing Field in Global Competition," in William Wallace, ed., *Global Manufacturing: Technological and Economic Opportunities and Research Issues*. Greenwich, CT: Jai Press, 1992, forthcoming.

Melcher, Arlyn. *Structure and Process of Organizations: A Systems Approach*. Englewood Cliffs, NJ: Prentice-Hall, 1975.

Merli, Georgio. *Total Manufacturing Management: Production Organization for the 1990s*. Cambridge, MA: Productivity Press, 1990.

Metraux, Daniel. *The Japanese Economy and the American Businessman*. Lewiston, NY: Edwin Mellen Press, 1989.

Miles, Lawrence. *Techniques of Value Analysis and Value Engineering*. New York: McGraw-Hill, 1961.

Miller, E. J. and A. K. Rice. *Systems in Organization: The Control of Task and Sentient Boundaries*. London: Tavistock, 1963.

Miller, Danny. "The Genesis of Configuration." *Academy of Management Review*, 1987, 12 (4), 686–701.

Mintzberg, Henry. "The Innovation Context," in Henry Mintzberg and James Bryant Quinn, eds., *The Strategy Process*. Englewood Cliffs, NJ: Prentice-Hall, 1991.

Mintzberg, Henry. "Planning on the Left Side and Managing on the Right." *Harvard Business Review*, 1976, 54: 49–58.

Mintzberg, Henry. "Patterns in Strategy Formation." *Management Science*, 1978, 24, 934–48.

Mintzberg, Henry. "Who Should Control the Corporation?" *California Management Review*, Fall 1986, 90–115.

Morgan, Gareth. *Images of Organization*. Beverly Hills, CA: Sage, 1986.

Naisbitt, John. *Megatrends*. New York: Warner, 1982.

Nakajima, Seiichi. *Introduction to TPM*. Cambridge, MA: Productivity Press, 1988.

Neilson, Eric. "Empowerment Strategies," in Suresh Srivastva and Associates, eds., *Executive Power*. San Francisco: Jossey-Bass, 1986.

Ohno, Taiichi. *Toyota Production System: Beyond Large Scale Production*. Cambridge, MA: Productivity Press, 1988.

Organ, Dennis. *Organizational Citizenship Behavior: The Good Soldier Syndrome*. Lexington, MA: Lexington Books, 1988.

Peters, Thomas. "Secrets to Growth: What Makes 'Best Run' Firms Run?" in Y. K. Shetty and Vernon Buehler, eds., *Productivity and Quality Through People*. Westport, CT: Quorum, 1985.

Peters, Thomas and Robert Waterman, Jr. *In Search of Excellence*. New York: Harper & Row, 1982.

Pinchot, III, Gifford. *Intrapreneuring*. New York: Harper & Row, 1985.

Pirsig, Robert. *Zen and the Art of Motorcycle Maintenance*. New York: William Morrow, 1974.

Porter, Michael. *Competitive Advantage*. New York: Free Press, 1985.

Porter, Michael. *Competitive Strategy: Techniques for Analyzing Industries and Competitors*. New York: Free Press, 1980.

Quinn, James Brian. "General Motors Corporation: The Downsizing Decision," in Arthur Bedeian's, *Organizations: Theory and Analysis*. Chicago: Dryden, 2nd Ed., 1984.

Radosevich, Raymond. "Strategic Implications for Organizational Design," in Igor Ansoff, Roger Declerck and Robert Hayes, eds., *From Strategic Planning to Strategic Management*. New York: Wiley, 1976.

Rand, Ayn. "What is Capitalism," in Ayn Rand, ed., *Capitalism: The Unknown Ideal*. New York: Signet, 1967.

Reischauer, Edwin. *The Japanese Today*. Cambridge, MA: Harvard University Press, 1988.

Robey, Daniel. *Designing Organizations*. Homewood, IL: Irwin, 2nd Ed., 1986.

Rogers, Buck. *The IBM Way*. New York: Harper & Row, 1987.

Rogers, Carl. "Active Listening," in Philip DuBose, ed., *Readings in Management*. Englewood Cliffs, NJ: Prentice-Hall, 1988.

Rollins, Fred. "Delta's Teamwork Approach to Labor/Management Relations," in Y. K. Shetty and Vernon Buehler, eds., *Productivity and Quality Through People*. Westport, CT: Quorum, 1985.

Sathe, Vijay. *Culture and Related Corporate Realities*. Homewood, IL: Irwin, 1985.

Savage, John. "Nucor's Keys to Quality Approaches," in Y. K. Shetty and Vernon Buehler, eds., *Productivity and Quality Through People*. Westport, CT: Quorum, 1985.

Scerbonski, Jacqueline. "Consumers and the Environment: A Focus on Five Products." *Journal of Business Strategy*, September/October 1991.

Schein, Edgar. *Organizational Culture and Leadership*. San Francisco: Jossey-Bass, 1985.

Schonberger, Richard. *Japanese Manufacturing Techniques*. New York: Free Press, 1982.

Schonberger, Richard. *Building a Chain of Customers*. New York: Free Press, 1990.

Shingo, Shigeo. *Zero Quality Control: Source Inspection and the Poka-yoke System*. Cambridge, MA: Productivity Press, 1986.

Stalk, Jr., George and Thomas Hart. *Competing Against Time*. New York: Free Press, 1990.

Stalk, George, Philip Evans and Lawrence Shulman. "Competing on Capabilities: The New Rules of Corporate Strategy." *Harvard Business Review*, March-April 1992, 57–69.

Sun-Tzu. *The Art of War*. New York: Oxford University Press, 1971.

Suzaki, Kiyoshi. *The New Manufacturing Challenge*. New York: Free Press, 1987.

Taguchi, Genichi and Don Clausing. "Robust Quality." *Harvard Business Review*, January-February 1990, 65–75.

Talbot, Michael. *Beyond the Quantum*. Toronto: Bantam, 1988.

Thompson, James. *Organizations in Action*. New York: McGraw-Hill, 1967.

Thompson, Arthur, Jr., Ken Pinegar and Tracy Kramer. "Wal-Mart Stores, Inc." in Arthur Thompson, Jr. and A. J. Strickland III, eds., *Strategic Management*. Homewood: IL: Irwin, 1992.

Tolousky, S. *Revolution in Optics*. Harmondsworth, UK: Penguin, 1968.

Trist, E. L. and K. W. Bamforth. "Some Social and Psychological Consequences of the Longwall Method of Coal Gettings." *Human Relations* 4 (February 1951), 3–38.

Vogt, Judith and Kenneth Murrell. *Empowerment in Organizations*. San Diego, CA: University Associates, 1990.

Walton, Mary. *Deming Management at Work*. New York: G. P. Putnam & Sons, 1990.

Waterman, Robert. *The Renewal Factor*. Toronto: Bantam, 1988.

Webster, Frederick. *Marketing for Managers*. New York: Harper & Row, 1974.

Welford, W. T. *Optics*. Oxford: Oxford University Press, 1980.

Williamson, Oliver. *Markets and Hierarchies: Analysis and Antitrust Implications*. New York: Free Press, 1975.

Wilson, Carl and Walter Loomis. *Botany*. New York: Holt, Rinehart, and Winston, 3rd Ed., 1962.

Woods, Powell. "The Teening of America: Communicating with a Turned-On, Tuned-In Workforce," in Lee Thayer, ed., *Organization Communication: Emerging Perspectives*. Norwood, NJ: Ablex, 1986.

Zemke, Ron with Dick Schaaf. *The Service Edge: 101 Companies that Profit from Customer Care*. New York: Penguin, 1990.

INDEX

ABOUT THE AUTHORS

BERNARD AROGYASWAMY is Associate Professor of Strategy and Policy at Le Moyne College. He has industrial experience, particularly in the electric power industry. He has published numerous articles in such journals as the *Journal of Management, Journal of Managerial Issues*, and *Production and Inventory Management*, and has contributed chapters to a variety of edited works.

RON P. SIMMONS is Vice President, Manufacturing, at DVC Industries. He has experience both as a manufacturing executive and as a consultant in the implementation of value-based systems.